The Art of Reading and Writing Haiku

A Reader Response Approach

The Art of Reading
& Writing Haiku

A Reader Response Approach

by

Dr. Randy Brooks
Millikin University

Brooks Brooks
Taylorville, Illinois

The Art of Reading & Writing Haiku:
A Reader Response Approach
by Dr. Randy Brooks

First Edition

Copyright © 2019 by Brooks Books
Printed in the United States of America

ISBN: 978-1-929820-17-7

Brooks Books
6 Madera Court
Taylorville, IL 62568

www.brooksbookshaiku.com
brooksbooks@gmail.com

For all of my
Global Haiku students
who have repeatedly surprised me
with their heartfelt readings and
playful creativity.

THANK YOU FOR SHARING
YOUR GIFTS OF DISCOVERY!

Table of Contents

Introduction

As a writer, editor, scholar and publisher of haiku since 1976, I have been an active member of the haiku community for over 40 years. Throughout these years, I have never ceased to be amazed by the blessings of this literary art.

First, and foremost, there is the gift each haiku offers if you give it a full imagined reading; if you let yourself enter into its space of perceptions; if you are open to its insight and feel the emotional significance of its moment; if you let it touch your own life memories and associations; if you let it come alive; and, if you let yourself come alive while holding it in your heart and mind for a moment.

Second, as you read more haiku and improve at the art of reading haiku, you become more aware of your surroundings and your own life's significant feelings or events. You start noticing things that you missed before. You stop to fully feel and perceive the moments you are living. As some of my students say, when you immerse yourself in this tradition, you get your "haiku eyes" and begin seeing and feeling things you missed before. You become more fully aware of the value of being alive; and, being a human, you get the urge to record those moments of perception and insight as new haiku.

Third, the haiku tradition is very social; it is inevitable that when a haiku touches us, we want to share our response with others. When we write a haiku, a moment of significant perception or realization, we are eager to offer the gift of that haiku to others for their enjoyment and response. When groups of people share their lives and insights through this literary art, they are drawn together into a community that values the art of reading and writing haiku.

As a teacher it was natural for me to seek ways to share my love of reading and writing haiku with my students. Throughout the 1980s and 1990s, I had been teaching haiku as a short unit within courses such as creative writing, Modernist poetry, and even first year composition. We would spend a week or two reading haiku in English and translations of Japanese haiku, and sometimes we would write and edit a few haiku before moving on to other units of study. My students loved reading and responding to haiku, and they immediately saw the value of learning to be more concise, as well as learning about the power of images in their writing. They enjoyed the idea that the reader is a co-creator of the significance when reading a haiku. But they never really understood the transactional blessings of being immersed in the haiku community, nor did they get enough engagement to fully understand the powerful integration of the art of reading and writing haiku. I realized that I needed to develop a program of haiku studies that would share the full blessings of this literary tradition with students.

Over the last two decades I have developed, taught and refined a semester-long course, Global Haiku Traditions, at Millikin University in Decatur, Illinois. My approach emphasizes two essentials: (1) students engage in the twin arts of reading and writing haiku as performance learning activities, (2) resulting in an understanding of what it means to be an active participant in a creative haiku community. My goals for this course are not focused on literary history nor the use of haiku as a means of cultural study. My goal is to simply invite my students into the joy of reading and writing haiku, in their own language and through translations from other languages. Of course, to be a good reader, my students need to understand where these traditions come from (so they need some Japanese cultural and literary history), but those subjects are ancillary to my primary goal of simply enjoying the arts of reading and writing haiku.

My pedagogical approach is to help students discover the art of writing haiku by reading a lot of haiku with them and asking (okay assigning) them to continually attempt to write a lot of haiku. We read haiku and write haiku and share our thoughts about haiku throughout the semester. Here are the kinds of questions I ask as we read an incredible number of haiku. *What's one of your favorite haiku? Read it out loud, slowly. Give it time to simmer in your mind and heart for a while. What did you feel in response to this haiku? Where did it take you in your imagined response? Why is this one so good? Where did it come from? How do you think the writer wrote this haiku? Why is this haiku so much better than other haiku? What do you notice when you read this haiku side-by-side with this other haiku? Which haiku do you enjoy reading over and over again? Find a haiku that you love every time you read it no matter how many times you've read it before. Why do you love that one so much? How is it written?* We do this over and over throughout the semester, simply enjoying favorite haiku that the students want to share with everyone in the class.

For the last two decades Millikin University has embraced "Performance Learning" as a distinctive approach to teaching and learning. Performance learning can be described as students "doing the discipline", which generates confidence and identity as someone who knows how to "do the discipline." For example, instead of merely studying history, Millikin students conduct historical research with primary artifacts or sources and write and present history for local communities, various museums and historical associations. Through this work for clients and professional colleagues, students learn what it means to be an historian.

In the Global Haiku Traditions course, I deliberately invite students to join the contemporary international haiku community by reading, writing, editing, sharing and publishing haiku. For a semester, my students are immersed in the life of being a haiku poet. I want my students to fully engage in the art of reading and writing haiku—bringing their memories, associations, experiences, and unique perspectives into the public sphere of this social literary art. I want them to be aesthetically serious and to have a lot of fun. For at least a semester (hopefully a lifetime), I want them to fall in love with haiku—how it is intended to touch others and what it is like to be immersed and engaged in the necessarily connected literary arts of reading and writing haiku.

Performance learning at Millikin University is also characterized as students performing for some intended audience or "third-party stakeholders" who respond to or benefit from these performances. These third-party stakeholders recognize the value of student performances in some way. In the Global Haiku Traditions course, I stress the importance of community in the classroom and beyond the classroom because art, especially the literary art of reading and writing haiku, is a very collaborative, social process. I deliberately construct the classroom as a space for performance—reading haiku out loud, discussing and sharing reader responses to favorite haiku, reading and competing with each other with original haiku, sharing original haiku with others beyond the classroom, and inviting others into creative collaboration as readers and writers of haiku.

In many ways, the Global Haiku Traditions course could be characterized as a continuous "kukai" in which students read, find, and discuss favorite haiku from haiku publications AND students read, find and discuss favorite haiku written by each other. Throughout the course, students select and respond to favorite original haiku submitted to each other through anonymous kukai contests. Two approaches to kukai are used— traditional and matching contest.

In traditional kukai, original haiku are submitted to the editor (me) who selects the best attempts for inclusion in the competition. These are placed on a page with no names, then students read, select, and share favorites. I often ask the students to write an imagined response to one or two favorites before the class meets to "give birth" to new haiku. During the kukai session, the students are directed to a favorite haiku which is read out loud and then several students talk about what they love about that haiku. Kukai is not an editing session, so edit suggestions or comments about why someone does not like a haiku are not allowed. The point of kukai is to find haiku that are loved Just the way they are. We say that when the haiku finds a reader who loves it, that is the moment it is born. After everyone has talked about why they enjoy that haiku, a vote is taken to determine how many students chose that haiku as a favorite. After the haiku is born, and only then, do we ask who wrote the haiku. When the newborn haiku is claimed by its author, we applaud (or snap fingers or tap pencils) to thank the writer for their gift. Then we look for another haiku waiting to be born. Authors of favorite haiku with the most votes receive awards of haiku books or recent issues of haiku magazines.

Matching contests work in a similar way—with the selection of matched pairs of anonymous haiku arranged in a tournament format. Each pair of haiku are discussed and fully appreciated, with one being voted on as the favorite between the two. The favorite haiku moves on to the next level of matched pairs in the contest until a grand champion is found. Then haiku authors are revealed so that all of the newborn haiku may be claimed by their creators. Most of the haiku in this anthology were first born in kukai or matching contests.

Receiving feedback on how their haiku is perceived by readers is an important part of becoming a member of the haiku community. The readers sharing their imagined responses "closes the loop" for the haiku writer who learns how effective or powerful or meaningful their work was for readers. It is also significant that students in this course inevitably share their original haiku and critical responses with others beyond the community of the campus classroom. Sometimes this is done by simply asking others, such as family members or friends, to read and respond to their original haiku. When students go home for fall break, Thanksgiving break or Easter break, I ask them to share a sheet of their best haiku with friends and families. Students ask these readers to pick out and discuss favorites. When students learn the collaborative art of renku (linked verses), they invite friends to become co-writers. Friends often help write haiku sequences or linked verses of haiku. It is natural for my students to want to share haiku they are reading and writing with others within their broader social network.

As you will see from student reading responses in this book, my students read a wide range of haiku from a variety of approaches. This is why I call the course "Global Haiku Traditions" instead of "The Haiku Tradition". Instead of indoctrinating students into one approach, it is my desire for them to see that there are many approaches and ways of pursuing this literary art. In a book review I once wrote that it has always been my contention that the haiku community needs to get past the beginner's mind of definitions and rules and get on with the celebration of the diversity of the genre that is rich and strong only to the extent that there is a wide range of practice, a surprising freshness of voices and perspectives.

We need to embrace and celebrate haiku writers who relish dense language and the naming function of words, haiku writers who live in the woods and tap into the biodiversity of ecosystems there, haiku writers who protest injustice and go to jail, haiku writers who resist the male ego dominance of English, haiku writers who meditate and seek the quiet voice within, haiku writers who celebrate being social and the significance of being in community, haiku writers who are religious within a variety of spiritual traditions, haiku writers who are all about people, haiku writers who write senryu and don't care about the distinction, haiku writers who are international citizens of the world using haiku to bridge cultures, and haiku writers who are so local nobody but friends at the local pub understand them. This diversity of writers and approaches to haiku is the strength and rich surprise of elasticity found in this literary genre.

The culminating assignment engaging students in the art of reading haiku is a formal reader response essay. The student essays focus on haiku writing techniques, haiku poetics, a thematic topic, or an individual haiku poet. Often students interview a contemporary haiku poet by email or in person as part of their research. Each student identifies a topic or poet of interest and seeks to read as many haiku on that topic or by that author as possible. To assist with this process, students have access to the extensive Decatur Haiku Collection of books and journals, which is cataloged as a bibliography on the Millikin University Haiku website. Students also are encouraged to visit the Haiku Foundation web site to explore the Haiku Registry and publications available online from the foundation's Digital Library. Several of the student essays are published on the Millikin University Haiku website and have been frequently cited in subsequent scholarship.

The course ends with a public poetry reading of each student's short collection of best original haiku. Family, friends, the general public and the Millikin University community are invited to this reading. In addition to this "finals" tradition, students in the course sometimes compete with each other through public impromptu "haiku cut" poetry slam competitions in locations such as the Decatur Area Arts Council, the Decatur Public Library or on campus. These playful competitions invite audiences to serve as flag judges, resulting in recognition of a winning haiku. At the end of the course, students also share their work by submitting to current haiku journals in which many students have been published. After the first ten years of teaching the course, a collection of student haiku called *The Millikin University Haiku Anthology* was published by Bronze Man Books, a university press that functions as a performance learning course for students.

In this book, *The Art of Reading and Writing Haiku: A Reader Response Approach,* I share my students' journey into the haiku community. I invite you to join this journey as a reader of their original haiku and their reader responses to favorite haiku. I hope the reader responses help spark your own reading and felt imagination of each haiku. May my students' creative work help you find your own "haiku eyes" during your brief immersion into the haiku community through this book. Welcome to the haiku community of the Global Haiku Traditions course. Enjoy the many gifts and blessings the art of reading and writing haiku have to offer you. Let the eye-opening begin!

Randy Brooks, PhD
Dean of Arts & Sciences and Professor of English
Millikin University
Decatur, Illinois

June 18, 2019

Chapter 1

The Art of Reading Contemporary Haiku

Sharing Haiku of the Day

How does anyone get interested in haiku and catch a glimpse of the haiku community? It usually begins with a friend or someone sharing a favorite haiku from a book or magazine. Or perhaps someone just got a new haiku published and they are eager to share it with others. Our first day of class at Millikin begins with a haiku. I ask students to close their eyes and imagine the following haiku that I read out loud:

> the sun coming up
>   five eggs
> in the iron skillet

> James Tipton, Bittersweet, p. 20

While they have their eyes closed I ask them where this haiku took them. What else do they hear, smell, or see? What kind of day is it? What do they feel? They turn to their neighbors and share their imagined reading of this haiku, then we discuss it as a group. In this way the Global Haiku Traditions class begins by careful reading out loud, a mindful response, and social sharing of the reader's response. This is the first lesson of the art of reading haiku.

Throughout the semester, we begin each class with this ritual of sharing a "haiku of the day". We close our eyes and quiet ourselves down to listen closely as a student reads the haiku he or she has found. After reading it out loud, we discuss various imagined responses and ask the finder of the haiku what they loved about it. Then another student is chosen to find the "haiku of the day" for our next class meeting. This is how we enter the haiku community each day.

Reading Haiku from *Mayfly* Magazine

On the first day of class we start reading and sharing responses to contemporary haiku. I hand out a recent issue of *Mayfly* magazine, a small magazine published twice a year by me and my wife, Shirley Brooks. My instructions are to read the magazine slowly—each haiku is on its own page to deliberately slow the reader down and to give the reader lots of white space to fill in the blanks around it. I encourage my students to enjoy each haiku, then pick out a favorite one. I encourage them to quietly discuss them with neighbors. After they have read most of the haiku, I ask them to select and share favorite ones. When one is called out, we all turn to that page, and I ask the student to read that haiku out loud very slowly. Then the student explains why it is a favorite. Other students talk about what they like about the haiku as well, so that we get a variety of responses. This continues as we enjoy most of the haiku from that issue of *Mayfly*.

This is the key to the art of reading haiku . . . find a favorite one, read it out loud, then share it with others to see how they respond as well. There's no need to talk about one's you didn't like. There's no need to complain about how one is written or how it could be edited into some other version of itself. I invite my students to just enjoy the haiku— and love it—just the way it is.

During that first class or as an assignment for the next day, I ask the students to write their imagined response to another favorite haiku from the Mayfly issue. At this point the students do not know much about the art of haiku, so they are simply responding to their immediate and mindful imagined response. This is entirely intuitive. Later, they will come to appreciate some of the techniques and aesthetics associated with haiku. At this point, it is pure first responses and secondary mindful consideration.

When students write a response to a favorite haiku, I ask that they begin by writing or typing the haiku exactly as it appears in the publication. Don't change punctuation, line breaks, capitalization or spaces in the haiku because each of these have been carefully chosen by the author. I also ask that they cite the author's name, publication title, and page number to make their selection easy to share with others. In formal essays students always include a works cited page with full citation for each haiku. This act of writing or typing the haiku helps students take it into their fingers and mind, carefully paying atten- tion to the exact choices of the poet.

Here are some student responses to *Mayfly* magazine haiku from the Global Haiku Traditions course.

> sleepless night
> the scent of her love letters
> in the fireplace
>
> Chad Lee Robinson, *Mayfly* 36, p. 15

I see a young man who has just lost the girl he thought was "the one". He knows it's better this way but the thought of how wonderful it all was is still keeping him awake at night. He sits in his dimly lit living room reading all the letters she had written him for the four years they went to different schools. With the stack at his side, he slowly reads the once meaningful words and one by one tosses them into the fire. The smell of the fire mingles with that of the letters and creates a feeling of bitterness which separates past from future. Leigh Ann Kitchell, Spring 2004

What a powerful haiku. There is definitely a surprise element to this haiku. At first, I thought that the author was enjoying the scent of "her" love letters, but the last line changes the entire tone. I envision a man in a hotel casino, possibly the honeymoon suite, alone. The woman that was supposed to be his wife has run off with another man. So, there he sits alone in the beautiful (but almost tacky) hotel room burning her love letters in the hotel room fireplace. I see a lot of color in this haiku — lots of red: the man in a red robe, the hotel room with red curtains and bed spread, red brick fireplace, and the red flames from the fire. Maureen Coady, Spring 2004

I really liked this haiku. I saw a man who has been out of this relationship for quite some time. He's had a few other relationships since this one but hasn't found one as good as her yet. He has just ended his most recent relationship only a few days ago and wants to remember what it felt like to be with that perfect girl. He can't sleep so he begins to read the letters from his "perfect" relationship that he has saved in a shoebox for many years. They are dusty and old, but still have the smell of her perfume encrusted on them. After reading them, he decides that he will never find that again and doesn't need to keep punishing himself. He then burns all of the letters in his fireplace, so he can never refer back and to clean the slate for him. Ben Kress, Spring 2004

after the funeral
just one toothbrush
in the rack

Anne LB Davidson, *Mayfly* 40, p. 11

The first line of this haiku sets the stage for the sad tone that carries through the rest of it. After reading it, I imagine a widow on her way home to an empty house. She is riding in the back of a black limousine. She is very elderly. The second line automatically made me think of emptiness. The word "one" contains so much power in this line. The third line works with the second to complete the thought. The widow is coming home to one less thing. I like haiku that expresses human emotions and ideas in terms of material things (such as the toothbrush in this haiku). Pat Steadman, Spring 2006

I really liked this haiku's attention to detail. The death of someone you love is a very large tragedy. It's interesting to think how such a huge tragedy can open one up to all of the little details of life. One might not normally notice the way that their toothbrush sits in a rack, but when the owner of the toothbrush is taken away it takes on a whole new meaning. When we lose someone, we tend to notice a whole new array of things, and old memories seem to flood quickly back. One might not be able to walk past a certain bench anymore or go into a certain room of the house. The single toothbrush in the rack is a small but strong symbol of love lost. Jamie Devitt, Spring 2006

Anne LB Davidson does an excellent job of conveying the depth of how hurt one can be after the death of a loved one or spouse. She does this by focusing on one of the simplest aspects and routines of our life, hygiene. It is a basic act that is so commonly looked over and has become such a routine that it is not noticed until something goes wrong or is missing. The toothbrush rack, for example, would not even be noticed or cared about in normal circumstances. Now, however, it is the epitome of loss and heartbreak, a constant reminder that nothing will ever be the same. After the funeral life will go on, the spouse will attempt to pick up the pieces and replace what they have lost. The thought is antagonizing and dreadful. I feel that the author has expertly chosen words and examples that clearly pass these emotions off to the reader through her use of an everyday object being disrupted. Erin Wyant, Spring 2006

S-shaped curves
of egrets and herons
different fonts

Pat Tompkins, *Mayfly* 48, p. 9

When I read this poem, I see in my mind's eye egrets and herons, standing in the shallow water of a lake or pond with the sun behind them so that they are only shadows. Because of the low visibility, it's hard to tell which are which, except for the different shape of their S-shaped necks. Despite their similarities, they are still identifiable by the unique 'fonts' of their necks. TJ Holmes, Spring 2014

This haiku brings me home to the East coast. It reminds me of laying on the top of my parents' boat in the middle of the Long Island Sound in the middle of the summer. I can feel the boat rocking back and forth with the lull of the waves, as well as the sun shining down on me. I can feel the heat of the sun on my forehead. As I lay there, I can imagine myself looking up in the sky and seeing all the water birds flying around in different curved shapes. They all have their own paths which in turn are their different "fonts." Jenna Farquhar, Spring 2014

apartment window
grandma's tulips
still bloom

Marjorie Sands, Mayfly 49, p. 7

With this haiku, I thought of my grandma. At home, I live with my grandma, mom and sister, so I am very close with my grandma since my mom works more than 40 hours a week. I always have wondered what would happen when my grandma was not around anymore. I truly have always believed that even when someone has died, they will always remain with us in some way. This haiku, to me, expresses this view in that the grandma may no longer be there, but her flowers that she loved and cared for are still with us. Another reading is that the grandma has given someone flowers for the apartment, because like me, they have grown up and moved away. These flowers remain with the person at their new apartment as a constant reminder of the love their grandma has for them. Allyson Staudenmaier, Fall 2010

our father
in the rear-view
mirror

PMF Johnson, Mayfly 49, p. 13

I really like this haiku because it takes me back to a simpler time: my childhood. When I close my eyes, I can picture my own father's face in the rear-view mirror, looking back at my brother and I in the backseat. I can hear his off-pitch singing voice, belting out an oldie tune as he always did on car rides. My brother and I would laugh as dad reached his arm back and would play a guitar or piano solo on our knees. Kelsey Meredith, Spring 2013

This haiku says a lot to me; it seemed very sad and depressing. I envisioned the writer being in the driver's seat, looking at his or her father in the rear-view mirror, where you never usually see your father. I imagined the father being an old man, needing his child to chauffeur him to appointments and to run errands, and I thought about the circle of life; how your parents take care of you in the first half of your life, and you must take care of them in the last half of their lives. It immediately made me think of my grandparents and how as the older they get, the more dependent they become on their children and grandchildren. Emily Crutchfield, Spring 2013

The haiku by PMF Johnson is intriguing. The imagery of a rear-view mirror harkens to leaving something behind, but why are they leaving their father? "Our father" makes me think first of the dad of two kids, one of which is obviously old enough to drive. They are leaving their father in the driveway because he did something to drive them off. However, "Our Father" is the beginning of a very common prayer we say in the Catholic Church, so in that aspect I think about people leaving the comfort and reassurance of their religion. Charlie Decker, Spring 2013

> reminded
> when I am with you
> . . . it rains

> Raquel D. Bailey, *Mayfly* 49, p. 14

This haiku makes me think of the people in my life that I could do without. The ones who are bad for me, who "rain on me". But at the same time, the people who I need and crave, the way that grass needs rain to grow. These are the people who have made me into the person I am today. The ones who have shaped me into a strong woman. Nothing can grow without rain. Kelsey Meredith, Spring 2013

I truly love this haiku above all others thus far, and I feel like this haiku will remain one of my favorites of the semester. Though I thought everyone's responses to this haiku were great, I would like to only talk about my initial reaction. When I first read it, I pictured a woman who knows that the man she loves is not good for her. She finds herself always wanting to go back to him but has to remind herself that it rains. Not a clean, refreshing kind of rain. The kind of rain that won't let up, locks you indoors, and prevents you from going out and having fun and doing what you want to do. It's the kind of rain that traps you, not wipes you clean. The ellipses make me think the woman is taking a deep breath in and sighing with remorse and regret, for even though she does not want to be lonely, she does not want to go back to inevitable sadness. I relate to this haiku a lot, because I have had people in my life who only bring storm clouds, not sunshine. I know the feeling of having to remind myself to not fall back into the same routine and tricks, because the storm these kinds of people bring is one that is relentless and uncaring. I now know, and I hope that this imaginary woman I made up will also know, that no matter how cheesy it may seem, after rain there are sunny skies and rainbows. And, if you think about it, you get to stomp all over the rain in rainboots. :) Courtney Burress, Spring 2013

This haiku shows how memories can affect us so much. I think of my boyfriend when I read this haiku because when I am at school, he is 4 hours away, which is the same number of years we have been together. He is one of my best friends and we have shared so many memories. It is hard to be apart and when we get to see each other I am so overjoyed. We have noticed the opposite of this haiku, every time we are parted it rains. The last two years when I have moved to Millikin it has rained. We like to think the sky is crying because we have to be apart. On the other hand, whenever we get to see each other it feels like old times but also like something new. This is just like rain because rain has been occurring for all time but every time it rains there is a sense of rebirth and new life starting. Madeline Knott, Fall 2010

moonset
he holds the last pearl of her
broken necklace

Raquel D. Bailey, *Mayfly* 55, p. 5

I love this one because it puts me in the mind of old times such as the 1920s. Women used to wear pearls commonly back then and that would be considered a fine piece of jewelry. I imagine an old black and white movie with a lady with a blonde pin up crying and snatching the pearl necklace her husband gave her off of her neck. She would be stricken with sadness from his infidelity and have her bags packed at the door waiting for him to answer her request or some sort of ultimatum. Before he knows it, she would be gone forever. He picks the necklace up several hours later, sad with his own failure to decide. He sits in a drunken stupor thinking about her, holding her necklace, wishing he had behaved differently. I like how the second line ends with "her". It is as if he was holding the last pearl of "her". Deja Finley, Fall 2014

This poem seems very similar to a fairy tale, almost a Cinderella tale, where a prince is standing in a forest after a long night, holding a pearl that is left behind from his princess fleeing. He knows that she still has affection for him, but she had to run from something. When she ran, her necklace broke and he caught one of the pearls, but the rest fell into the mud. He is lost without her and feels that he needs to find her again. I find that this poem makes me feel like the adventure is just beginning for this prince and his lady; however, it has considerable potential to fail if he cannot find her, or if she has lost her fondness for him. Danna Herbach, Fall 2014

briefly her eyes unglue from the iPhone fireflies

Carl Seguiban, *Mayfly* 57, p. 3

This haiku made me remember the many summers I spent as a camp counselor for a Girl Scout camp. At this camp, the girls would not be allowed to have electronics, especially cellphones, for the entire week of their stay. There were always a couple of girls who had a difficult time with the separation from their cellphones. However, one of the nights at the camp we would take them to a miniature village that was named the Fairy Village because the fireflies like to fly right around the houses making it look like a bunch of little fairies dancing about. After that night the girls would forget about the cellphones and begin to appreciate the nature that was surrounding them. Mikayla Shaw, Fall 2014

This haiku is so simple but is such a perfect way to describe the interaction of teenagers and young adults of this generation. I'm imagining a group of friends who are all hanging outside in someone's backyard, just talking and sharing Buzzfeed articles or other people's posts on Facebook. Then, one girl looks up for a second to swat away a mosquito and sees the big, beautiful sky with all the stars twinkling back. She awes at it for a second, but a notification brings her back to her phone. My image of this poem just goes to show how technology oriented we are that we cannot even put down our phones and enjoy the nature around us. Olivia Cuff, Fall 2014

in the wheelchair
tilting her head back
to feel the rain

Carl Mayfield, *Mayfly* 57, p. 10 and Mayfly 58, cover

I enjoyed this haiku because of the sense of freedom it provokes. I have always been best friends with my grandma and while she doesn't like the rain, reading this made me think of when she finally sits down in the afternoon with a cup of tea. She feels relaxed and at ease while enjoying a moment with herself. I love the imagery this haiku paints; the light raindrops falling onto a damp earth, the relaxation of the body, and the human appreciation for nature. What a beautiful haiku. Katherine Viviano, Spring 2016

This haiku made me think about a cancer patient going into remission. When patients leave a hospital, they are often wheeled out. I imagine a cancer patient who has been in the hospital undergoing chemo for a long time and is finally able to leave. When she leaves the hospital for the first time, it is raining but she doesn't care. She just tilts her head back and feels the rain. She is relieved and happy that she can feel the rain again because she felt trapped in her room. Erica Forbes, Spring 2016

I feel pain and sorrow. I see a young woman experiencing a tragic accident leaving her in a wheel chair. She has a severe paralysis—everything below her neck is paralyzed. She's angry. She had a life ahead of her, and her family doesn't know what to do with her, so they leave her outside in the middle of the rain. I think the rain symbolizes her tears. For so long she's been stuck feeling anger, bitterness, and hatred. She's questioning why this happened to her, and then all of a sudden, she feels the rain on her face. It's a bittersweet moment because she can feel; the feeling is more than that of just rain, but it's to feel again in general. The rain kind of washes away a lot of the negative energy surrounding her and mixes with her tears and kind of heals her. She can still feel, she can still find happiness through the pain and misfortune. Francesca Rios, Spring 2015

sunrise . . .
    learning again to color
outside the lines

Julie Warther, *Mayfly* 58, p. 4

When I read this haiku, I visualize so many warm colors, including different shades of orange, yellow, red, pink and purple. When the author says "outside the lines" I picture a sunset that has all the colors blended together and it doesn't really fit the sunset structure most people think of. I also think about how all sunsets are different, even though they are similar. When the author uses the word "again" I think about how we think children are the only people that color outside the lines, and you get better at coloring in the lines as you get older. In this case, coloring outside the lines is what makes the sunset beautiful and makes it art, even if that means messing up when a child colors the page. Emily Mihalkanin, January 2016

I particularly liked this haiku because of the strong visual imagery conjured in my head when I read it. This haiku instantly catches your eye because it is different: it has punctuation and does not line up on the left border. I thought the shift of lines was really important because of how such a simple change reinforced the theme of the haiku itself. I also imagined a painting of a sunrise, which no one can ever perfectly capture the beauty of, and just saw it fading into a real sunrise. The simplicity of the image in my head and the poem itself simply resounded with me in a way I can't exactly put into words. Cori Grzenia, Spring 2016

I absolutely love the imagery and message in this haiku. I love to paint, especially sunsets, so it strikes me especially nicely in the sensation I immediately feel. It tells the story of waking up to a new day to start over and try again, one of the bravest things a human being does. It breathes a sense of renewal, perhaps a person feeling like themselves again, or feeling like their life is so confusing that it can feel like painting without directions. If you think about it, that's what we are all trying to do, and I think this sums up the human experience beautifully. Genevieve Breitbach, Spring 2016

> dad's bench
> a goldfinch takes
> his place

> John McManus, *Mayfly* 58, p. 12

After reading this poem, I envision a bench in a garden in the backyard of a home. The narrator who sees the bench has just arrived home for the first time after losing their father, perhaps even returning from a funeral. They walk to the backyard to surround themselves with memories of the garden. Oftentimes people do not feel the importance in objects until their owners are gone, and they become the vessel for memories. So now, it is as if he or she is seeing the bench for the first time. Never before did they notice the beauty of the bench, the garden, or the goldfinches. Whitney Gray, Spring 2016

This haiku is my favorite because it represents a rebirth or a new generation with something good to come. It describes a "goldfinch" taking his place on the bench so we can assume that the father has passed and what was his "bench" is now taken by another spirit. It also represents very sad but hopeful feelings, as well as a feeling of being anxious for the future. This makes me feel at peace and hopeful for a new beginning with many opportunities to come. Emilio Tejada, Spring 2016

From this poem, I imagine a stone bench that was in some way dedicated to a person's father. This could be a bench where they had a lot of talks with each other or a bench that was placed on their property or gravesite in memory of the father. I see the son or daughter looking at the bench and noticing a goldfinch appear while walking by on the property or gravesite, and I feel as though the son or daughter believes that this goldfinch is a representation of his or her father's spirit. From this action of the bird, the children can feel a presence of their father and I get the sense that they are relieved to see this goldfinch on their father's bench. The beginning of the poem makes me feel like they are missing their father and it's a sad feeling, but then when the goldfinch appears, it is like they are reassured that he is watching over them even when he is gone. Heather Doyle, January 2016

> midnight call
> his car
> a pumpkin

> Helen Buckingham, *Mayfly* 60, p. 4

This isn't necessarily a good midnight call. Maybe Cinderella isn't all that excited about meeting her prince. His car isn't a pretty carriage, it's just a pumpkin, and this "call" isn't born out of romantic love. More like a one-night-stand. It's a very interesting subversion of fairytale tropes. Alexa Duncan, June 2016

I can picture the car. It's a small, two-door, white sports car, with black tinted windows. They drove together to the restaurant, talking about the night, how it went, joking about the goofy things one of their friends said. They order their food, but they agreed that they needed to be home kind of early tonight, so they would leave at midnight. That's early, right? The hours pass, and they're laughing and talking with friends, enjoying them-selves and each other's company, not realizing that midnight is upon them. They get up (together), get their checks (together), each forget they had to pee (though they probably didn't do that activity together) and leave . . . together. Their friends exchange knowing looks, thinking they understand. They get in the car and head back home. He pulls into the parking lot next to her building. He's in the middle of a sentence, so she doesn't get out. But then she has something to say, and they keep talking until they realize neither of them made it home early . . . they're still sitting in their pumpkin. Marah Kittelson, Spring 2016

depression lifting
a scatter of stars
in dusklight

Billie Wilson, *Mayfly* 60, p. 14

This haiku stood out to me the first time that I read it in class because it reminded me of Van Gogh's "Starry Night" and times of depression and hardship that he faced towards the end of his life. Looking at it again, this haiku really speaks to me as a new begin-ning, a time of transition (dusk) as the fog of depression lifts to show the stars. The stars show that there is hope and happiness in little places in your life. You've made it through the darkness! Alyssa Becker, Fall 2016

I love the word choices in this haiku. The word "lifting" is both figurative and literal in that it lifts to reveal the scatter of stars. "Scatter of stars" is such a great phrase. It has an alliteration that rolls off the tongue and it shows the perfect image of how a sky full of stars actually looks. I grew up near the light-polluted Chicago, so what I think a starry sky looks like is similar to what you'd see in movies, and not what it actually is. The real thing is imperfect, and that makes it more beautiful than a picture-perfect movie scene. Then, "dusklight" changes the image completely. I've never seen stars when it isn't completely dark outside, but I imagine that when mixed in with the colors of a sunset, they look hazier and covered. With this word, it makes more sense that a person with depression would barely notice the stars until it lifted. Natalie Smith, Spring 2016

I really liked the hope in this haiku. It reminds me of someone I know who has depres-sion. When things get bad, we can all kind of tell, but when things get good, we can all kind of tell too. It's so amazing when things get good because they're able to see the world again. They see the good instead of the bad and it's like they're free again. The dusk light represents when things first start to lift, it's not completely light but it's also not completely dark. There are still hints of sadness, but the person is able to see the good things again, even though some bad still remains. Corrin Littlefield, Spring 2016

well-worn faces
Halloween night at
the nursing home

James Babbs, *Mayfly* 65, p. 7

The first line alone feels very unfinished and unsure to me, but coupled with the second line, makes sense. The first two lines together give me the image of a Halloween party with young, lively, beautiful people. The 'well-worn faces' are the extravagant costumes that the youthful guests are wearing. The faces could be make-up or masks. Whatever they are, they are what the haiku says: worn well. The second line also left me with some anticipation. Halloween night at . . . what? Where is it? A club? Someone's house? Nope, the nursing home. This changes everything. Now these well-worn faces can mean one of three things. The first is similar to my initial thought. There are simply fun beautiful elderly people wearing fancy costumes at their nursing home. This idea brings me more joy than the other two. The second meaning is that the author is referring to some really beautiful old people. While entirely possible, my third idea seems more likely. These well-worn faces are not worn well but are in fact well worn. They have been effectively worn creating lines from laughs, worries, and tears, and spots from the sun. This interpretation brings me less joy than the previous ones. It isn't entirely bad! I just find more joy in seeing a whole bunch of elderly people in fancy costumes, making the most out of their Halloween night. Isabella Loutfi, Fall 2018

I decided to read this haiku poem line by line. The first line made me think about the people who put on a happy face for others, like a sort of mask of emotion. After reading this line, I could already tell this poem would have a more serious tone. At the mention of Halloween, I felt that my mask metaphor became even more justified. However, the last line altered my translation a little bit. By adding the setting of the nursing home, I realized that this could be referring to the many faces, emotions, and struggles that all people will have gone through by the time that they are old. It also makes me think about how many older people who are in nursing homes become depressed at the fact they are no longer able to do things that they used to do, and that they aren't able to celebrate more youthful holidays like Halloween where children go trick-or-treating and young adults go to costume parties. I picture a gloomy nursing home with cheap Halloween decorations hung on the walls; maybe one resident is putting on a happy face/front on the phone while talking to their daughter on the phone about the rest of the family's Halloween plans even though the resident has now lived out their days of celebration and is now feeling lonely and constrained. Isabella Spiritoso, Fall 2018

Reading Haiku by Aubrie Cox

In addition to reading *Mayfly* magazine at the beginning of the Global Haiku Traditions course, students enjoy reading haiku by one of our most successful alumni from Millikin University, Aubrie Cox. She first took the course in 2008 and continued haiku studies at Millikin for several years, eventually serving as my teaching assistant in 2011 when her first collection *Tea's Aftertaste* was published. Here are some student responses to haiku by Aubrie Cox from class kukai or her chapbooks.

morning snow
on her bottom lip
a drop of blood

Aubrie Cox, Spring 2010

I loved this haiku because the first image that came to mind was of Snow White. I saw a pale girl, her skin glistening like snow, with lips as red as blood. Then I saw this girl all bundled up, stepping out into fresh snow, and her chapped lips cracking to perfectly let one drop of blood spill out. The image of the bottom lip also made me think of a soft surface, parallel to the image of soft snow resting on the earth, untouched. Susie Wirthlin, Spring 2010

I love the contrast in this haiku. It starts out with something beautiful and ends with something sad and scary. It plays well on the emotions, and I never expected the last line to be anything like that. It also leaves so many questions. Perhaps the girl just fell and cut her lip. Perhaps she is biting her lip in frustration. Perhaps there isn't any real blood, but the blood is a metaphor. The snow may be a substitute for cold emotions. And why is there blood on the bottom lip instead of the top? The exciting thing is that I don't have the answers. It is such a cryptic haiku that really makes you think. Nathan Bettenhausen, Spring 2010

confessional
alcohol breath
from his side of the grate

Aubrie Cox, Fall 2008; *Tea's Aftertaste*, p. 21

When editing the *Millikin University Haiku Anthology*, I remember running across so many of these "misbehaving in church" haiku. It seems to be a common subject for college students. I enjoy the twist in this one—it appears that the confessor is not the drinker! It could easily be paired up well with a haiku I have read about the priest tipping back communion wine! Melanie Mclay, Fall 2008

This haiku makes me think of a man down and out of luck. He's in a rough place in life and he doesn't know how to make it better. I sense that he used to be a church goer and hasn't been to church in a while but has decided to go back and see if he can find answers by doing a confessional. The man uses alcohol to cope with his feelings. He wasn't planning on drinking before his confessional, but his nerves got to him. The man may have needed liquid courage to even go through with the confessional. He needed liquid courage to face his sins, and to face them aloud with an audience. It's hard because he feels like he's facing them alone. Jenesi Moore, Fall 2018

used bookstore
with love
from no one I know

Aubrie Cox, Fall 2010; *Tea's Aftertaste*, p. 18

I love this haiku because it captures a special quality about print books, especially in a day and age when most things are becoming electronic. It gives print books a timelessness, with the idea that they can be passed on from person to person and that artwork can be shared by complete strangers, and yet they are connected on some level because they both read that book. It's just funny to think about, when you buy a used book, who else has read this book before you, and what they got out of it. I like that this haiku captures that idea. Morgan Oliver, Fall 2013

This haiku reminds me of when I was younger in school and they would pass out textbooks for the year. We would always anxiously wait to see whose name would be in the book we would get, because once you received the book you would have to write your name in it. You almost felt like that it connected you to that person in some way. You always hoped it would be one of the "popular" kid's name in your book. Then there is that disappointing feeling when you get a book with a name you do not know. Michelle Holsapple, July 2016

wilted lilacs . . .
your hand
slips from mine

Aubrie Cox, *Tea's Aftertaste*, p. 15

This one is a good example (to me anyway) of what a haiku is all about. It perfectly ties nature to humans. When I think of wilted lilacs, I think of something or someone dying. I lost my mother about 5 years ago. She loved lilacs and the last two lines remind me of her passing. The ending in my head has her smiling back at me, and her eyes saying, "until we meet again." Michael Means, July 2018

I loved this haiku because the first line "wilted lilacs" reminds me of dead flowers you don't want to throw away. It is such a nice feeling to walk into a room filled with fresh flowers that may be from someone you love. I often have a hard time throwing flowers away because I love them so much and I don't want to get rid of them. I wait until I really can't hang onto these dead flowers anymore before I throw them away. The rest of the haiku refers to a relationship slipping away. While the first line is relating to flowers, the flowers could be representative of the relationship itself. It was beautiful and happy at first, but the relationship is fading. Naomi Klingbeil, Fall 2018

distant galaxies
all the things
I could have been

Aubrie Cox, *Tea's Aftertaste*, p. 19

When reading the first line of this haiku, I began to envision the milky way, with millions and millions of stars, planets, and projectiles scattered throughout its belt. I was viewing this image from a third person perspective, as if I were floating throughout outer space. I saw purple and orange light waves scattered throughout the belt, as well as a few explosions. As I read on, the phrase "all the things I could have been" instantly shifted my perspective as if I were within the molecular level. I myself was existing as an atom of some sort. I was no longer in outer space, but amidst millions of other small particles and atoms buzzing around and about. I was now observing these small components that every "thing" in the universe is made up of. Then I envisioned the atoms coming together to form images of different things. At first, a human was formed from millions of matter particles. Then it diminished, and the atoms began to form an image of my father's veterinary clinic back home. And so, this continued, and I realized that I was imagining all of the things that technically could have existed if I were an arrangement of different atoms than I currently am. Logan Bader, Fall 2018

I have to look up when I read this haiku and be so very thankful for all the ways things have turned out for me. I truly have been blessed. Things could have turned out so differently than they did, but through grace and many prayers from amazing grandparents and parents, things are amazing. This haiku also reminds me that things are so much bigger than me. I strongly believe that without those prayers and guidance that things would be a lot different, and not in a good way. Michelle Holsapple, July 2016

The reason I like this haiku from Aubrie's collection is because it reminds me of the times that I randomly day-dream and think this exact same thought. It's crazy to think how big our solar system is sometimes and that we are just a tiny little pawn in this big game of chess. We can be anything we want to be in this life, although limited some. There is always that thought that, "what if I was doing this right now?" or "what if I had done this instead of that?" These are questions that have people pondering their decisions all the time, but it is also thrilling to think that you could be making a decision that could impact you for quite some time. Alex Koulos, Fall 2013

> father-daughter talk
> my fishing lure
> caught in the moon

> Aubrie Cox, *Tea's Aftertaste*, p. 25

When I read the first line, I automatically pictured my younger self sitting on our front porch at home looking up at my dad as he's telling me an old funny story and I'm just whole-heartedly eating it up. I love my dad so much and I've always been a "daddy's girl". We hang out all the time together whether it's canoeing or singing or even just being completely goofy together. That first line made me feel so warm and happy inside because for a brief moment in my mind I was back at home with him. The next two lines really set the stage for me though. Not only were we sitting on the front porch but now it was nighttime, and our front light was on and there's a full moon. The fishing lure caught in the moon is my dreams. The dreams I've had that my dad has always supported me to follow and pursue no matter what might get in the way. If one can reach for the moon, why wouldn't they. And the "talk" we are having is about him going back to the mistakes he's made in his life and not wanting me to make the same mistakes he did. He helped me cast that line and is the support pushing me to the moon. I also hear the cicadas and the frogs in the pond at our neighbor's house, but all of that is just background noise to what my dad has to say. Ahhh I love this poem – I'm still crying writing this summary. Hannah Haedike, Fall 2018

I really enjoy this haiku by Aubrie Cox because it brings back memories of going fishing and having various conversations with my father as I have grown up. My father taught me many different outdoor things and this haiku allows me to reflect on all of the moments we shared. I was the last child and he treated me as his little boy because he never got the opportunity to show a boy the things he loved and enjoyed. Although I sometimes got annoyed being shown all of the boy things, I really enjoyed the time I was able to spend with my dad and the different things he taught me. This haiku allows the reader to picture a fishing lure stuck in the far away moon. I took this as the conversations and journeys that the daughter and father would take throughout their lifetimes and the various discussions and activities that the two would go to that would make their relationship what it is today. Codi Gramlich, Fall 2013

the old lady dies
everyone comes
to the estate sale

Aubrie Cox, *Tea's Aftertaste*, p. 30

This haiku goes from sad to sadder. The first line states a fact: an old lady is dead. There is not much emotion behind this statement. It is simply stating what has happened. The next line: everyone comes, implies a bit more emotion. It sets the reader up to think that the last line would say something like: everyone comes… to her funeral. Everyone comes… to say goodbye. Everyone comes… to mourn. But instead it says everyone comes to the estate sale. Everyone comes to buy her things. To get a discount price. To buy antiques and knickknacks. To scrounge through what was once her life. It takes such a cold and drastic turn in just four words that my jaw dropped when I read it. Melanie Wilson, Fall 2018

I really loved this poem. I like how you expect it to end one way based off of the first two lines, but then the third line defies that expectation. After reading lines 1 and 2, I imagine that the event everyone is coming to is her funeral because maybe she has become beloved by many over the years. However, line 3 reveals that the large mass of people actually just shows up to her estate sale. The poem left me feeling sad for the woman even though I don't know whether she was a good person or not. I guess it doesn't matter who she was because the thought of someone's passing being viewed as only an opportunity to make material gains is a sad concept to me in general. Isabella Spiritoso, Fall 2018

autumn leaves
new neighbors
take down the tree house

Aubrie Cox, *Tea's Aftertaste*, p. 32

This haiku brings out the feelings of a lost childhood. It makes the child inside me sad to hear of a treehouse being torn down. This haiku is full of change beyond just new neighbors. This haiku shows a change out of childhood, also likely the loss of a friend. I like the word "leaves" in the opening line. Obviously, there are leaves in the tree, but I feel like it is talking about more than the tree. The old neighbor, likely a friend, left, childhood left, the fun of the treehouse left. "Leaves" seems to have a double meaning. Eve Greenwell, Spring 2015

I liked this haiku because, for me, the "autumn leaves" line is not only an image. While, yes, it does create an image of flaming red maple leaves dripping with water on a mist-filled October day, it also connects to the symbolic meaning of the season. Autumn is the time of year when things begin to die and go dormant. Like the season, new neighbors are moving in—signaling the end of the "season" of the old neighbors. And, even further, the demise of the treehouse, bringing about the end of a period of child-like joy and play, perhaps? Overall, the play gives me an odd sense of hope because, along with being a season of death and dying, autumn leads to winter, and then to spring—the season of rebirth. There is hope in a possible relationship with these new neighbors even though they have torn down a relic from the old ones. Daria Koon, Fall 2018

overgrown bridge
I tread lightly
through my childhood

Aubrie Cox, *Tea's Aftertaste*, p. 35

When reading the very first line, I picture the bridge to Terabithia—a wooden bridge that almost has a curved center, but it's overgrown with beautiful flowers and vines. There are wood railings on the side which keep people safe as they cross the bridge and the bridge is definitely over a stream or a creek. The stream has various rocks, causing little ripples which I hear with each step I take across the bridge. For me, the bridge is what's leading back into my childhood. It's a metaphor for going back into the past and that's why I'm treading lightly. The past is known, but it's also foreign to who we are in the present. With each step, I'm reminded of a place I visited in my past. This could also be taken very literally, in the sense that this author is visiting her childhood home which had a bridge. That bridge is now overgrown, representing the time which has gone by and she's reminiscing on her childhood days when she would play and run across this bridge, but it's bittersweet which is why she's handling it lightly. But, if you noticed, I switched back to talking about the author rather than making it a personal experience with that specific interpretation. And I really like the fact that art can be personal for everyone and represent a different story and meaning for everyone— so, I shall stick to my bridge to Terabithia meaning. Hannah Haedike, Fall 2018

What I really liked about this poem was the imagery. It made me feel sort of nostalgic picturing a bridge, possibly placed over a creek in a woodsy backyard, that the narrator used to play on. It takes me back to my childhood and the times that my brother and I would go and play in the creek in our backyard. The fact that the bridge is overgrown leads me to believe that the bridge has been abandoned for a while and forgotten. I begin to imagine the strong sense of nostalgia and warmth that the narrator must feel when they walk over that bridge and remember the days that they walked over that bridge in their childhood; maybe the bridge was used as a shortcut to walk to a friend's house, or possibly to school. In the vision I've created, I see green leaves above my head, green moss and vines growing over the natural wood bridge under my feet, and clear water flowing below the bridge over smooth mossy rocks. I hear the rustling of wind through the leaves in the trees and I feel the breeze through my shirt. This poem creates a full scene in my mind. Isabella Spiritoso, Fall 2018

Chapter 2

The Art of Writing Contemporary Haiku

A Continuous Kukai

In many ways, the Global Haiku Traditions course could be characterized as a continuous "kukai" in which students read, find, and discuss favorite haiku from haiku publications AND students read, find and discuss favorite haiku written by each other throughout the semester. Through this process of seeking and discussing favorites, my students develop both the art of reading and the art of writing haiku.

Throughout the class students write 8 to 10 "haiku attempts" in a journal for each class period. They submit these attempts to me, and I select the best of their work for anonymous kukai. We have kukai frequently throughout the semester. Here is a quick version of our kukai process.

(1) Students receive a sheet with all of the selected haiku without author names.
(2) Students read the kukai selections and mark their favorite ones.
(3) Students share favorite haiku—reading it out loud and talking about why they love it. Other students join in the reader response discussion, sharing their imagined responses and what they love about the haiku.
(4) We have a show of hands counting how many people love that haiku. (Yes, students may decide to vote for it after hearing the shared discussion even if they did not mark it as a favorite before).
(5) Then we ask who wrote this haiku and celebrate the "birth" of their haiku with applause of some sort: tapping of pens, clapping, snapping fingers, etc. A haiku does not exist until it finds a reader who loves it.
(6) The 3 to 4 top vote winners receive a haiku publication (books or issues of haiku magazines) as a reward.

In kukai, participants are not allowed to say disparaging words about a haiku. Kukai is not an editing session. It is not a writing workshop seeking improvements to flawed haiku attempts. It is simply finding and enjoying haiku that we love—just the way they are written. After the oral kukai process, I ask students to write about their favorite 2 to 3 haiku. These written responses are posted on the class web site along with the names of authors for haiku that have been loved and "born" in kukai.

Often students write their 8 to 10 haiku based on prompts related to perceptions that students are currently experiencing. However, "open topic" haiku are always welcome. I encourage students to get a journal and to just write haiku whenever haiku arrive, but most of the students follow the prompts. At the beginning of a semester, one of the first prompts is to write haiku about times of transition: waking up, dawn, dusk, summer's end, going back to school, or changes in consciousness. Here are some of the haiku shared and born in kukai related to this prompt.

Favorite Haiku on Times of Transitions

changing the clocks
I fall back
into old habits

Aubrie Cox, *Out of Translation*, p. 19

This haiku makes me giggle a little. It reminds me of every time something new happens—like a new year, clocks changing, or something of that nature—we promise ourselves we will stop doing something or start exercising. But each time we fall back into old habits. We always seem to want to stay in our comfort zone even if we are not fully happy with what that is. We seem to always be more comfortable with not changing and being not fully happy with ourselves. Michelle Hosapple, July 2016

back to the future
familiar faces
in my new hometown

Mackenzie Martin, Fall 2017

This haiku begins with the mention of the famous movie series, *Back to the Future*, and from there uses it as a play on words. It is relatable to all college students, because it describes their journey of going home for the first time, maybe Thanksgiving break, after being away at college for a while. The faces are familiar and comforting, but the hidden line here is that you are almost mortified by the faces, wondering if ending up back in your hometown is your eventual future. On the flip side, maybe your hometown is already so distant and old to you that you feel disconnected to it, as if it is a "new hometown." Mackenzie Martin, Fall 2017

old faces
I used to know
their smiles

Hannah Haedike, Fall 2018

This haiku brought me back to my hometown on a break. I imagine being at our local restaurant everyone loves and running into old friends. Maybe it has been months or even years since we have spoken; but at one point in time, we spoke every day. It's weird seeing them on social media or running into them at a local restaurant and not knowing really anything about their current situation. Naomi Klingbeil, Fall 2018

morning chill
you usually made
the coffee

Francesca Rios, Spring 2015

I like this haiku because it speaks to regret. I like the cold feeling of loneliness. I like the memory of what was. The phrase "usually made" shows that it was a habit, not something that both sides of the partnership hoped for or expected. Lexy Bieber, Spring 2015

the rain slowing
my body rests
against yours

Betsy Quigg, *Millikin University Haiku Anthology*, 32

I feel like cuddling inside during a rainstorm is one of the best feelings in the world. It's quiet, and you can feel the other person's skin and heartbeat while listening to the rain tapping on the window or hitting the roof. You don't close your eyes and experience the other senses, like the smell of their cologne and the warmth of your skin touching theirs. Aundrea Marsh, Fall 2015

I liked this one because it can be a comforting or a sexual haiku. The rain slowing can be literal, or it can mean a shower of tears slowing. It would be comforting because I know, personally, I like to be held after I've cried. The comfort of leaning on someone helps calms me down and it's nice. The literal way puts an image of two people either actually outside in the rain, or inside next to a window where they can hear or see the rain. As the rain slows, the bodies resting together calm and breathing slows down. I just like the calming effect and the play of slowing and resting. Kari Thornton, Spring 2010

deleting Facebook friends
draining the water
from macaroni

Alec Campbell, Fall 2014

I like this haiku because at first glance it seems like it is about two very different topics, but after a closer look these topics are connected. Deleting Facebook friends is getting rid of something that is no longer needed, just like draining water from macaroni to leave only the desired pasta. Also, these events form a visual of a person so casually doing both of these tasks as just going through the motions, unaware of the irony of these events going together. Trista Smith, Fall 2014

I absolutely loved this haiku ever since I first read it. I just went through deleting over forty of my Facebook friends. Sometimes you just need to take control of your life and filter what you see on this social media site. Certain people can be so negative and do not have a place in your life. I love that he connected this action to macaroni because I adore food. Rebecca Coutcher, Fall 2014

seeing his face
first time in years
delete

Hannah Ottenfield, Fall 2018

For this haiku, I imagined a girl around my age scrolling through Tinder. Nothing about it is particularly out of the ordinary until she sees an old ex-boyfriend. She hesitates as she remembers the time they spent together. They were young, fifteen or sixteen, and they used to spend every second together. They'd go out to the movies, out to eat, to the park, to family gatherings, everything. And now, they're basically strangers. For a minute, it's hard to resist the urge to swipe right. But she knows better than to let an old flame rekindle—she swipes left. Sophie Kibiger, Fall 2018

break up text
she cuts bangs straight
in a mirror

Randy Brooks, Fall 2018

I liked this poem because of the emotion it brings up without using emotional phrases or words. By juxtaposing a break up text with cutting her bangs, the reader fills in the gap with what led her to do so. I personally interpreted it as an impulsive decision brought on by a heartbreaking message. I also find it interesting in movies and other media, the trope of someone getting a haircut after a breakup is common. That idea in the haiku can connect to many even if they have not experienced it personally. Rachel Pevehouse, Fall 2018

Chapter 3

Reading Selected Haiku of Peggy Lyles

The Open-Handed Gift

In the first third of the semester students read and respond to collections of selected haiku by outstanding contemporary haiku authors. A collection of selected haiku features the best haiku by a single author, usually written over several decades. I explain that these collections are often edited by a team of readers reviewing an author's published work and selecting their favorite haiku to be included in the book. Then the author and editor make final selections and arrangement of the haiku for an ideal reading experience—planning an order to the haiku and avoiding undesirable pairings of haiku on a page. Since authors usually have only one or two collections of selected haiku published in a lifetime, such books often provide excellent introductions and prefaces discussing the author's approach to writing haiku. Therefore, these collections of selected haiku are an ideal way for new readers to gain an understanding and appreciation of different approaches to haiku. As students read each collection, they are asked to write reader responses to favorite haiku before we share and discuss the haiku together in class. The students are also asked to write original haiku in response to the author's work. Sometimes students are prompted to address similar issues or to try particular techniques or approaches evident in the author's collection of haiku. The first collection students read in the Global Haiku Traditions course is *To Hear the Rain: Selected Haiku of Peggy Lyles*.

Reading Haiku by Peggy Willis Lyles

Peggy Lyles' collection is an excellent introduction to the art of reading contemporary haiku. In her preface she describes haiku as "open-ended and open-handed poems, capable of receiving, being, and giving all at once. Expressed in simple language, they invite the reader to participate as co-creator. Sometimes they seem to leap from heart to heart" (p. 9). Peggy Lyles provides more specific guidance on reading haiku: "How do I want you to read these pieces of the story of my life? Slowly. Individually. More than once. Preferably aloud. Above all, I want you to read them with assurance of their essential honesty, and faith that what you find in them is what they mean and are. I hope the poems link to your sensory perceptions and affirm a connection between what Robert Frost called inner and outer weather. I hope they touch your sense of wonder, stirring responses that make the sharing mutual. I hope they spark the desire, new or renewed, to write and share your own haiku" (p. 11). Here are examples of student responses that show they have taken her advice to heart in their reading and writing of haiku.

lingering heat
the third-grade classroom
one desk short

Peggy Lyles, *To Hear the Rain*, p. 30

This one is very vivid for me. I can feel the heavy, hot air in August and see myself walking into the class. There's always that awkward staring to begin with because it's like you're an alien from another world. Then the situation gets worse as you search for a seat and realize the class is one desk short for you. It creates that unwanted, awkward tension. I like this one because I have had similar situations every time I've moved schools. Kari Thornton, Spring 2010

Reading this haiku brought me to my mom's classroom. I look around the room and can see colorful posters hanging from the walls. Each desk has a nametag and several books sitting on the top awaiting the students. I imagine my mom hunting down a custodian to get an extra desk for her and contemplating how she is going to rearrange the seating arrangement to accommodate the extra student. I can see the sun shining through the window, and even with the air conditioning on in the room, you can still feel the heat from outside. Allyson Isenhower, Spring 2018

I cannot help but imagine myself in this situation as a future teacher. When I read this, I can almost feel the heat building up inside me. Hot classrooms are a problem in many schools that don't have air conditioning. The line "lingering heat" makes my skin feel sticky with sweat. The third-grade classroom where I imagine teaching is not only hot from the obvious lack of cool air or breeze, but also because I have worked so hard to prepare for the first day of class. Of course, I am one desk short; the first problem of the long grueling day arises. However, how will I handle this situation? Will I let this heat of frustration linger for the rest of the day and rub off on my students or do I clear my brow of sweat and forge on to solve the problem? Alyssa Becker, Fall 2016

for her mother
bluets
roots and all

Peggy Lyles, *To Hear the Rain*, p. 19

This haiku brought a really vivid picture to mind after I looked up what bluets were and reread the poem. In my mind, I saw a young mother sitting on the porch steps of a house out in the country. She's relaxing in the sun while she watches her young daughter, a toddler, playing in the yard. Her daughter brings the once rooted flowers to her mother, bursting with pride at the gift she brought. She has those tiny, chubby toddler hands clasped around the flowers. It's a beautiful moment between mother and daughter. I can see the colors clearly, feel the sun on my face, and hear the summer breeze and the happy gurgling of the child. I am flabbergasted that I get all of this imagery from three lines of text and seven words. Marah Kittelson, Spring 2016

I imagine a little girl running through the neighborhood on a Saturday afternoon. She is on the search to find her mother the most beautiful flowers that she has ever seen. She comes to the back of a house that has a garden full of different flowers. She sees the ones she wants her mother to put in a vase on the dinner table. She starts picking these flowers by hand and is thinking wow I can't wait for my mom to see these. She gets home and into the kitchen and says mom these are for you. Mother says these are beautiful, but honey where did you get these. She said from the neighbor's back yard. Her mother says we must go and apologize for this. The little girl asks why? Her mother says because you have brought me not just the flower but the roots and everything; they will no longer be able to grow these again if we don't give part of them back. Jacqueline Davis, November 2014

I love this haiku, because it brings back the innocence of childhood. I imagined a little girl of five or six, her blond hair in messy disarray and her smiling face streaked with dirt, clutching a fistful of wildflowers that she plucked for her mother. I pictured tangled roots with dirt clods hanging precariously from them, the stems of the flowers bruised in the girl's grasp. Despite the flowers' perhaps ruined appearance, the mother accepts them with a smile and a swelling heart, touched by the girl's display of love. It is not the appearance of the flowers that makes her happy, but the adoration and thoughtfulness of her little girl. Mackenzie Peck, Fall 2014

> yellow leaves
> a girl plays hopscotch
> by herself

> Peggy Lyles, *To Hear the Rain*, p. 33

I like this poem because it shows the independence of the girl who can have fun without the company of others. Peggy Lyles places "yellow leaves" as the first line because it forces you to picture a warm and peaceful day during the fall season. The second line lets you know what she is doing as the last line says how she is doing it. You wonder who she is playing with but then soon find out she's alone. Briana Curtis, June 2016

I remember in elementary school, way back before me and my friends could drive, I loved to spend clear, crisp autumn afternoons playing outside in the yard. I live in a cul-de-sac, which makes for a perfect bicycle path around and around my neighborhood that is still close enough for my mother to watch me play. I was very intrigued by the fact that the line 'by herself' stands on its own at the end. I have always been one to enjoy pockets of alone time throughout the day, so being by myself is an enjoyable thing. Some people might be tempted to bring in a hint of sadness and loneliness to this one, since the girl is by herself. I just imagine myself on those afternoons winding down after school and enjoying myself and being outside. Laura Scoville, Fall 2010

> family graveyard
> a boy finds his middle name
> on the oldest stone

> Peggy Lyles, *To Hear the Rain*, p. 30

I love how not only in this poem, but in many of her poems, Peggy Lyles writes about family bond. In this poem, she writes about a boy whose middle name is the same as the name of a very old family member from a different generation that he probably never met. What is cool about this is that even though the boy and the old man never met and came from practically different worlds, they are still bonded together through family. It is amazing to think that two people who are completely different in every way can have absolutely nothing in common except a name and blood. This poem shows how strong familial bond is and how it can connect people in a way that nothing else can. Isabella Spiritoso, Fall 2018

This was the first haiku to pop out at me because it immediately created a clear image in my head as well as resonated with me emotionally. I imagine a gloomy sky, with dark grey clouds as if it is about to rain. A little boy is walking among gravestones, observing each one, until he comes upon one that has the same middle name as him. To me this haiku is almost like a connection of life and death. The "boy" is young and doesn't understand much about death, yet he is somehow connected to this person that came before him. I also thought that this haiku provided an overall mood of nostalgia and wonder. Trey DeLuna, Fall 2017

Upon reading this, I was transported to Litfchfield, Illinois. There's a cemetery there that houses most of my deceased family. As a child, I would wander through the stones, playing with spiders and touching the engraved dates and letters. I looked for names I knew and found plenty. For me, this haiku evokes big trees full of evergreen tones; I see wolf spiders that are bigger than my child-sized palm; I hear my father tell stories of those who lay under the grass, and I realize that cemeteries are silent homecoming parties for both the living and the dead. I don't mean that in a morbid sense. Simply, I understood at a young age that death is not always a terribly alienating thing. I learned to find peace with the presence of death, and to me, this haiku represents a child coming to terms with that same notion. Taylor Hagerdorn, Fall 2014

> oval frame
> a woman curves
> around her child

> Peggy Lyles, *To Hear the Rain*, p. 44

A frame holds the mother and the mother holds the child. This haiku almost made me think of a Russian nesting doll but in the sweetest most meaningful way. The author seems to be combining shapes and making different shapes work together to build a larger image and moment. I like how this haiku works by building the image slowly with each line. First you get the picture of the oval frame, then the curves of a woman, and finally those feminine curves and shapes encircle her most precious possession, her own child. It is the ultimate spiritual comfort and physiological perfection to make this haiku intimate and relatable as child and mother. Jessica Brooks, January 2015

This haiku is about a pregnant woman. The oval frame is her stomach expanding as the fetus grows inside her. I like the phrasing of this haiku, "a woman curves around her child" shows how the mother is changing, growing, adapting to her child. Not that the baby grows inside her, not that the fetus imposes itself in the uterus. "a woman curves around her child". These phrases show the sacrifice and selflessness a woman makes when she has a child. Not only is her body curving around the baby, but her whole life will change when the baby is born. She will always come second to her child. Her life will shift and curve to fit the needs of the child. Melanie Wilson, Fall 2018

I loved this haiku. I am very close to my mom, and this made me think of her. The two of us are interested in a lot of "fun" facts about everything, and one of them that we like to focus on is the six-second hug and how that influences the release of dopamine and other happy chemicals in the brain. Every day when she gets home, we stand in our kitchen and give each other at least a six-second hug before we do anything else, and reading this haiku took me directly into my kitchen, and I could almost feel her arms around me as I read it. In addition, it also reminded me of a necklace she wears almost every day. It is an oval with two dots at the top representing a mother and child. At the bottom of the oval are two gemstones, hers and mine. The oval represents the mother and child embracing. This was another image that accompanied my reading of the haiku. Daria Koon, Fall 2018

mother-daughter
small talk
snap beans

Peggy Lyles, *To Hear the Rain*, p. 48

I really like this haiku because I picture a mother and daughter spending quality time together, either gardening or cooking a family dinner. It reminds me of my relationship with my mom. She and I garden together; I help her water her plants when I am home for the summer. I also help her cook sometimes, and vegetables such as beans are something we eat often. Although my mom doesn't grow beans in our garden, she does grow green peppers and tomatoes. The one thing in this haiku that I cannot connect to is the small talk part. I would imagine that the small talk is indicative of a distant or frayed relationship between the mother and daughter. The second line leads me to believe that the daughter must be older, married and maybe with kids and something happened to distance her from her mother. Morgan Vogels, Fall 2016

I see a mother and her teenage daughter sitting on the back porch of their farm house. There is a large metal pot between them that they throw the beans in for dinner. The daughter has not helped her mother out a lot lately and has reluctantly sat down to help with the beans. The mother feels sad because she can feel the disconnect between her daughter and herself. They struggle to maintain a conversation, but they both realize that anything would be better than silence. It's a warm summer evening, and both women have sweat beads forming on their foreheads. The beans offer a crisp crack with each snap. Jenna Pelej, Spring 2007

When I was twelve, my mother passed away. I fortunately have many memories of having small talk with my mother about everything. We were close and had been through a lot as a family. I do, however, have a few younger siblings. The first line immediately made me think of how my sister does not have many memories with our mother. The haiku does not say anything about the relationship at this point, but I often think about this anyway. The next lines further enforced my thoughts that my sister will never have an opportunity to have those memories with my mother. By this I mean she will never have the small talk memories about silly things like what partners she likes, what dress to wear to homecoming, or bigger topics like what she should do with her life. This haiku broke my heart. Zachary McReynolds, Fall 2018

Saturday
he whistles as he turns
the children's pancakes

Peggy Lyles, *To Hear the Rain*, p. 56

The sun is pouring through the windows around the small kitchen. The light gives everything a yellow tint but seems to make everything happier. He's standing at the stove, whistling and smiling. His face shows no signs of wrinkles; it looks like he'll stay young forever. The children are sitting at the table, being as patient as they can be. Mom stands in the corner, where the counter top and the fridge meet. She's just watching, taking in her family and remembering this moment. She sees her husband happy, making pancakes for the family they created together. She sees her kids, extremely excited for the meal they are about to share. She smiles to herself with the knowledge that this is one memory she'll never forget. And she never did forget it, as it was one of the last happy memories of her husband. Corrin Littlefield, Spring 2016

This haiku made me think of a family of four. The kids just woke up to the sweet smell of bacon. They come downstairs and see dad is making pancakes and are overjoyed. They don't waste any time in running around the house playing tag. Mom is sitting at the table reading the newspaper and drinking her first cup of coffee. This poem also makes me think of when I was a little girl and when my dad would make me and my sister breakfast in the morning. It would always be such a beautiful morning, waking up to the bright sun, and the smell of breakfast being made. The author really gives you an image of what she wants you to imagine while reading this poem, without saying a lot. Alyssa Rodriguez, Spring 2018

When I was young Saturday meant no school, cartoons, and pancakes for breakfast, made by my father. The word Saturday sets this tone of carefree elation, as I would have felt at the thought of having no school for a whole two days. When we were younger, I think the days seemed longer. For some reason, Saturday seemed the longest, and the most fun. Because my dad made our breakfast, this haiku makes me think immediately of him; he is also an expert whistler, and I remember him often whistling the theme to the "Andy Griffith Show". The second line is interesting, because it seems to me that the person described could be turning in response to children's inquiries about when the pancakes are ready or turning merely to have a conversation with a child as he cooks. In the same way, he also cheerfully turns the cakes on the griddle. Because of this dual meaning of the word "turns", I believe the man in this poem to be a kind, loving care-taker. My own father is this way. Sarah E. Kisly, Spring 2013

> snowed in
> the wedding-ring quilt
> lumpy with children

> Peggy Lyles, *To Hear the Rain*, p. 64

This reminds me of weekends at home with my kids when we don't have anything to do. Instead of everyone waking up early for school or work we actually get to sleep in. No alarm clocks going off, we all get to wake up on our own. Typically, our youngest daughter, Chloe, who is 7 years old, will be the first one to come in. She creeps in, climbs in bed with us, takes turns snuggling me and then rolls over to give her dad a turn. We start to stir around as our son, Jeric, who is 14 years old comes in. He picks a spot to get under the covers as well. By that time everyone starts getting a little more awake and is moving around. We spend a little time just being together and enjoying not being rushed. My husband and son usually start teasing one another with a poke or a pinch until it will progress into a full-on wrestling match. This is when my oldest daughter, Kenzie, who is 17 years old, finally comes in to see what woke her up and decides to find her own spot in the bed along with our family dog. What was once a peaceful bed is now a wrestling ring with 5 people and a dog. The covers always end up on the floor and the girls are always literally kicked out of the bed. We head down to make breakfast at that time. In a busy life it is nice to have times like this when it is just us. Stacey Longfellow, July 2013

This particular haiku made me feel many different emotions. The first line of the poem left me feeling cold to the bone. It took me back to a couple times as a child that we got snowed in and no matter how high we turned the thermostat it was still just plain cold. The second line left me with a much warmer and kinder feeling. My grandma has always been known for her great quilt making. They really are pieces of art. I can remember her working hours on all different shapes and colors of materials placing them together like puzzle pieces. The last line of this haiku left me with a full smile across my face. My children are 11 and 13 years old. They still, to this day, will sneak into our bed on mornings that we sleep late. We all twist, turn, grunt and laugh until everyone finds their place. Elbows kissing kneecaps, it really is a special time! Kimberly Hanners, November 2012

traffic jam
my small son asks
who made God

Peggy Lyles, *To Hear the Rain*, p. 57

This haiku makes me think of the chaos and noise that surround early morning, rush hour traffic jams. In a moment filled with frustration and stress, the little boy's voice cuts through with a calming innocence. I almost hear a powerful silence when I read the little boy's question in the third line. Alternatively, I think that the traffic jam could be symbolic of being "stuck" because answering the little boy's complex, yet simple question is an incredibly tall order. Either way, the haiku helps remind me to take in each moment and be present where you are because the rush and chaos of life around you can be so distracting that you accidentally ignore special, small moments. Brittani Allen, November 2014

I could not help but pause my reading for several minutes after coming across this haiku because of how strongly it resonated with me. The first line sets up a rather hectic environment—cars honking, irritable people in their cars, possibly running late for some engagement or other. A small boy enters the scene in the second line, someone who is likely not concerned about running late or escaping traffic. Children it seems tend to ask questions that adults no longer think to ask, and generally do not know how to answer—such as, "who made God". This haiku caused me to reflect on how adults often become preoccupied with day to day troubles, such as traffic, and often neglect the big picture and big ideas. One thing I really liked about this haiku is the contrast between the "small son" and "God"—a small person asking about a big idea. The haiku ends there, but I imagine a flustered mother in her car, grappling with complicated answers to her son's simple question, still amid honking cars—a moment of reflection in the middle of what might be a highly stressful day. Emma Prendergast, Spring 2012

This haiku was extremely near to my heart, as a Christian. As I began reading, I envisioned the line of rush hour traffic leading out of a large city—cars backed up as far as the mother's vision allowed. A mother and son sit together in the silent car. She is consumed with the stress of the day—hoping her old, blue Mazda will make it home once again—while he sits silently, swinging his legs, and gazing out the window at the adjacent cars. Then at the perfect moment, he turns to his mother, with the most inquisitive eyes, to ask "who made God." With the silence broken, the mother cannot help but to smile and forget the stress of the day. Reading this haiku, brought back memories of my own childhood questions and discussions with my mother. She would always take time out for my questions. I can feel the warmth of her smile. Alida Duff, Spring 2004 clay on the wheel I confess my faith

Peggy Lyles, *To Hear the Rain*, p. 60

This haiku is different than a lot of the other ones I have read in that it is formatted in one single line, giving it the feeling of being rushed. I am religious, and so the picture that this poem brings to me is one of an adolescent person literally confessing their faith. There is a song that has the lyrics, "You are the potter/ I am the clay. Mold me and make me/ this is what I pray." That is the song that I hear and that this poem reminds me of— the young person knows that they are not perfect, and they have impurities that need to be worked out. They are only the clay, and they are inviting "The Potter" to shape them into what they need to be. I like that it has a rushed feeling; I think it captures the nervousness and sense of relief that people have when they finally confess that they are not perfect and accept the change. I literally picture a lump of clay on a potter's wheel being spun around and molded into a person, the wet clay running over the potter's fingers and pooling on the wheel. I hear the whir of the wheel and the squelching of the clay as it is shaped. Hailee Peck, Spring 2012

I just recently began learning how to throw on the wheel, something I had not attempted since my sophomore year in high school. Right now, it's very frustrating and taking a while to figure out, but I think that's an incredible element of faith. Faith requires trusting that things are going to work out, and in the ceramic's world, faith is understanding that it's going to suck for a while before it can get better. Taryn Pepping, Spring 2016

This haiku reminds me of the darkest and saddest times of my life. Divorce, a new life, starting over, me and my sons. Broken, torn, confused, and all alone. This is where I found intimacy with God and my relationship with Him truly began. My faith made me the woman I am today, and I know nothing is impossible with Him. Isaiah 64 tells me "He is the potter and I am the clay. He will restore and remold everything that was taken away." Ocamie Outlaw, November 2014.

summer night
we turn out all the lights
to hear the rain

Peggy Lyles, *To Hear the Rain*, p. 45

I love this haiku a lot because of the fact that I can relate to this on so many levels. I love it when it rains in the summertime. There is something about the way the rain hits the ground that is really calming. The sound is soothing. Then, there is the smell of the rain. It's not a strong smell, but more of a light, earthy smell. To me, summer nights and rain make me think of a clean slate. This poem makes me think of someone sitting by a window and drinking some tea while looking out of the window. It feels almost as if the world has stopped for a moment, there is a stillness. Alyssa Rodriguez, Spring 2018

Summer night! Right off the bat, I am reminded of my childhood and my adolescence, where having wonder for all things was commonplace. The idea of "summer night" is fiercely open-ended, with room for love under the moonlight, serious heart-to-hearts, and walks along a beach's dark horizon. "We" promises partnership in the haiku and offers refuge for the narrator's other person/people. I seriously fell in love with this haiku's spirit—turning off the lights is an extremely juvenile delight and savoring those delights for special moments past one's childhood is enlightening. And, finally—the sound of the rain washed over me. I can close my eyes and hear it. Unobstructed, unashamed, and unmonitored. Melting into a sound of nature requires a heightened awareness, and it unapologetically begs for a focused mindfulness. Furthermore, this acquired awareness is being shared between people, on a summer night, where the rain could go on forever. Kala Keller, Spring 2017

I really love summer. Every time I hear the phrase "summer night" I think of the emotional connection I have to boating at night. Night boating is so peaceful; it is my way of connecting with nature. As I read about turning out all the lights, I pictured a family turning off their technology and enjoying the company of each other, something I've recently recognized as valuable. While turning off the lights doesn't affect the ability of someone to hear raindrops, the metaphor is that of truly focusing on the beauty that is nature, especially a warm summer rain. From this haiku, I can smell the warmth of summer air and feel the moisture of a warm summer rain. Adam Peters, Spring 2015

> winter night
> he patiently untangles
> her antique silver chain

> Peggy Lyles, *To Hear the Rain*, p. 65

This haiku makes me envision an older couple walking in the evening, possibly after dinner or church. I can feel the love between the husband and wife, and that love is illustrated by the care the husband takes to untangle his wife's necklace from her scarf. The colors are not very vibrant, but more muted tones of gray, white, black and silver. The winter night line provides the temperature setting of the haiku, but I also thought of the 'winter' stage of one's life, which was how I decided it was an elderly couple. I also thought it could be an older couple because of the antique silver chain, possibly a gift from their courtship a long time ago. Jenna Pelej, Spring 2007

Winter nights are so vividly cliché and warm in my head. Deep reds and browns, a fire, hot chocolate and peace. I really enjoy tasks that require dexterity and a gentle approach; to me, undoing knots in necklaces is so rewarding and calming. The antique silver chain makes me wonder: who does the chain belong to? What moments did the chain witness? Is it part of an heirloom? Is she young or old? What is her relationship to the man? I see many combinations, but particularly a young woman, reclined on a couch with a book. The man, her significant other, has warm evening light in his eyes as he picks at the knot in the chain. He cares for her immensely, so he performs his task willingly and with the utmost care. Taylor Hagerdorn, Fall 2014

I imagine a man alone in a warm house on a cold night in January. The windows are dark and snow clumps on their sills, but I picture a fire crackling at the hearth to heat the room. The antique silver chain gleams dully in the dim firelight. I can imagine the feel of the twisted chains between the man's fingertips, the ache in his back from bending over the necklace, and the stiffness he feels from sitting in the same place for too long. The chain gives off the smell of metal, similar to the way one's hands smell after handling coins. I read this as a poem of silence. The night is quiet and calm, and though the fire crackles, so intent is the man on his task that he does not notice. Natalie Perfetti, Spring 2009

into the night
we talk of human cloning
snowflakes

Peggy Lyles, *To Hear the Rain*, p. 67

"Into the night" is a better start to this haiku than something like "into the morning" would be. At night, the kids are asleep, and the adults can talk of heavier things. Night is stillness and mystery and darkness. Everyone is on a more level playing field in the dark, making the human cloning aspect of this haiku that much more appropriate. The snowflakes are also important to this juxtaposition. Every snowflake is supposed to be unique, but when you pair that idea with the idea of human cloning, you get a really cool comparison between the two that helps bring new life to the haiku. However, since humans aren't cloned (as of yet), we have more in common with the snowflakes. We are all unique and we all have differences that complicate our lives in more ways than one. But that's okay. In the night, we're all a little like human clones. The dark makes us the same. Alexa Duncan, June 2016

This haiku stood out to me as a biology major. People tend to settle down at night after a busy day. Families gather in a common place and just talk. Their talks range from minuscule subjects to present day conflicts and fantasies. Successful human cloning will be amazing and frightening all at once. I found the last line ironic. The word snowflakes may not necessarily be talking about the weather. I have read that no two snowflakes are ever exactly the same. This is foreshadowing no two humans will ever be the same even when successfully cloned. Nurture vs. nature will change the outcome of how a human is molded. Kailey Hurst, January 2016

This haiku by Peggy Lyles seems much more serious than her other poems. It makes me think of the serious conversations I've had with my son that just go late into the night and you can't remember where they even started. The language "we talk" means to me that this is a relaxed discussion, an exchange of ideas—not a heated debate. Human cloning is such a controversial subject with many negatives and some potential huge positives. At first thought, human cloning sounds so boring with everyone being the same. However, human cloning can also represent the potential for new organs for people who need transplants and hope for children who were born with disabilities. Snowflakes at the end reminds us that we are beautiful, special and unique, just as each snowflake is beautiful, special and unique. Cindie Zelhart, Spring 2007

attic sun
from Grandmother's gown
a grain of rice

Peggy Lyles, *To Hear the Rain*, p. 69

I like this poem a lot. I see a young girl and her mother up in the attic of an old house. The grandmother has maybe just passed away and her daughter and granddaughter are cleaning out the attic when they discover grandmother's wedding dress tucked away in the very last box. Suddenly the only things in the attic are the mother, the daughter, and grandmother's old, slightly yellowed wedding dress. The moment is quiet, fragile—and then a single grain of rice falls from the folds of the skirt to the wood floor below. And then the tears follow. This poem reminded me of my own grandmother, whose wedding dress I have in a box in the back of my closet. This poem took me to another place and made me happy and sad at the same time. Nicole Wells, Spring 2018

My grandmother passed away last year. My family has spent months sorting through her estate and reflecting on the sentimental items she left behind. Precious keepsakes saw her through sixty years of marriage, two children, six grandchildren, and ten great-grandchildren. All of these lives were made possible because of the love of two people married in a small country church in the middle of the great depression. The writer's technique transports the reader to an attic dimly lit by the filtered light of the sun. The simplicity of the poem's first line captures the dust motes, musky scent, and creaky floors. Following the break, the writer shares a discovery—a gown. But not just any gown, a wedding dress. Falling from the dress is a single grain of rice. The rice symbolizes the blessing of fertility and good fortune bestowed upon a newly married couple. The fulfillment of this blessing brings into existence the finder of the memento—the grandchild. Jennifer Yeakley, July 2017

This haiku made me smile because it seemed so peaceful and the emotions it evoked were really warm and safe. I could see a young woman going through things in her attic randomly, but then stopping at the discovery of her grandmother's dress. The woman holds the dress up to herself, remembering the time her grandmother told her the story of her wedding day. While she is holding the dress up, the grain of rice falls to the wood floor. The rice is an additional memory of that special day; a little piece of the celebration. To me, the sun represents the love of the grandmother. Jenna Pelej, Spring 2007

> dress by dress
> the story of her life
> day lilies close

> Peggy Lyles, *To Hear the Rain*, p. 83

When I read this haiku, I picture myself as an old woman looking through my closet. Each dress holds a memory. I picture dresses from school dances, dresses I wore to important events throughout my life, a wedding dress, and the dresses I will wear when I am an old woman. I love dresses and wear them all the time when the weather allows it, and I will take any excuse to dress up. As I look at each dress, I am reminded of different times in my life when that dress was something I wore, or in the case of a wedding dress, I reflect back on my wedding day. The day lilies are closing, so it must be night time. I picture myself looking at my dresses with a fond memory of everything, putting on my pajamas, and going to bed. Courtney Burress, Spring 2013

I read this poem two ways. My first reading was of a girl going through her closet, looking for a dress to wear when she goes out that night. As she goes through her dresses, she is reminded of all the stories that the dresses hold. The bad first date dress, the "drank-a-little-too-much dress," the bridesmaid's dress. Every dress has a story, and depending on those stories, (along with the style) chooses what she will wear. The other reading that I had was darker. I read it as a family going through a recently deceased relative's closet, seeing the dresses and thinking back to all the memories of her in those dresses and their stories. The last line of the haiku is the reason why I like this reading because I think of a sense of youth and beauty when I read it, bringing out that this woman was beautiful and filled with youthful joy and that her life has come to a close. Nicholas Sanders, Spring 2015

I felt a very real connection to this haiku as I think of my Grandmother. It has been one year since she has been gone. My grandmother was a very elegant woman. She always looked beautiful when she had to get dressed up. She had a closet that was as long as the wall in her bedroom and it was full of clothes. We found clothes from twenty years ago in this closet and I think even longer than that. My mother and I had to go back to her house to find a dress for the funeral. The moment I walked in the house I could feel the pain of how much I would miss her. I walked up the stairs of her house and stopped at her bedroom door. I looked around to see all of her things just as she had left them. The tears began to swell in my eyes as I looked at pictures next to her neatly made bed. I opened the closet doors and saw the clothes neatly hanging in her closet. The minute the doors opened the smell of her scent hit me like a cool breeze. I stood there looking at the history of my grandmother's clothes. I could see her in the clothes as I ran my hand over them. Clothes she wore at Sunday dinner, clothes she played bridge in with her friends. As the tears ran down my face, I wrapped myself into one of her favorite dresses. This dress was a beautiful navy-blue dress that she wore to my wedding. She was so proud of this dress when she found it. The day of my wedding she was glowing in that dress. I put the dress up to my face hoping for a hint of her perfume. Holding that dress made me think of my wedding and how upset she was that the church would be decorated with white lilies. She was from England and they believed lilies were the sign of death, but I thought the church would look elegant. She thought it would look like a funeral. This was the only time that the two of us ever disagreed. I knew she could have a mind of her own and that it would all work out and that the wedding would be beautiful. Years after the wedding we would still bring up the white lilies just to tease her. When I see lilies today it makes me think of my Grandmother. I stop and laugh to myself because I know she would want me to think of a rose or violet instead. I have many lilies of different kinds planted in my yard. I guess you could say we are all like day lilies, our lives come to a close and another one opens. Amy Eller, September 2010

> piano lesson
> her braids outdo
> the metronome

> Peggy Lyles, *To Hear the Rain*, p. 32

This haiku is filled with so much excitement and happiness. I think of this as a young girl, sitting at a piano with her legs struggling to reach the floor, as she plays the piece that she has been learning. However, her excitement is getting the better of her, because she is rushing. We can tell this because her hair is swaying back-and-forth faster than the metronome. This is such a simple painting of excitement, but it remains quite elegant. It brings me back to when I first started to learn the piano, and I would constantly hear comments about how I need to stop rushing. Nicholas Sanders, Spring 2015

This haiku brings a smile to my face. It brings to mind the image of an enthusiastic little girl with her hair braided into pigtails, her head bobbing and braids swinging as she plays. I can hear an upbeat, maybe playful, tune being hammered out on the keyboard with a few wrong notes here and there, disregard for written dynamics in the music, but none of the mistakes are prominent enough to overshadow the little girl's smile. It's a cheerful scene of a child who is doing something she loves and putting everything she has into it, even if she has yet to master it. Natalie Zelman, Fall 2014

I began taking piano lessons when I was in first grade and reading this haiku put me smack dab in the middle of one of those lessons. I picture myself in the piano room of my teacher's house, surrounded by keyboards, pianos, plants, and pictures. I'm sitting at the "practice piano" in braids that my mom put in my hair that morning. When I was in these lessons, I usually was so excited about what I was doing that'd I'd forget when I was supposed to play fast or slow, and everything I played kept getting faster and faster. When I read the last line of the haiku, "the metronome", I could practically hear Mrs. Tallman saying "Lizzy, slow down..." as she turned on the "click, click, click" of the metronome. Liz Ciaccio, Spring 2006

an open window
somewhere
a woman's wordless song

Peggy Lyles, *To Hear the Rain*, p. 20

I liked this haiku because music has always been a part of my life. I hear it in everyday things, like people speaking or an object falling. When I read this, I can feel the breeze coming through the window and hear the world going on around me. I also love to sing, and I tend to just sing whenever, so I'm sure there have been people who've listened without knowing it was me or understanding. It can transport you to other places, and it's interesting to see all of the different aspects that can be seen through this haiku. Sabrina LeBlanc, January 2018

The open window made me feel the breeze and the fresh air associated with the necessity of clearing one's head. People sing songs to express what speaking will just not emote. I love the idea of a wordless song because I think it represents that situation when someone is alone, and speaking isn't for them, but a song would suffice and yet there's no one to hear. It is that inner monologue that is just as beautiful and eloquent as a song, yet it is wordless. The open window is the perfect setting and the "somewhere" lets it be accessible for everyone. Andrea Burns, Spring 2017

When I read this haiku, I picture myself outside just going through my daily routine of a walk. Then I hear a melody hummed by a woman. I cannot tell where it is coming from, nor does it matter. The song relaxes me and soothes my cares away. I think the "open window" represents new opportunities. Something just ended and there is a difficulty but somewhere there is an open window. To me, the woman is my guardian angel reminding me that there are more good times to come. It does not matter when or where this time is to come. All that matters is that it is out there "somewhere". Courtney Gerk, Spring 2012

shimmering pines
a taste of the mountain
from your cupped hands

Peggy Lyles, *To Hear the Rain*, p. 23

I really love how this haiku focuses on the senses of the body. The first line creates a vivid image of pine trees that "shimmer" in the sunlight. The second line speaks of a drink of cold mountain water, which is being held in cupped hands, which invokes both taste and touch. Together, the lines form a simple but effective haiku that encompasses the reader in familiar senses. I was just in Colorado last weekend, and I was able to visit the Rocky Mountains, so this particular haiku brought back fresh memories that I have from that trip, which is enjoyable for me. When I read it, I could feel the crisp mountain air, and smell the pine trees. Lane Caspar, Fall 2017

I immediately place myself in this haiku. I have travelled out west to many national parks and have great imagery of these places. I see the colors of the pines and their surrounding elements. The dark, everlasting color of green. The brown earthen dirt and the pine cones resting on the ground. The orange-ish fallen pine needles. I can smell the crispness of the pines. I can feel the pointiness of the needles themselves. The pines are glossy and shimmering from a bright sun, or possibly from a heavy snow that has covered and frozen the trees. The mountains are also glimmering in the background and are capped with snow. The sun warms the mountain and releases water from the rocks. Potentially a spring resides at the base of the mountain. Or a pool of water resides there from the melted snow. I feel the chilliness of the water. I sense purity in this experience as I become a part of the environment. Nathan Heppermann, January 2017

The imagery in this haiku amazes me. Not so much the expressed imagery, but how open the words are allowing myself to, in my mind, create beautiful scenery: the man kneeled on his tired knees, quenching his thirst from the stream, flowing through the ever-so gorgeous mountains, surrounded by dark green pine trees, with bits of snow on the mountain tops, and the sun pleasantly illuminating the horizon. As the preface stated, this haiku is "capable of receiving, being, and giving all at once" (Peggy Lyles). I take from the haiku, interpret, and build my reading of it into something unique to me, something I relate to. Matt Swofford, Spring 2013

> a damp fern
> strokes my ankle
> dark eyes of the doe

> Peggy Lyles, *To Hear the Rain*, p. 18

This haiku takes me to the late summer evenings I have experienced ever since 1st grade. I have always been a long-distance runner, and every summer I would go on runs training for the fall. Often times I would run in the evening as the sun was descending to avoid the heat of the day. I ran through the woods that marked the edge of my neighborhood and would often see wild life. Deer, squirrels, and, my favorite, foxes were all present while on my runs. The woods were darker and damper than the rest of my neighborhood, even on the hottest, driest days. Often times, I would come back home with wet socks. Whenever I got lucky enough to encounter wild animals on a run, I felt very blessed and I never wanted to disturb their homes, being raised under similar beliefs as many native American tribes. I would try to connect with the animals, and at the very least show them I was not a threat. Alexander Erickson, Fall 2016

I felt drawn to this haiku because I am an avid hunter. I've felt the dew from a plant as I stared down the eyes of a deer. It puts me in a place of focus and concentration. I see dark colors, it's an overcast day with many shadows from the trees. I hear the breeze blowing and I'm holding my bow in my hand, waiting to make my move as soon as she looks away. I feel the dew from the ground, but I also feel the doe's stare. It's intense and unwavering. Eli Cook, Spring 2015

> reaching for green pears—
> the pull
> of an old scar

> Peggy Lyles, *To Hear the Rain*, p. 86

I guess you could read this poem literally, as in there is a scar on the arm or hand that is reaching for the pears, but the reason that this poem resonated with me is because I took it metaphorically. To me, as I'm picking the green pears, the colors or the smell remind me of someone I lost, or someone that hurt me. I'm alone in this scene, and I try to ignore the yearning, almost nauseous feeling in my chest as I pick the pears. This would be a seemingly easy task for anyone who did not have an associated memory with pears. In real life, I have felt this way when walking by certain places or eating certain foods that remind me of a past relationship or a family member that has passed away. The scars are healed over but get pulled at when you're reminded of the original cut that caused the scar in the first place. Rachel Humphrey, Spring 2018

When I read this haiku, there are many things that stirred in my thoughts. I think it is interesting that Peggy Lyles chose to place "—" after the line where the reaching is occurring, almost as if you can feel the scar stretching. The scar in this sense makes me think of a physical scar. However, I also believe the scar could be an emotional scar. An old scar could be from a failed attempt at a relationship in the past or a difficult emotional time where you later healed. When reaching for something green, or new, the pulling scar reminds you of that troubled time and tries to hold you back, maybe scaring you from foraging ahead. Alyssa Becker, Fall 2016

I can see someone reaching for a fruit and a scar just being torn. I have a two-foot scar down my back and when I read this I can just feel myself reaching for something and having my scar pull. The numb feeling came across my back. It was not a painful pull, but just enough to notice. When reaching out for that pear I can just see the pear and then my eyes are drawn to what my back looks like. The scar moves with every pulse that occurs. It is almost like the pears are ripe and perfect, just the color to pick. Then the scar that is pulled is old and no longer new and it creates a connection between the pear and the scar; they are both being pulled. Shannon Hackl, Spring 2007

I brush
my mother's hair
the sparks

Peggy Lyles, *To Hear the Rain*, p. 93

My Mama's fine blond hair is one in a million. My mother has taught me so much, she has poured herself into my life, praying for me, loving me, and being my best friend. When all 3 of my mother's children left for college, she decided to get more involved in the community. My Mama was the chairman of a fancy dinner party for our community. In preparation for that big day, she got her nails done, bought a new outfit, and was on a diet for weeks. I went home from school early on her big day. After she showered, we talked, and I brushed her hair. The relationship that my mother and I share is rare. We laugh more, cry more, and share more about our lives than any two women I know. The way we love each other is truly blessed by God. She may just be my mother, but sparks fly when we are together. Maureen Coady, Spring 2004

This haiku shows a reversal between mother and daughter. I see a mother who has finally reached the age where it is simply too difficult for her to lift her hand to brush her hair. In the old days, this mother used to brush her daughter's hair and tie it in ribbons before school, but now it is her daughter's turn to take care of her. Both the mother and the daughter are quiet as the girl brushes her mother's hair. There is a true bond between these women, and the love between them grows as the daughter nurtures her mother the way her mother used to nurture her. The idea of old age in the mother makes me see silvers and whites within her hair, perhaps she is wearing a nightgown and preparing for the morning with her daughter. Her hair is long. She stares through old eyes at her daughter in the mirror as the daughter delicately brushes her hair; her wrinkled hands are folded on her lap and she waits patiently. Kersten Haile, Spring 2008

This past summer my grandmother died of cancer. It came on very quickly and we lost her after a month. She was put into the hospital and never was able to leave. She used to make me smile every morning when my mother and I would visit with her because the first thing we had to do when we got in her room was make sure she looked presentable. I know this probably had to do with either how she was raised or even just her being born in the early 20th century. My mother would sit on the edge of the bed and brush her hair for her. This haiku reminds me that after we were done her expressions were totally different from when we first arrived. Her eyes would light up after she had her hair brushed. The sparks in her face would connect and it was like she wasn't dying anymore. Lyndsay Lemanczyk, Spring 2009

> a handprint
> on the hospice window
> fingers widely spread

> Peggy Lyles, *To Hear the Rain*, p. 94

As a nursing major, this one got me. Hospice gives a somber feeling, like death is inevitably near. The handprint on the window gives me the sense of a patient sitting in their wheelchair, gazing out the window and into the world. Placing a hand on the window, desperately wishing their life was not almost over; to be young again. Leaving their print on the window, are they still alive? I imagine a beautiful day outside, the sun is out, birds flying, trees moving slowly in the wind. The world is still going on around them while these patients are cooped up in the hospital surrounded by illness and death. Megan McGurr, January 2016

This haiku provided me with an image of hopelessness. I imagine a thin hand, pressed against a window on one of the top floors of a hospital. The window is covered in frost, and the terminally ill patient can feel the cold through the glass pane. I imagine someone that knows they don't have much time left alive and wishes to be healthy and back in the outside world. They are reaching for something that they know is incredibly unlikely to ever happen, but still can't help but to hope, despite the terrible circumstances. Georgia Martindale, Fall 2017

I have two different perceptions when reading this haiku. The first image is of my grandfather. My grandfather has been diagnosed with two different types of cancer, leukemia and bladder cancer. I picture him at his house and sitting in his favorite recliner. I picture him getting up and going to stand in front of the window, placing his hand on it and asking God to care for his family once he passes away. The second image involves my grandmother. Instead of my grandfather standing at the window in their home, it's my grandma. Her fingers are tense, as she is worried how she will go on without my grandpa. Karlee VanDeVelde, January 2015

> dinner party
> glancing up from grace
> to the flood mark on the wall

> Peggy Lyles, *To Hear the Rain*, p. 95

For this haiku, I saw a group of maybe 10 to 15 people all sitting around a huge table, laughing and talking over a wonderful home cooked meal. These are all very close friends who just enjoy spending time with one another, sharing stories and reminiscing. The host, who I picture as a woman in her mid-forties, is very grateful for all of these wonderful people in her life and then she looks up to see that flood mark on the wall. While that mark leaves awful memories of a very scary and troubling time, it also shows that fate was kind to them, and they were able to move on and still find happiness. Sydney Brangenberg, January 2017

This piece really stood out to me for a few reasons. Because it is a dinner party, I'm imagining sitting at a table, feeling a fancy tablecloth, smelling great home-cooked meals. I also come from a Catholic family, so saying grace is a very common occurrence whenever we all actually sit down at the table to eat together. The most effective part for me, however, was the last line. To me, the flood mark represents things that are random occurrences of misfortune that will continue to happen to good people no matter how much praying gets done because that's the way life is. 'Life is random, and life is unfair' is how that line came across to me. Additionally, I connected with this realization of random misfortunes because I have abandoned my belief. In doing this, I had some troubling times examining my mind and the world around me. The author seeing the flood mark symbolizes that point in my life where I was questioning and examining my faith. In short, I connected with this haiku on a very personal level and this piece is my favorite one I have read so far. Austin Evans, Spring 2014

Something about it caught my attention. I get a different emotion from each line, but together they all work. The first line makes me feel happiness and I think of people laughing, talking, and drinking wine. From the second line I get a feeling of awkwardness or uncertainty; one of the guests possibly does not have a strong faith or is struggling with their faith at the time and they look up, almost as if they were looking for an escape. The third line is kind of sad to me. The flood mark is almost a scar on the wall; a permanent reminder of a great flood the house experienced. When I put it all together, I get a picture of a person who is going through a rough time but goes to his friend's dinner party out of politeness. He wants to leave and even looks up during grace for his escape. When he sees the flood mark on the wall, he is comforted because he realizes that even when things go bad, such as the flood to the house, you still can remain standing and come out okay. Jenna Pelej, Spring 2007

> dog-eared script
> I prompt a wise man
> from the wings

> Peggy Lyles, *To Hear the Rain*, p. 118

This haiku may mean something quite different to someone not raised in a Christian household, but I can only assume that it is referring to the time-honored tradition of Nativity pageants; a celebration where the entire congregation comes together to clothe some children in semi-convincing bathrobes and have them pantomime the story of the night of the birth of Christ. Ours were always outdoors, on the snowy hill beside the chapel. The teenagers were even privileged enough to lead around real sheep and donkeys, lent to the ward for the occasion. The stench of the animals was apparently part of the package. This haiku reminds me of the nights I spent as a shepherd, clutching a cup of steaming apple cider for warmth, listening as my father's voice, recorded years ago, recites the familiar story once more. Kaia Ball, Fall 2016

All I can think of is a children's church Christmas pageant. They never go well. There's always one kid who pees or won't sit still or starts to cry . . . I've directed these before. Even though the haiku doesn't suggest frustration, I feel it. Maybe it's just because I don't like directing children in anything or maybe it's the subtle hints like the word "prompt," like this particular wise-man doesn't quite know his lines or is so nervous that he forgot them. The thing about these Christmas pageants is, no matter how bad they actually go, everyone loves them in the end because they're a tradition that warms the heart. They remind us of the Christmas story and put everyone in the holiday spirit that is so easily lost in the shopping and commercialization of Christmas. Heidi Zapp, Spring 2013

An Introduction to Writing Haibun

In addition to writing short responses to favorite haiku by Peggy Lyles, I ask my students to write a different kind of response to a favorite haiku. In this case, the student enjoys a memory from their childhood or past that has been triggered by one of Peggy Lyles' haiku. Then they write a descriptive extended piece (about one page long) attempting to "put us there" in feelings and sensations of that remembered experience. After writing this extended memory, the students analyze key images used in the short memoir and write 3 to 5 haiku based on that experience. The final haibun is edited, polished, and shared, ending with a single haiku. Ideally the haiku obviously stems from the prose, but expands or adds to it in some intuitive way.

Here is an example of a memory writing by Hannah Haedike that was triggered by this haiku by Peggy Lyles:

shimmering pines
a taste of the mountain
from your cupped hands

    Peggy Lyles, *To Hear the Rain*, p. 23

Neighboring Planets

Every year my family goes to Colorado. We either go hiking in the summer or skiing in the winter. I remember the first time I summited Long's Peak with my dad when I was 12 years old. We left at 4am and the first few hours were just hiking through forests and it was beyond beautiful. It was like walking through Mirkwood (which is a forest from The Lord of the Rings*). I could hear the leaves ruffling and the distant chirping of birds and waterfalls and creeks in the background. When you're climbing a mountain, you still see the peak in the distance as if you're on a neighboring planet unsure of how you're ever going to get to the summit. It was daunting to attempt a 12 to 14-hour hike as a 12-year-old, but adventures were everything to me and still are. Seeing the world from a new perspective is what I live for and being on top of one of the most well-known 14ers in Colorado was exactly the adventure my 12-year-old-self wanted to do.*

Along the way, we came to a cross roads. We could either go left and venture on to Chasm Lake, which is a glacier lake about 12,000 feet above sea elevation, or we could go right and continue our summit of Long's Peak. We knew if we decided to stop at Chasm Lake there was a chance afternoon showers would roll in and we wouldn't have the opportunity to summit Long's Peak, but we did it anyway!

Chasm Lake was a sight more beautiful than anything I had ever seen. The water was viciously deceptive, looking only inches deep, but was truly around 6 feet deep at the "shore". I was young and hot from a long hike and wanted to jump in, but the thing about glacier lakes is that they are incredibly dangerous to swim in. The water usually doesn't go above 50 degrees, but I was quite unaware of that and decided to get a little wet. Luckily, I had taken most of my heavy clothes off, but man was I freezing afterward. I thought I was walking into the lake, but no I plummeted and my whole body was submerged. I got out at as fast I could, and I remember my dad was bragging to the park ranger about how his brave and adventurous daughter went into the lake and the park ranger got so upset at him for letting me do it because most people fall into a state of hypothermia and I was quite lucky that didn't happen to me. Once again, I defied the odds without necessarily trying to.

Without my dad's grace and willingness to hike with me and go on these crazy adventures, I never would have fallen in love with the mountains the same way I have today. Every time we go to Colorado in the summertime, we attempt to summit a new mountain. From the cupped hands of my parents, I have been able to taste and see and feel experiences in a way that wouldn't have been imaginable without them providing me with the opportunities in the first place.

the mountains call
my name
afternoon showers

Hannah Haedike, Fall 2018

Reader responses:

My favorite haibun was "Neighboring Planets" by Hannah Haedike. I loved the detail she included throughout because it made the story much more personal and honest. She went in depth with the physical details of her surroundings and explored her inner feelings genuinely, which sucked me into her story. I appreciated the optimistic and reflective conclusion, which tied together the whole story and explained its significance to her life today. Rachel Pevehouse, Fall 2018

I like this haibun because it reminds me of how my family goes on vacation every summer, most of the time to somewhere new. We always drive everywhere (my dad insists that spending time together in the car is most of the "family" part of "family vacation"), and the past several years we have driven through one mountain range or another to get to our destination. One of my favorite parts of the mountains is the winding, curving roads, especially the passes (even though I'm petrified of heights) that go up, over the mountain tops, rather than through the mountain via tunnel or around the base of the mountains. Another of my favorite things about the mountains is the uncertainty of the weather; I love that a rainstorm can just pop up out nowhere, at any time. When reading this poem, I pictured riding in the car through the mountains during a rainstorm, and that image is just super peaceful to me. Haley Vemmer, Fall 2018

Pool Toys Left Behind

I remember my grandparents' house back when I was younger. My brother and I would swim in their pool when we stayed the night. As soon as we got there, we would run inside and put on our swimsuits. Then we would run to the pool. Usually the sun was still out, so the wood deck from the house to the pool was scorching hot. My brother and I would race across the deck and jump into the pool. We would swim and play and swim some more until my grandma would call us for dinner. She would drag us out of the pool or bribe us with the threat of no ice cream. On nice nights we would sit outside as it started to get dark and eat dinner on the floor of the gazebo. In every other opening around the gazebo my grandmother hung a different wind chime. We listened to the clanking of the wind chimes as we ate and watched the sunset, and later the moon reflection bounces off the water of the pool. Once we were done, we would go inside to get ready for bed, leaving behind the pool toys floating on the calm water.

cool night breeze
wrapped tight in a towel
dinner is served

    Caitlyn Latshaw, Spring 2017

Reader responses:

This is sort of funny because I had a great aunt and uncle who had a huge swimming pool. I would spend all afternoon and evening in the pool. I wouldn't get out until the hotdogs were ready to eat. Life was so much easier when all you had to worry about was who was going to put my floaties on and to be careful not getting a splinter on the wooden deck. Amanda Donohoe, Spring 2017

This haibun transports me back to my childhood. Some of my favorite memories are from when I used to swim in my pool with my friends. We would start the afternoon off by doing "tricks" into the pool, trying to outdo one another's cartwheels. The heat would fade once the sun slowly disappeared behind my house, and then we would climb out, grabbing our towels and sitting on the deck. If it was a special occasion or if I asked ahead of time, mom let my friends stay for dinner. That image clearly comes to mind with this haiku. I can feel the breeze brush past me while I sit on the deck munching away. Emily Chudzik, Spring 2017

•

Deeper into the Mirror

In 2007 my life changed forever. I was in a car accident that required the jaws of life. I could not walk, and 10 years later I still have back pain. Worst of all, this accident made it unbearable for me to look at myself in the mirror. In the accident, a truck hit my side of the car and glass shattered, slicing my face. I had over 30 stitches in my face to remove glass pieces from my forehead. My face was so swol-

len I couldn't recognize myself and did not want to be seen. At such a tender age, I remember crying when I looked at my reflection wondering if I would ever look the same. I remember the first time I saw my face in this state I had tears falling down my face and literally stepped closer to my bathroom mirror because I could not believe it. I had to look deep inside myself for confidence and comfort. I had to realize that beauty was really within. I was still the same person. I just did not look the same. I remember lying in bed (unable to walk) with a mirror on my nightstand. I rarely looked at it because I hated the way I looked and every time I did see myself, I cried and thought about the song "reflection" from the movie Mulan. Weeks later the swelling went down but I still had scars on my face. As a young woman I still felt ugly and hid for years, until my freshman year of college. Then I had an even more traumatic accident, and that's when I realized I had nothing to hide, I had nothing to be ashamed of, they were scars and told a story. People could look at me and see a chapter of my life story without me having to say a word to them. Now I can look at myself with my scars and feel and believe that I'm beautiful.

she traces a story
the fingerprints
over his scars

Yunek Moore, Spring 2017

Reader responses:

I think that this haibun is beautiful. Many of us face traumatic events in our lives—oftentimes at a young age. Some of these traumatic events may cause physical change or internal change. Or both. This haiku explores the inner and outer changes that occur when someone experiences something incredibly traumatic at a young age. Many times, when facing such events, we are able to move on. Our emotions may come back as a reminder of the events, but it can be easy to let that go away. However, when there is a physical change due to such events, there is a constant reminder of the event. That makes it even more traumatic in my opinion. The fact that this narrator couldn't even look in the mirror without breaking down is devastating. I love how honest and open this haibun is. This event caused so much change in the person, and they had to deal with that all on their own. Even though there was an outer change in the person, they really did stay beautiful on the inside. That's why I appreciate the idea of looking deeper instead of closer. Yes, this person is changed from the event, but they are still themselves on the inside. They may look closer and closer in the mirror and not see themselves, but if they look deeper and deeper then they will find themselves again. Jordan Oelze, Spring 2017

I liked this haibun because it expressed feelings of looking into the mirror and not getting the image that you want to look at. This is a great haibun about self-esteem and I think a lot of people have low self-esteem. The ending adds a positive experience instead of a depressing one because the mood went more sublime. I enjoyed the story and was very intrigued by it. Olivia Gonzalez, Spring 2017

•

Kukai - Favorite Haiku on Childhood

In addition to writing "extended memory" haibun in response to favorite haiku, I ask my students to try writing haiku similar to topics or approaches evident in the most recently read selected haiku collection. Often Lyles' haiku bring to mind various memories from childhood. Therefore, several students write haiku by recalling significant events or feelings from growing up. Here are some of their resulting haiku on childhood:

pigtails bouncing
lone watermelon seed
stuck on her chin

Alexis Iffert, Spring 2002

My overall favorite haiku gives us such a sweet and innocent image of a young girl in pigtails. She is walking around with a slice of watermelon. She looks so happy. She is out enjoying the perfect summer day. It is bright. It is warm. All of a sudden, as she is wrapped up in the perfection of the day, a single watermelon seed misses her mouth and gets stuck on her chin. She walks around for minutes before she discovers it. She only notices it because it starts to dry a little and she can feel it resting below her lip. The image is just enhanced by the fact that the subject is a little girl with pigtails. That makes the haiku that much easier to envision and identify with (but then again, maybe that's because I was once a little girl). Shannon Kroner, Spring 2002

bubble mower
side by side
we cut the grass

James Hartnett, Spring 2005

Wow, this is a really great haiku. I get such a perfect image from this one. I definitely remember the bubble mower, and how many times do you see a young child side by side with mother or father mowing the grass. The "we" is the child and parent mowing and that picture reminds me of my nephew that used to mow with my dad. He loves doing this with "Papa" and this is a Hallmark picture of a boy looking up to his favorite person in the world, so innocent and ready for dad or grandpa or whoever to show him the ropes of this crazy, fast moving world. Cory Hodges, Spring 2005

deep in the jungle
dog at my side
mom calls us in for dinner

Brad Tubbs, *Millikin University Haiku Anthology*, p. 34

I love the story that this haiku tells. A small child is out in the backyard among tall grass (maybe some giant sunflowers) with his or her dog making up great adventures when they are interrupted by dinner, and the game is abandoned as the smell of mom's cooking reaches them. Or maybe the child calls back and asks for five more minutes, like so many children do when they are on an adventure. This haiku also reminded me of the beginning of the movie "Up" when little Carl and Ellie meet and pretend to travel to South America. The haiku leaves off when the child must make a choice: listen and go in, or just blaze one more trail? Alex Buchko, Spring 2013

The first two lines leave you with a sense of an adventure that lies ahead. I feel that the cut lies between the second, and third line. It is in the third line that the imagery is drastically changed. The initial image of a fit man, and his companion, ready for some Indiana Jones-esque adventure, is quickly replaced by a small boy and his terrier playing in the back yard. The third line floods you with childhood nostalgia. On another level, having two sons, I also imagined them playing in the backyard, and my wife calling them in for dinner. Thomas Friend, July 2017

The imagination and youth captured in this poem is what drew me in. There are few fonder memories of my childhood than the ones where I played imaginary games with my friends. We would pass hours and hours of time in the backyard pretending we were tigers, princesses, whatever we wanted to be. However, like clockwork, Mom would always call us in for dinner at 5:30, and the magic would be lost. No matter how much we tried, you could never get back the magical game we had going on before dinner. I liked the idea of this boy in the "jungle", which is probably just his backyard, adventuring right up until dinner. It connects with my childhood so vividly and deeply. Molly McCullough, Spring 2013

    church bulletin
    I still draw
    in the margins

    Brian A. Blankenship, *Millikin University Haiku Anthology*, p. 35

I laughed as this haiku brought me back to when I first started going to "big church." I was in that transitioning period where I did not belong in children's worship any more, but church with my parents seemed weird as well. Instead of taking notes, I would doodle along the margins and sometimes even in the open space. I did this at least throughout junior high and perhaps even into high school. Despite being a teenager, I still enjoyed the art of doodling everywhere. Debbie Vogel, Spring 2014

This haiku brings back many memories for me. Before my parents divorced, we went to church together every Sunday. My mom and dad would sit on the outside and my brother and I would sit between them. My mom was the one who pushed us all to go and was usually caught up in the sermon. Meanwhile, my dad, my brother, and I would be drawing on our church bulletins. The pews all had mini pencils in them, so you could fill out prayer cards. We used them to play a favorite game of ours. One person would draw something—something very minuscule like a curvy line or an odd shape— then they would hand the bulletin to the next person. That person would then have to finish the drawing. They were always so creative, and no two drawings ever looked the same. It was always exciting to see what the other person had come up with after you'd started them off. Kelsey Meredith, Spring 2013

    football field
    he seems so small
    mom can't look

    Julie Trimble, January 2009

I can sympathize with the football player in this haiku. Although I never played competitive sports in school, I did for a short time take martial arts classes against my mother's wishes. The short duration was due to me breaking my nose. In contrast, I was the biggest kid in the class. This haiku also inspired a strong visual image for me. It is easy to imagine a smaller kid being tackled by big linemen with a mother in the stands averting her eyes. J. Mark Issacs, January 2009

My son, Drew, played football in high school, and I can totally relate to the feelings evoked in this haiku. There were many times during a game where I had to get up and visit the concession stand or go to the restroom because I was so nervous that he would get hurt. Did my not looking work? No, he still got hurt, but thank goodness he suffered no serious injuries. Lauri Torbert, January 2009

> muddy hands
> the little girl lets
> her prince go

> Randy Brooks, Spring 2015

As I said in class, this one was my absolute favorite haiku I read. There is something about the imagery and playfulness of this poem that takes me back to my childhood. I remember catching frogs by my dad's house, because we had a pond in our subdivision. I was afraid to scoop them up, but once I did, I cupped them in my hands and took them down to the pond to let them go. The muddy hands remind us as readers of how messy and dirty kids get, which reflects their carefree, no-worry spirit. The word choice of "prince" is very specific and adds that idea of imagination into the haiku, reminding us that kids are full of playful imagination. Instead of saying "lets her frog go" or "lets her friend go", the word "prince" suggests there could have been much more behind their relationship. The language is simple, but the idea is effective, and paints a setting of a mucky river with a little girl in a pink tutu, leaning down and feeling the cold, fresh water as she places her frog in the stream. Kendall Kott, Spring 2015

> in the park
> the swing
> makes me a child again

> Brett Coffman, Spring 2008

> tiny town—
> kingdom
> of the daffodil

> Andy Jones, Spring 2008

These two matched haiku are rather whimsical, nostalgic, and simply magical together. Swing sets sometimes seem like time transports really. The feeling of going through the air and falling back down can entrance anyone at any age. When I was younger (and I imagine now if I went back to the playground), I loved jumping out of swings; I'm still obsessed with free fall. That feeling of being made into a child again takes one back into the past and thinking of all the games one used to play and all the worlds one made in their imagination as a child. This is a magical world that only they and their friends could enter and make their town their kingdom. Very sweet and nostalgic. Aubrie Cox, Spring 2008

the angry child shouts
I'll run away . . .
after lunch

Kassie Knoll, February 2010

I believe each of us has been this child at one time or has had a child who has said those very words, "I'll run away". I can picture a small child upset with her parents and thinking they are the worst parents on earth. She would be much better somewhere else. The child heads to her room to pack her little pink bag, which of course includes some of her most precious items . . . that special teddy bear, possibly a well-worn blanket and money from her piggy bank. She heads to the kitchen to pack some snacks, so she won't get hungry. As she heads toward the door, she looks back to see if her mom or dad is watching. Surely they will stop her and beg her to stay home with them. No one says a word, so the small child heads out the door and looks around. She walks to the edge of the yard and looks back one more time, hoping someone will stop her. She is now more upset than ever because her parents don't even care. She walks a few more steps and sits down at the edge of her property and tears begin to pour down her cheeks. Moments later, she feels her mother's arms around her and remembers how comfortable it feels to be in her mother's arms. Suddenly, she doesn't even remember why she is angry and just wants to go home. Hand-in-hand mother and daughter walk back into the house, all anger forgotten. Tammy Maxwell, February 2010

I ran away once as a child. My mother told me that I could not play in the hose, so I ran away. I ran all the way under my back porch. From there I could see the other kids playing in the sand and on the swing sets. I did not want to do that, and I was going to show Mommy. She would be sorry when she found out I was gone. That I wouldn't be around anymore to tell her when the big kids peddled their bikes up town without permission or when daddy got in the cake before supper. She would miss me all right. She would miss the way we cuddled up at night to watch TV. Her lap sure would get lonely without me. I stayed under that porch for at least an hour until I smelled the grilled cheese. It is not fair she knows they are my favorite. Sandy Fitzgerald, February 2010

prison sentence
bail set at
one more bite of chicken

John Spaw, Fall 2013

This poem allows readers to connect and imagine different experiences from their past. Every child has encountered a meal where he or she refuses to eat something that is placed in front of him or her. We have all been given different consequences if the food is not eaten, however, the fight will still continue until someone gives in. Usually the parent will tell the child to take one more bite and they can be done. However, some children push their limits to try and get a treat or sometimes get into trouble for not obeying their parents. In this poem, the only way to get out of trouble is to take one last bite and be done. Codi Gramlich

pitter patter on the roof
we play Scrabble
in our princess gowns

Therese O'Shaughnessy, Spring 2013

This haiku was definitely my favorite. I really enjoyed the imagery as I could easily see
the girls in their princess gowns. A little too old to be playing dress up, but still excited
to wear the dresses and act younger than they are. The Scrabble game makes it clear that
they are old enough to understand what they are doing, and therefore the whimsicality
of the princess dresses in relation to the seriousness of the Scrabble is very interesting. I also enjoyed the word choice in the first line. The use of "pitter patter" helped to
give me a feeling and sense of the space that this haiku is in. I can hear the rain on the
rooftop, and I feel as if I am with these people. This haiku helped me to put myself in the
position of the writer. Molly McCullough, Spring 2013

game of street whiffle ball—
waiting for
the car to pass

Emily Chudzik, Spring 2017

I chose this haiku as my favorite because it brought me back to my childhood. I lived in
a cul-de-sac, so my friends and I would always play in the middle of the street because
it wasn't too busy. Every once in a while, you would hear someone yell "car" and we
would all immediately clear the street by picking up the bases and the bats. Chase
Smith, Spring 2017

I really like this haiku because I felt it captured that moment perfectly. As I read the
poem, I was able to put myself on the side of the street waiting on the car to pass so we
could continue playing the game. Most haiku that I have read have done a great job of
painting a picture of the scene and what is going on, but I felt as though this particular
haiku actually put me in the street. I felt the annoyance and anticipation as the car drove
through the middle of our field. Caitlyn Latshaw, Spring 2017

grand dragon
settles in to bed
i love you mom

Hannah Ottenfield, Fall 2018

This haiku made me think of a book called *My Father's Dragon*. My mom used to read
it to me when I was little. It's told from the point of view of a little boy recounting his
father's journey to a faraway island with his pet dragon. Along the way they meet a
whole bunch of random jungle animals and eat a lot of fruit. It's a very odd book, kind
of like a longer, less scary *Where the Wild Things Are*. The book had a lot of illustrations
and a map of the island in the front cover. The dragon was blue, yellow, and red and
was kind and gentle, just as a children's book dragon should be. My mom and I would
read a chapter every night, and then she would tuck me into bed. This haiku is just very
specifically familiar to me because of this book. Isabella Loutfi, Fall 2018

5-hour car ride
I'm not touching you
monkey butt

Alissa Kanturek, Fall 2018

I liked this haiku because it reminds me of family vacations. I have two older siblings and growing up, I always sat with my sister in the middle row in the car because I was small. My brother, who is the oldest and biggest sibling, always got the backseat to himself. Trying to annoy my sister and I, he would prop his bare feet up on our seats behind our head. He would shove his feet in our faces jokingly. I called him names back and would tattletale to my parents in the front seats. I could see myself saying "monkey butt" as a young child. Although my brother liked to mess with my sister and I, we always knew it was in good fun. Honestly, the fact that he did mess with us made those trips more enjoyable. My siblings and I have always had a good bond, and we still annoy each other out of love today. I would not trade the memories of my family vacations for the world, and I really wish I could turn back time to enjoy those days of stinky feet and cramped car rides again. Emily Sullins, Fall 2018

snow angels in the yard
one less
than last year

Sophie Kibiger, Fall 2018

I loved this haiku because it gave me a very strong emotion when I read it. There is an entire storyline that could exist behind this haiku. Did someone die? Has there been a divorce? Where is the person who made the extra snow angel last year? It spikes curiosity and is a really good haiku. Jenesi Moore, Fall 2018

This is a very sad haiku. My immediate reaction was that a child has died and is no longer there to make snow angels with the rest of the family. Or, perhaps, one of the children has moved out or gone away to college. Either way, there is a sense of somber loss in this haiku. I think the author did a good job of only telling a piece of the story, so the reader is able to fill in the details for themselves. Melanie Wilson, Fall 2018

Kukai - Favorite Haiku on Mothers and Fathers

Haiku by Peggy Lyles also evoked several new haiku about mothers and fathers. Here are a few favorites from related kukai.

arguing over the dress
mother and daughter
on the mall escalator

Shannon Kroner, Spring 2002

When I first read Shannon's haiku, I began softly giggling to myself. I have pretty much lived with Shannon for almost three years now and have had the opportunity to meet her mother on several occasions. Therefore, it was easy for me to picture the scene she was illustrating in her haiku. I laughed at the sight of Shannon bickering with her mother as they head up the escalator over something so simple as a dress. The relationship that they have is one that epitomizes the stereotypical mother/daughter relationship. They get along just wonderfully, yet they definitely have their moments of dispute and petty arguments. I think the best part of this haiku is that I feel pretty confident in predicting the ending. Shannon convinces her mom to buy the dress for her and they live happily ever after. Alexis Iffert, Spring 2002

messy lumps
in my ponytail
mom in the hospital

Xiu Ying Zheng, Spring 2003

I like this haiku because it reminds me of when I was younger. When I would get ready for school, my mom would always help me get ready. I loved her to do my hair. When I had longer hair, I would get up early because I would have her French braid my hair. When I read this haiku, I imagine a girl like myself who depended on her mother to do her hair in the morning. However, her mom could not help her this particular morning because her mom was in the hospital. The little girl tried doing her hair by herself, but her hair didn't look as good as when her mother does it. Miranda Baker, Spring 2003

Sunday morning
my ex's mother
hugs me

Faith J. Martin, *Millikin University Haiku Anthology*, p. 64

I was married for 23 years and attended church where all my ex-husband's family attended. When we divorced, it was very difficult for me to attend the church, and I had started going late so they wouldn't see me, or sometimes I would go to a different service to avoid them. My brother-in-law at the time was a Pastor at the church, and I pulled him aside one Sunday after church and broke down. I had decided to find another church because I felt it was just awkward. The words he spoke that Sunday morning will forever be with me. He said that I was his sister and that would never change, and if I was going to church for the family then I was going for the wrong reason and I needed to search my heart why I was at that church. The next Sunday I walked in and went towards the coffee bar area when my former mother-in-law met me half way, threw her arms around me, told me she loved me and missed me. I hugged that woman so hard and we both stood their crying like little girls. I now sit down and talk with them every Sunday, and I am glad that I did not leave that church. I am no longer a member of the family, but we are still church family. Christine Lourash, July 2016

Reading this haiku, I got such an awkward feeling from putting myself in that situation. It's a Sunday morning, so I picture the two seeing each other after a church service where the mother is all overly cheery and annoying. She goes in for the hug and there's nothing you can do about it . . . you're trapped. I can see the person being hugged cringing in the middle of the hug, which is undoubtedly one-sided. I wonder what goes through the mother's head as she does this. "Hello, there's a reason your son is my ex . . . don't you think there are some weird feelings between me and you?" Liz Ciaccio, Spring 2006

placing my graduation cap
on the child's head
you're next

Uriah Walker, January 2016

I see a single mom struggling to balance life. There are many late nights she stays up crying and pleading to God. She needs help and knows she cannot complete her degree without his mercy. Though she goes to bed late and wakes up early she will forever have "hope" which is tattooed on inside of her foot. Whenever she hangs her head it is a reminder to stand tall and never give up. The mom feels blessed from all the support she has had throughout her time completing her degree. She is overwhelmed with happiness that her young daughter gets to see her graduate. Kailey Hurst, January 2016

chirping gaily
a language of their own
mother and daughter

Marah Kittelson, Spring 2016

This reminded me of my mom, my sister, and I. My sister and I can be pretty sassy to our mom, but she can be equally sassy back. Sometimes she even starts it. This reminded me of us bickering over nothing but it's too perfect to just stop. It also reminded me of the bond we share. I wouldn't trade the relationship I have with my mom and sister for the world. They are the people I go to when something goes wrong or goes right. I will call my mom and ask her a question, say I'm going to go, and then stay on the line because I remembered three other things that I wanted to tell her. Corrin Littlefield, Spring 2016

mom and me
drinking on the porch . . .
we do that now?

Isabella Loutfi, Fall 2018

This poem is cute. I like the use of punctuation and how it adds inflection to the poem. The ellipses after the second line is almost like a moment where the writer is trailing off in their own thoughts before they come back with a direct question in the last line. I feel that this punctuation plays well into the subject matter of the poem; it is a slightly strange and baffling time when your parents begin to allow you to join in on "adult" activities with them. This poem made me smile. Isabella Spiritoso, Fall 2018

ashes in the lake,
my father and I
drift apart

Tyler Lamensky & Garrett Derman, Fall 2010

In this haiku I get a sense of sense of relationship, and space (figuratively and literally). Literally, I imagine someone sprinkling their father's ashes in a lake, whether it be a weekend or vacation getaway, or just a place the speaker's father loved. It's a sense of closure, and as the ashes float along the lake, the speaker feels the separation from his (or her) father, which may or may not parallel their relationship when the father was alive. Aubrie Cox, Fall 2010

Kukai - Favorite Haiku on Grandparents

old jazz record
my grandfather taps his finger
to the static

Aubrie Cox, Fall 2010

What I love about this is the many different ways it can be interpreted. At first glance I think that the record is old and broken and the grandfather is too senile to notice, but another reading is how the grandfather knows the song so well than even when there is more static than music, he is able to pick out the melody. Garrett Derman, Fall 2010

This haiku fits perfectly with my own grandfather—he is obsessed with jazz music, but has absolutely no sense of rhythm, so his clapping, tapping, or swaying is always off, never quite right. My grandfather is also starting to suffer from dementia, which gave me a unique reading of this haiku. This grandfather could be losing his memories, memories made when this old jazz album was new, but now these bright memories are nothing more than static. Susie Wirthlin, Fall 2010

ginger bread cookies
eggnog
my grandma's a racist

Amanda Donohoe, Spring 2017

This haiku immediately stood out to me because the third line takes a dramatic turn. I was not expecting that line to exist the way it does because of how innocent and sweet the previous lines are, but it really tells a story. The first two lines set the scene of Christmas time where grandmother and grandchild are innocently baking cookies. But the third line shows how the conversations may have taken a different direction when the narrator admits that his or her grandmother is a racist. I connect to this because I am able to spend quality time with my grandparents, but at the end of the day, my grandparents grew up in a completely different time and culture, which is why they think the way that they do. Brittany Walsh, Spring 2017

valentine's day
nursing home
dinner with grandma

Darien M. Sloat, Spring 2013

I love this haiku because it is so sweet. I love how this person chose to spend their Valentine's Day with their grandma. I love how it brings the focus of Valentine's Day to a love other than romantic love. It is so sweet how this haiku brings a whole new meaning to Valentine's Day. I am really close with my grandma, so I can relate to this person. Amanda Lee, Spring 2013

This reminds me of the importance of family, and how we should think of the feelings of others rather than our own. It makes me think of selflessness and being there for the ones we love in their time of need, even if it means making a sacrifice. However, even though this haiku doesn't state the intent of the visit, I visualize the dinner occurring out of love and a desire to do so, rather than obligation. Matt Swofford, Spring 2013

the print on her shirt
checkers
I used to play with papa

Madeline Delano, Fall 2017

This is the haiku that stuck out most for me. The first thing I notice is the use of the word "checkers" in the second line. This word applies to both the line above and below it. In one sense, it is saying that she has a checkered print shirt on, or that she used to play checkers with her papa, or both. It was a very interesting and clever thing to do. I also really enjoyed this haiku because the feelings of nostalgia it brought to me. "Papa" is often used by children, or in this case a little girl. I pictured my sister back when she was younger, playing with my grandpa. Now that we are all grown up, we never experience these things as adults, and it is very sad. Haiku like these allow those memories to come back. Trey DeLuna, Fall 2017

This haiku makes me think back to when my grandpa, dad, brother, and I would play checkers. We would gather around the steel checkerboard that my grandpa made and play for hours. All of us would be telling jokes, laughing, and trash talking of course. I remember smelling the dinner my grandma was cooking while we were playing. When dinner was done, she would yell, "Beans are on! Be quick before it gets cold!" Another note on this haiku is that I really liked the transitional word "checkers". At first, it is talking about a pattern on a shirt and then transitions to the game of checkers, which I find to be very clever and creative. Austin Taylor, Fall 2017

helping the nurse
flip him over—
bare butt

Stephanie Dietrich, *Millikin University Haiku Anthology*, p. 165

This haiku makes me think of a daughter or wife helping the nurse flip their dad or husband. I think the man has a terminal illness and the roles are reversed with the daughter and the wife just doing what has to be done. As a CNA I can smell the hospital and know the feeling of flipping someone's family member with their help. I've seen my share of bare butts. Most elders in nursing homes are only bare when they can no longer take care of themselves. This is why I see this man as having a terminal illness and not having too much energy left. Yunek Moore, Spring 2017

I found this haiku to be a humorous memory from three years of hardship my father endured a couple years ago. He went through two years of chemotherapy and underwent three surgeries—colon, liver and lungs. He was able, though, to maintain his sense of humor throughout. During one of his hospital stays, wearing a dreaded hospital gown, he was embarrassed when he flashed a crowd of people when going on his daily walk. When it happened a second time, he didn't mind because he thought everyone should have the pleasure, as he said, of seeing his bare behind. Elizabeth Braden, Spring 2006

cherry popsicles
grandma and grandpa
compare red tongues

Isabella Loutfi, Fall 2018

This haiku is absolutely adorable. I love it when older couples are still playful and madly in love in their relationship. Too often I see older couples who don't even look at each other during dinner or talk before bed. This haiku just reminded me that in some relationships, love never dies. Jenesi Moore, Fall 2018

This poem is extremely cute. The first line immediately gives a sense of sweetness by mentioning a treat like "cherry popsicles". Then, the next line mentions "grandma and grandpa," which gives me a feeling of warmth, as I am close with my family. Finally, it is revealed that the grandma and grandpa are comparing their red tongues from the cherry popsicle. This action is playful and youthful, which makes it twice as heartwarming to know that the grandparents still act young and silly together after all these years. Isabella Spiritoso, Fall 2018

grandma's garden
salt on
a sun-warmed tomato

Whitley Sapp, Spring 2019

I don't have a personal memory of picking food from a garden with my grandma, but I do have a personal memory of picking flowers! My grandma and I have always been close from my beginning. I vividly remember going into her backyard on nice Spring days, picking the pink roses which lined her backyard fence. I actually to this day, still have a rose I'd dried, kept in a little jar. I really liked the words grandma and sun-warmed in this poem. It seems as though grandmas always make us warm and fuzzy on the inside which I believe the sun-warmed tomato is a symbol of. For my grandma and I, she is just the sweetest elderly lady, so I believe that dried pink rose is a symbol of the sweet friendship we still have even after her rose bushes are all dried up. Breana Bagley, Spring 2019

My grandmother had a very positive effect on my life; Going over to grandma's house always meant that there was something she would try to feed me. Out in the back yard we worked together in her garden to grow some delicious produce that provided much more value than a sugary snack. The same value that I found in this haiku. The first line in this haiku opens my mind up to amazing memories leading into the second line that gives me vivid imagery making my mouth water just thinking about it. Finally, the language of sun-warmed puts you in the location and provides that imagery that haiku are supposed to incorporate. Mason Bruce, Spring 2019

Chapter 4

Reading Selected Haiku of Wally Swist

A Poetics of Walking

Another collection my students read early in the Global Haiku Traditions course is *The Silence Between Us: Selected Haiku of Wally Swist*. In the preface, titled "The Poetics of Walking", Swist explains his approach: "Haiku for me has been a path, a way of life, a vehicle through which I see the world anew daily and newly many times during the day. For me it has meant to learn how to look, and to paraphrase the American lyric poet Mary Oliver: 'the more you look, the more you find'" (p. 15). He suggests that "It is in walking that the best haiku can be created" (p. 16). Students enjoy reading his work and imaginatively joining him as he walks through the landscape. They also enjoy writing haiku by "going outside" and looking at what they find. Inevitably, they notice that Swist's haiku are consistently seasonal so many of the haiku they write in response to his approach convey the seasonal context of where they find haiku.

Here are some of the student responses to favorite haiku by Wally Swist.

> summer pasture—
>   a child emerges
> in the old man's eyes

Wally Swist, *The Silence Between Us*, p. 117

This haiku is by far my favorite one in this whole book. I love the idea of a little old man returning to a pasture where he used to play with his siblings in the summer. As he looks out at the pasture and watches his own grandchildren play and have fun, suddenly something changes, and his eyes become fogged over with fond memories. All at once he is that little boy, running through the field again. He's reminiscing about a time in his life when everything was easy, and he was carefree and happy. It's a beautiful, touching moment we can easily relate to. Everyone has places that embody happy childhood memories. One place that holds my childhood is my friend Leah's family farm. I spent almost every day of every summer there until I was 13 or 14 years old. When I go back there now, I'm suddenly a seven-year-old hiding in the basement when my parents arrived to pick me up at the end of the day so that maybe I could stay just ten more minutes. Nicole Wells, Spring 2018

This haiku brought a smile to my face when I read it. My grandpa is 95 years old and is losing his memory at a rapid pace. He does not remember any of his grandchildren's names. In fact, he only remembers my dad's name because my dad is his main care-taker. Sometimes my grandfather comes over to dinner and he gets confused where he is and why he is there. But the minute someone starts talking about Ukraine, the country he was born in and lived in until he immigrated to the United States, his eyes light right up. He starts singing the songs he sang in the choir there when he was in his late teens. He tells us stories of how he had to survive on one loaf of bread a week. He remembers. He remembers his childhood years so well and you can see it in his eyes with the way he talks about it. So, although a country is not as specific as a summer pasture, this haiku made me think of my grandpa right away and the memories he has been able to pass on for generations. Maria Klek, Fall 2017

new buds
the ferris wheel
takes another turn

Wally Swist, *The Silence Between Us*, p. 56

A young boy and girl are on their first date at the fair. They call themselves "buds" as neither wants to admit their feelings of wanting to be anything more than such to the other. This date, like any first date between young high schoolers, is filled with awkward silences. Another awkward silence approaches as they wait for their turn on the ferris wheel. The boy looks up, laughs nervously, and makes a joke as the ferris wheel continues to turn. The girl returns the boy's nervous laughter and jokes back. Maybe this date isn't going to be a disaster after all. Ben Maynard, Fall 2017

I love the feeling of new beginnings and hopefulness that this haiku brings about. This haiku reminds me of spring and how it feels to be looking forward to the great things to come. It also brings to mind the pale, pastel colors that are common during Easter and the springtime as a whole. I also love how this haiku talks about new beginnings from a couple of different viewpoints. The new buds can represent the new season that is ahead, and the new revolution of the ferris wheel is the beginning of more time spent with the person that you are with. Anna Harmon, Fall 2016

shining in the heat
the laborer's back
sticky with sweat

Wally Swist, *The Silence Between Us*, p. 50

When reading this haiku, it reminded me of my dad working on my aunt's van in our garage. My dad is pretty much the mechanic in the family, so he works on just about everyone's car whenever they need something done. I imagine "shining in the heat" as it being a scorching hot day in the summer and he's laid out on his scooter, sweating bullets. There's kind of a musty smell in the air, and it's so hot the heat makes your mouth dry. I imagine it just being the most uncomfortable kind of weather to be working on a van this day, however, knowing my dad he's determined to get the job done anyways. Almost finishing up, I can see my dad complaining about his back hurting from constantly leaning over and checking out the engine. Alyssa Rodriguez, Spring 2018

I instantly felt the warmth of the sun and thought of my father. He started working at a very young age and I look up to him for working so hard in his life. He pulled a large part of his family's income at 7 years old. To this day he works at our restaurant without resting much. This haiku helps me imagine the times he worked outside for so long that he glistens with sweat. Alex Herrera, Fall 2017

silence after our argument
   crumpled cigarette pack
uncurling

   Wally Swist, *The Silence Between Us*, p. 29

This haiku reminds me of things much bigger than myself. Sometimes we can feel that what we are going through is the most important thing taking place, but life goes on. We could be mourning a loss and the people next door to us could be celebrating a promotion. Pain does not stop time—it can't even prevent a small occurrence such as the uncurling of an inanimate object. In the midst of an argument life happens . . . physics occurs. Christa Hunt, June 2016

I liked this haiku because, to me, it documents the pain that is felt after an argument and how that demands to be felt through the destructive habit of smoking. I especially like how "crumpled cigarette pack" is slightly indented, which emphasizes the almost-awkward post-argument silence. "Uncurling" is a powerful way to end the haiku because it is so open-ended. What is uncurling? The relationship? The cigarettes? I think the haiku can be representative of unresolved issues. Mackenzie Martin, Fall 2017

   Christmas day:
   at peace
   peeling potatoes

   Wally Swist, *The Silence Between Us*, p. 30

I imagined the mother peeling potatoes on Christmas Day. It is a very quiet and snowy morning. I can smell the turkey cooking in the oven that is seasoned with celery, carrots, onions, and paprika. Mother is humming a popular Christmas song, "White Christmas", while she peels potatoes for Christmas dinner. The pot on the stove is full of water, on low heat, for a slow boil because the mother is taking her time to peel the potatoes. Everyone else in the house is sleeping because it is about 8am in the morning and this is a day to enjoy the time of joy and cheer on Christmas Day. Olivia Gonzalez, Spring 2017

While reading this haiku, I picture an old woman, peeling potatoes in the midst of a chaotic Christmas day party. In the middle of all the craziness going on, the old woman is contented and calm, simply peeling the potatoes. I have an old great aunt who taught me how to peel potatoes. This reminds me of her because peeling potatoes was a bonding experience between us. My family members would sit in a circle, peeling potatoes and telling stories. I relate to this haiku because I feel like this was a calm, relaxing experience with my aunt. Renee Sample, Fall 2016

This haiku made me feel tranquil and warm. Christmas time always brings about that peaceful, cozy atmosphere, but to incorporate the peeling of potatoes adds an element of togetherness. I picture being at home with my family gathered around the kitchen, some sipping hot chocolate, some washing the potatoes, some peeling, and some just gathered around to enjoy the conversation. Deadlines are non-existent, no one is hurrying through life, but rather they are enjoying their time in the moment with those they love. This is lovely. Katherine Viviano, Spring 2016

dropping a handful of change
at the toll booth
a missing child poster

Wally Swist, *The Silence Between Us*, p. 33

This one really caught my attention. I imagined a heartbreaking scene. A family is in their minivan on the highway; everyone is excited for where they are traveling to. They slow to a stop as they gather change to throw in the toll collector. The dad is in the driver's seat, and as he reaches out the open window to throw the change in, a poster on the wall next to the tollbooth catches his eye. It has the smiling face of a young boy on it. He reads the word "missing." His stomach drops, and his heart breaks. His mind immediately jumps to his own kids, sitting in the car behind him. What would he do if he ever lost them? As they pull away from the toll, he feels extra grateful for his family sitting next to him. Lauren Bartel, Fall 2015

I liked this haiku because it reminded me of the saying, "Over seven billion people experienced today differently." For example, to you it is just any other day. I picture myself driving to work like I do every day, probably frustrated and annoyed with the inconvenience of stopping at the booth. I may huff at my normal everyday routine while someone else's life is falling apart and heartbroken for their lost child. Whitney Gray, Spring 2016

Christmas eve
leaning against the chain-link fence
the trees no one wanted

Wally Swist, *The Silence Between Us*, p. 69

When reading this haiku, I immediately think of Charlie Brown. As a child and still today, I love Snoopy and Charlie Brown. I used to watch the Charlie Brown Christmas Special each year, and I always would appreciate that Charlie went out of his way to get the one tree that no one wanted but he felt was special. This haiku makes me think of that story and how no one wants those trees left over besides a guy like Charlie Brown. Kalli Farmer, Fall 2017

This haiku leaves me feeling sad. I am really big into the foster care system, and I want to be a foster parent when I graduate. Even though haiku do not usually use metaphors, to me this haiku represents kids in foster care who may feel like these trees—left behind, alone, small and bare, not full of life. These emotions would be heightened during times such as Christmas and that's immediately where my mind went when reading this. It makes you want to pick those trees and fill them with life as much as you can. These words left a really powerful meaning in my heart. Bailey Welch, January 2018

We're driving home from our Christmas Eve celebrations and my daughter is very awake. She keeps talking about Santa and how excited she is for tomorrow. She tells me at least three times that she loves her new dollie and is going to take her everywhere. My husband and I smile because it truly feels like Christmas. We pass the grocery store on the way to our house and I notice all of the unwanted trees propped up against the fence. My daughter asks why there are so many trees left over, and I tell her that every-one already had one and they are just extras. She says, "Oh," and then starts smiling. "At least they all have each other," she says with a huge grin on her face. I smile because of how she sees the beauty in it, instead of the sadness. Corrin Littlefield, Spring 2016

morning star
the hospice patient
lingers

Wally Swist, *The Silence Between Us*, p. 78

This is easily my favorite haiku in the book. When we read it in class, I was immediately struck by how beautiful it is, how elegant. I picture the dawn of a new morning, with a star still shining in a pink sky. The star is holding onto the night, just as the hospice patient is still holding onto their life. The star lingers, the patient lingers. It's such a beautiful image, and it's very quiet, but deeply effective. Alexa Duncan, June 2016

This is not going to be a super happy reflection, fair warning. Over the summer, my boyfriend's grandmother died. She had been living with them for the past 14 years and had been slowly declining in health but not mental capacity. He was her absolute favorite, so whenever she was having a bad day it was his job to cheer her up. He helped her eat and got her where she needed to go, and then went off to school. His mom had been hiring help for a while, and of course my boyfriend was their favorite as well, as he knows how to make people feel important and happy. So, for the past year and a half, I had spent a lot of time at his house. I was there to witness the defeat and sadness that fell upon everyone when they realized she wouldn't make it too much longer. Slowly, she became bedridden and silent, and was unconscious most of the time. Hospice was there, but the nurse was absolutely awful and would sleep through morphine doses and the times when she needed turning. So, because his mother was an absolute wreck and needed to sleep, my boyfriend and I sat by her bed one night and rotated her when needed, gave her all of her medications, and talked about how great she was while playing solitaire to distract us. We didn't think she would make it through the night, but she did. The following day was the same routine, and she passed at 12:45 am the next morning. They called me to come over, and my always strong and happy boyfriend was sobbing. His mom was curled up in the hospital bed crying to her mom, praying that she was happy and not sick any more, and it was heartbreaking. He told me he opened the window when she passed. So that's the memory this poem brings up. Taryn Pepping, Spring 2016

sharing my good news
his handshake
slackens

Wally Swist, *The Silence Between Us*, p. 85

When reading this haiku, I got the vibe that the person who was shaking the hand of the other telling the good news did not truly care to see them do good in life. I imagined it as two men who were shaking hands, and the body language of the guy who slackened his handshake told me that he was in competition with the other. I would consider someone like this to be fake, because he is still shaking his hand like they are friends or acquaintances—yet when he heard the good news it seems as though he did not want what was best for his friend or acquaintance. Kaitlyn Foster, Spring 2018

I felt melancholy when I read this haiku because I have experienced almost this exact situation to a T. I have had many moments in my life where I give someone good news, like making it into a school faraway, or getting a role in a play which means my time will be taken up. In this instant, while the person is happy for you and shaking your hand, they are also upset because this news causes them to not see you as often. I have also been on the other side of the news and have felt happy for someone but also upset that the person I love will not be able to be by my side as often. Lauren Montesano, Spring 2016

> closed mental hospital
> swings creaking
> among windblown weeds

> Wally Swist, *The Silence Between Us*, p. 107

This haiku gives me chills. The words are very deliberate, in the fact that they take you to some kind of horror movie/show about a closed mental hospital. I like this in the fact that I imagine the swings to be creaking due to spirits still lingering, blowing as aimlessly as the weeds. It's important to me that Swist wrote about weeds versus a plant like a flower because he insinuates that nothing quite as happy or bright as a flower could grow around such a distressed place. Mackenzie Martin, Fall 2017

This haiku left me with a creepy feeling, which I found interesting since we have not read a lot of haiku with that kind of feeling. I live by one of the "most haunted" abandoned mental institutions in the state so this haiku stood out to me for that reason as well. The creaking swings give an eerie feeling about whether the closed mental hospital is haunted or not. However, the fact that there are weeds and run down is also sad. There was a lot of history that occurred on that swing and within the walls of the hospital, good and bad. Now it is left, abandoned and alone. Erica Forbes, Spring 2016

This one was sort of eerie. I just pictured an old abandoned building that all the kids told ghost stories about. I am picturing this as one of the earlier mental hospitals where they sent people that couldn't help having the mental illness that they had but were sent here basically to rot and to be treated badly because others blamed them for their sickness. The swings creaking actually makes me think of the lost souls that may have died while being here, with them sitting on these swings rocking, forever cursed to stay in this place because they weren't accepted. These people were left here by family members that they had loved but, in return, had been abandoned by. Maybe it is fitting that this place be abandoned as well, sort of as pay back for all of the "patients" who had come through those doors. Sydney Brangenberg, January 2017

An Introduction to Reading Matched Pairs of Haiku

As students read haiku by different authors, it is inevitable that they discover connections between haiku. I encourage this and explain that the Japanese have a long-standing tradition of discussing pairs of matched haiku. I ask the students to find an interesting matched pair of haiku with one by Swist and the other by another author we have read. I ask them to write the haiku side by side, then enjoy reading them together. In this case, in addition to intuitive responses, I ask students to consider and discuss how each of these haiku were written. What are the strategies evident in arrangement, line breaks, language choices, and other techniques? Here are a couple of examples of student responses to matched pairs.

dry mountain streambed:
    a red admiral settles
on the dusty rock

Wally Swist, *The Silence Between Us*, p. 101

shimmering pines
a taste of the mountain
from your cupped hands

Peggy Lyles, *To Hear the Rain*, p. 23

Both of these haiku present a nature scene in which I picture contrasting mountain-scapes. In the first haiku, it seems to be very dry and dusty. The fact that there was a "dry streambed" hints that this was once a beautiful valley but has dried out over the years. I do not know what a red admiral is, but with the use of the word "settles", I can picture a red bird settling into its nest on the "dusty rock", overlooking the dryness of the landscape. Although the scene is dry, Swist phrases the haiku very elegantly and delicately, so it is still a beautiful picture because there is still life in the parched scene. The next haiku was more so my favorite because I like the elegant diction, demonstrated with the words "shimmering", "taste", and "cupped". Although "taste" and "cupped" are not traditionally considered as elegant words, they are viewed as more elegant when put in a beautiful scene like this. The "shimmering" of the pines indicates the wetness or moisture on the pines, which leads the audience to further conclude that the rest of the scene is just as beautiful and green and full of life. Peggy Lyles excellently portrays drinking water from a mountain stream without implementing the word "water" or anything related to it. From personal experience in the Balkan Mountains, the mountain water is the greatest tasting water I have ever tasted, and it makes sense why someone would want to write a haiku about it. The haiku makes me think of how good the air in the mountains and nature smells, due to all the trees. It is a very refreshing haiku. Masha Kostic, Fall 2017

alone . . .
she hangs fresh mistletoe
just in case

R.A. Stefanac, *Mayfly* 48, p. 15

scraping across snow
    the unlocked gate
glazed with ice

Wally Swist, *The Silence Between Us*, p. 81

I chose to match these two haiku because they both were about winter. Both have excellent word choice, such as "alone", "fresh", "scraping", "unlocked", and "glazed". These words help the reader to get a clearer image when reading the haiku. In the first haiku, the ". . ." after alone helps the reader pause, and it almost feels like the author is thinking about how they are alone, not fully aware of the concept yet. In the second haiku, Swist tabs space on the second line for a pause. I think he did this because the first and third lines are describing the gate, but that second line is about the actual physical gate, so he wanted to separate it visually. Morgan Bettner, Spring 2018

a handprint
on the hospice window
fingers widely spread

Peggy Lyles, *To Hear the Rain*, p. 94

morning star
the hospice patient
lingers

Wally Swist, *The Silence Between Us*, p. 78

The first point of similarity between these haiku is the obvious theme of a hospice patient. Both convey a sadness centered around the main individual who is in hospice care. Digging deeper into the writing technique, the second similarity is how Swist and Lyles constructed the first line. The images "morning star" and "a handprint" instantly give a solid foundation for the rest of the poem to follow. Neither of these two lines contain verbs, leaving the beginning of the haiku open to interpretation. Both lines contain three syllables as well. The second lines of each haiku introduce the word "hospice" for the first time. Again, the lines do not contain verbs. Both poems are written from an objective view. The authors are not themselves the hospice patients. The poems also signal the desire for being outside and away from the confines of hospice. In the first poem, when Swist says "morning star," he is taking readers to the sky where the star is outside the boundaries of the hospice. In Lyles's poem, she mentions a window, where the hospice patient has been looking out of. Both poems convey anticipation and a want for freedom. Emily Sullins, Fall 2018

illuminating
the silence between us . . .
firefly

Wally Swist, *The Silence Between Us*, p. 103

lights out
. . . the firefly
inside

Peggy Lyles, *To Hear the Rain*, p. 108

As I was reading through the book *The Silence Between Us*, I was curious when I would come across the title poem. Once I found this poem, I knew that I would be using it for my mirrored poem because it instantly made me remember the similar poem from Peggy Lyles. Though it was the word "firefly" that caught my attention in Swist's poem and made me think of the poem by Peggy Lyles, I realized after rereading both of the poems again that both of the authors use similar techniques in their poems even though they are about two different things. Though I am using these poems for comparison, it is a bit ironic that the beginning lines of each are complete opposites. Swist begins his poem by immediately introducing an idea of light, while Peggy Lyles begins her poem with a feeling of darkness and the unknown. The authors both use ellipses for a pause in their poems. I believe Swist uses his ellipses to capture the essence of the silence, while Peggy Lyles uses it to draw out a moment of anticipation for the readers after giving them a dark canvas to begin to picture the poem. One difference is that Swist takes this pause at the end of the second line, while Peggy Lyles takes the pause before the second line. What is also interesting is how the both authors use this punctuation right before introducing the firefly to the poem; it is as if the firefly illuminates right in that moment and so that is when it begins to appear. Isabella Spiritoso, Fall 2018

in one corner
of the mental patient's eye
i exist

George Swede, *Almost Unseen*, p. 82

closed mental hospital
swings creaking
among windblown weeds

Wally Swist, *The Silence Between Us*, p. 107

In both Swede's and Swist's haiku, neither attempt to put a positive spin on issues of mental health care. Swede's is a bit brighter whereas Swist's is gloomy. With Swede's haiku, he is elucidating that the mentally disabled person has someone special in their life. However, it turns a bit darker with the line "i exist". To me, it seems to say that this person does not, in fact, truly exist. Is this person only alive in the eyes of the mental patient? Or is this particular person also mentally disabled/depressed, and they can only exist through the other person? With the Swist haiku, the scene is actually so dark and cold that it produces goose bumps on the arms of the reader. There is an absence of life with this haiku—in fact, the mental patients that used to inhabit this hospital seem to have been gone for a while. All that's left are the weeds. Rather than the last line, I think that the most haunting line of this haiku is "swings creaking", because it is this line that illustrates for the reader the eerie feeling of this place, a closed hospital. Mackenzie Martin, Fall 2017

winter night
he patiently untangles
her antique silver chain

Peggy Lyles, *To Hear the Rain*, p. 65

going over and over
what my wife said—
petals of the rose

Wally Swist, *The Silence Between Us*, p. 36

These haiku share a lot in common with each other. When I read the Swist haiku, I instantly remembered this one by Peggy Lyles. Both of these haiku paint a picture of a devoted husband, simply taking time he needs to work at something (in my head, I imagine it to be marriage). In this first haiku, the word "patiently" shows a sense of dedication. Whether or not the wife is alive or not doesn't matter, and neither does the current standing of their relationship. To me, this action shows a lot of care towards this woman whose chain he's untangling. There is love and loyalty behind the action. In the second haiku, the first two lines could definitely give off a negative connotation, as we often go over the meaning of critical words people say much more than their compliments. However, the last line of the haiku brings a sweetness to the haiku. The fact that Swist chose to say "the rose" instead of "a rose" shows that there is some sort of significance to this flower. I imagine this rose being one that appeared on a date or a wedding, where loving and dedicated words were exchanged that were influential to their relationship. At the moment this haiku is written, I imagine the man reliving these words as he struggles through a hard time. The words remind him of what is important and why he must continue to love as fiercely as he can, even when things get rough. As a woman, it is rare to witness tender moments like these in men, and I think that is why they pulled so strongly at my heartstrings. Alissa Kanturek, Fall 2018

Christmas day:
at peace
peeling potatoes

    Wally Swist, *The Silence Between Us*, p. 30

mother-daughter
  small talk
  snap beans

    Peggy Lyles, *To Hear the Rain*, p. 48

I think these two haiku are a matched pair because of the repeated use of couplet words. The lines each have two words, which make them both fall into a natural rhythm. They also use rather plosive consonant sounds, which gives the rhythm a crisp and clear beginning and end. The word choice in both haiku give the reader a sense of nostalgia (whether positive or negative). They are arranged so that the last line specifies what kind of food is being fiddled with. I think this is nice, because it leaves the sense of touch for last, which solidifies the memories brought about by the other two lines. However, I will say that the haiku by Peggy Lyles has a more somber voice and adds a darker inflection than the Swist. I chalk that up to the use of the word "peace" in Swist's haiku, but the contrast is still evident otherwise. Kyle Kite, Spring 2017

Kukai - Haiku from Being and Looking "Out There"

As students read and responded to Wally Swist's haiku, they noticed how he drew on his experiences of walking and noticing his surroundings in nature. As a corresponding prompt, I asked students to write haiku from being "out there" rather than simply writing haiku from their desks. Here are some of their resulting haiku that were born in kukai:

midnight . . .
I mosey
along the train track

    Kersten Haile, Spring 2008

I like this haiku because it makes me think of one of my favorite activities: walking. Not walking as in walking from one class to another, but walking with nowhere to go, at my pace. Most of the time this walking is with my dog when I take her out, a task I do at the beginning and end of the day. I like walking her more at night because there's no one out, and it's peaceful. It allows me to take a break from homework and breathe in some fresh air. It's kind of like my personal break time to relax. It also frees my mind to think about anything else that I need to get done or how I need to manage my time. Brett Coffman, Spring 2008

star-studded sky
the gleam of stepping stones
across the frozen creek

Angie Hawk, Spring 2005

I really enjoyed the language in this haiku. I like things that shine, and this haiku used a
lot of words that represented things that shine and sparkle. I can imagine the sky twinkling and creating a reflection off of the frozen creek. I also see stepping stones stuck
in the middle of the creek with ice on top that gleams from the reflection of the stars.
I almost imagine the stones looking like the top of turtles' shells stuck in the ice. The
picture created in my mind is very peaceful and because the images are so clear I feel
as if I had been there before or seen this same place sometime in my life. Sarah Bassill,
Spring 2005

a horse's breath
warm on my hands
the smell of fresh-cut hay

Alizarin Salmi, January 2016

Reading this haiku, I can feel the horse's breath and warmth on my hands. It makes me
feel right next to the horse which is such a great place to be. I can smell the hay, very
fragrant since it's fresh-cut. I like the simplicity of the haiku, beginning with the breath.
Betty Harnett, January 2016

cold, clear stream
shoes and socks
atop a rock

Amanda Young, *Millikin University Haiku Anthology*, 19

This is one of my favorite haiku because it gives me a calming visual. When I was
younger, I had a creek in my back yard, and I used to go down there with my brother
and friends every day after school and play in it. We would take off our shoes and socks
and leave them on the rocks or hill and come back for them when we were done. The
creek was always cold, but we didn't care, and it was hours of entertainment. I can
picture my creek, even though it wasn't so clear, and my shoes and socks atop a rock.
Lexi Doss, Spring 2018

This haiku by Young was one of my favorites from the Millikin University Haiku Anthology because it is so calming. The cold and clear stream I can picture perfectly. I also like
the rhyming of socks and rock in the last two lines. I'm not sure if the author did this on
purpose but it worked well. I get a good imagined vision of someone sitting on the rock
just getting ready to take their shoes and socks off before they put them in the stream.
Chase Smith, Spring 2017

snowy path
I fit my footprints
inside his

Kristin (Boryca) Kozlowski, *Millikin University Haiku Anthology*, 109

Through this haiku I draw on my experiences as a child when I would play in the snow with my dad. The juxtaposed pictures this creates includes a path of fresh snow that my dad is trudging through. I am jumping from footprint to footprint behind him, enjoying trying to be just like my dad. I also love the challenge of trying not to step into the fresh snow. Furthermore, this haiku contains a deeper meaning of trying to follow a man's path of hardship, but not deterring from the path because you care about him. Alyssa Becker, Fall 2016

This haiku creates a playful image of a couple. There are two people who have been spending the day together inside on a cold winter day during a blizzard. They decide to go for a walk after the blizzard stops and are the only people outside. The snow is pristine, and it is like they are the only people in the world. The boy walks ahead of the girl to block the wind (because she is cold) and she walks behind him. Although she is older (maybe in her 20s or even early 30s), she still sometimes feels childish and it is one of those moments now. She matches her footprints to his and tries to step exactly where he did. Beth Ann Melnick, Fall 2010

> wind from the lake
> biting my ears
> not a taxi in sight
>
> Aubrey Ryan, Fall 2003

During high school, my friend Robin (from another town) and I made it a tradition to take the train into downtown Chicago for some Christmas shopping. Eventually, it also became tradition to miss at least one train in the morning going to downtown (there has been more than one occasion where we've watched our train pass us while we're stuck in our car at the intersection), as well as at least one train on the way home. Oftentimes, we'll be all the way up on Michigan Avenue when one of us looks at the watch and goes, "oh crap, we have twenty-five minutes to get all the way back to the train station!" So, there we are, standing outside in the freezing cold on a December evening, cold wind off the lake numbing our toes and coats pulled tight around us, just TRYING to hail a cab so we can get back to the train station and make it home before it gets super dark and our parents get super worried. (This is back before everyone and their dog had a cell phone, remember.) In any case, we were never really good at hailing cabs. We'd usually have to walk until we found one that was hanging out by the curb to climb into. Let me tell you, sometimes we were grateful that those cabbies drove like crazies. Jenny Schlutz, Fall 2003

> he tucks her feet
> beneath his warmth
> snow flurries
>
> Skya Gentle, Fall 2012

I like the image that this haiku creates. There is a definite loving relationship between these two individuals. Not only does he know that she is cold without a word from her, he moves to help her. There is something about the tenderness of this relationship that I really enjoy. Danielle Davis, Fall 2012

cold feet
I steal the blanket
back

Lexy Bieber, Spring 2015

I enjoyed this haiku because it makes me think about every cold winter day that I am stuck inside. My entire family fights over the blankets because not all of them are long enough. I myself am six foot five and there is only one blanket that we own that covers my entire body. From the haiku, I get an image of me sitting on the couch with my blanket that I have to keep constantly pulling down to keep my feet warm because I have just come back inside from shoveling the drive way. Alex Cardascio, Spring 2015

I imagine a wedding. A young bride tossing and turning on her wedding night realizes she has cold feet. I saw the blanket less as a blanket; it's her life. She steals her freedom back, she's backing out. I also really like the way this one reads as well with just one word in the third line. It's a very subtle end. "I steal the blanket . . . back" is how I read it. Even though I know it goes together, I read it with a longer pause than between the first two lines and I think it makes it sound really unique. Francesca Rios, Spring 2015

winter night
the newlyweds watch
their first snow

Logan Bader, Fall 2018

I imagine a cozy cottage all decorated with Christmas lights. This couple just had a December wedding, and tonight is the first night home from their honeymoon. They watch the snow fall outside while they curl up on their couch with hot cocoa. The Christmas tree is in the corner, and a Christmas movie plays on the tv in front of them. They talk about their snow day traditions as children and wonder what traditions they will start together as a family. Maybe they will do snowball fights or find a hill to sled on each year. The newlyweds smile and giggle, excited for the many winters ahead of them. Emily Sullins, Fall 2018

This haiku was inspired by where I see myself in the near future. Over winter break, I am planning on proposing to my girlfriend when I am with my family again. We were experiencing snow in Decatur when I wrote it, and that got me thinking about many "firsts" together as a married couple. First snow, first Christmas, first snowman, and so many more first things that we will be doing united in marriage. I love reading this haiku when I am missing her and when I want a quick smile. It is safe to say that I cannot wait for Christmas break! Logan Bader, Fall 2018

snow-caked
heels click together
there's no place like home

Isabella Loutfi, Fall 2018

I like this haiku because of all the different parts and meanings it has. I personally do not enjoy winter or snow, so I am always glad to get back home and go inside. I like the image of clicking heels together, and the allusion to *The Wizard of Oz*. This can be interpreted as clicking one's heels together like Dorothy in the movie, wishing to go home and get out of the snow. Or as stomping the snow off of your feet as you walk into the house. Melanie Wilson, Fall 2018

snow day
my red nose
doesn't glow

Emily Sullins, Fall 2018

This haiku is just fun and cute. I love the reference to Rudolph the Red-Nosed Reindeer. I also appreciate how it is combined with a relatable sensation—the red nose many have during the winter months. It has a fun and unique voice that creates a feeling of light-heartedness. Rachel Pevehouse, Fall 2018

spring morning
I shave my legs
for no one

Alyson Ludek, *Millikin University Haiku Anthology*, 17

I liked this one because I can 100% relate. I don't know how other women feel, but I think you can shave your legs for two reasons: either for the sake of appearance or the simple pleasure of that smooth feeling. So maybe this girl is just enjoying a peaceful spring morning by herself, taking time to take care of her body, for no one else's sake but her own. This haiku also made me think of prom; specifically, my senior prom. I do love shaving my legs for dances, as it makes me feel pretty and polished. But it was a floor-length dress, and I didn't have a date anyway. So why did I shave my legs? I laugh. It's just one of those things we learn to do but never know why we do it, isn't it? Such an interesting thought in such a concise image. Alex Buchko, Spring 2013

I love this haiku because there is such a sense of empowerment in it. I think every girl has this sensation at some point in their life. For me it came just after finally getting over a failed relationship. I woke up one morning and decided to shave and get all dressed up, not because I was spending a day with some guy but because it made me feel good about myself. There is a slight chance that this haiku could be interpreted more depressingly, however, the first line, spring morning, evokes sunshine and new life—happy sensations. Overall, this haiku reflects self-respect and inner peace for me, two things that are essential in order to truly be empowered and take command of your life. Samantha Parks, Fall 2010

she picks a daisy
just in case
spring cleaning

Rachel Humphrey, Spring 2018

This poem to me has so much hope. I love the fact that it is the idea of this girl picking a daisy almost as a new moment in her life, a fresh flower to signify her coming into a new time, just in case someone is to come around. Elizabeth Pillow, Spring 2018

When writing this haiku, I really wasn't thinking about the meaning of it, and just went with my gut and instinct on what to write. However, it became one of my favorites because of its simplicity. Eventually the meaning to me personally became clear. I think the girl is cleaning her soul and refreshing her life. She is choosing to be happy. She is hopeful for the changes in her life that she is making. Rachel Humphrey, Spring 2018

spring shower
watering the grass
on the new grave

Allyson Isenhower, Spring 2018

This haiku was one of my favorites because of the meaning that it holds in my heart. My grandpa passed away last year in early spring. His grave had just been created, and the top of it was just dirt. For the first few weeks it was only mud when it rained, which created an ugly scene that mirrored how I felt inside. However, eventually grass began to grow. The grass that grew was not enough to cover the entire place, but it was a start. This spring when I visited, the grass was growing like crazy, and it finally covered the nasty muddy image that so vividly remained in my head. Allyson Isenhower, Spring 2018

the water still cold
to our bodies—
summer lake

Pat Steadman, Spring 2006

I like this haiku because of the contrast of hot and cold between the first and last lines. It is a hot, summer day, but the lake water has not absorbed enough of the sun's heat to warm up. The shock of cold water on hot skin is a universal sensation—something most everyone has experienced. Also, I like the way the middle line uses "our bodies" instead of "my body" This makes the experience one for everyone, not just for the author alone. Melanie Mclay, Spring 2006

flip flopping
my pillow
sticky summer night

Rachel Humphrey, Spring 2018

This is one of my favorite haiku because it is so relatable. During the summer my parents like to turn off the air conditioning and open the windows, so it gets so hot and sticky. Those are the worst sleeping conditions, so I keep flipping my pillow to the cold side and laying against the wall trying to find something cold. Lexi Doss, Spring 2018

When I read this haiku, I imagine a very hot and sticky summer night. There is no air conditioner to cool this night down, all there is are fans and even those aren't helping. It's so humid it's suffocating. All you can do is toss and turn in bed. You're irritable at this point. You're desperate to feel some kind of cool air just to be able to get some sleep. The only thing that seems to be helping is flipping your pillow over every now and then to feel the coolness of it. Alyssa Rodriguez, Spring 2018

Chapter 5

An Introduction
to Haiku Poetics

There Aren't Any Rules?

Although students often ask me to explain "the rules" for writing haiku, I resist because I want them to understand that high quality haiku do not come from a list of rules. They come from writers who devote years of practice developing their expertise in the necessarily conjoined arts of reading and writing haiku. Practice and reader's responses provide a social means of developing a deeper understanding of haiku poetics, not a list of "do's and don'ts". I explain that one of my ultimate goals for the class is for each student to develop their own understanding of where the best haiku come from and why some haiku are better than others, according to their own preferences as readers and writers.

However, after reading a few collections of selected haiku by excellent writers, students are starting to formulate their own understanding of haiku poetics—their own values for excellence. For those who still might wish for a more explicit discussion of aesthetic goals and practices, I ask my students to read Gail Sher's "Guidelines for Beginning Writers of Haiku" which is published as the last chapter in her book, *One Continuous Mistake: Four Noble Truths for Writers* (Penguin Books, 1999). Sher explains that "successful haiku work on three levels: 1. the surface, literal level pleases and is enticing; 2. underneath, a deeper layer of meaning emerges; 3. finally, if a reader is receptive, the haiku will create the space for a moment of enlightenment" (p. 179). I ask students to compare Sher's step-by-step guidelines with the author prefaces in the selected haiku books by Peggy Lyles and Wally Swist. As you can see from the following readers, the students soon discover that while there are different approaches to writing haiku, there are also several aesthetic goals in common.

Here are two student summaries:

> *I found that Peggy Lyles and Gail Sher actually had a lot in common to say about haiku, how it should be written and read. They both discussed the importance of being succinct and to the point and that the reader must play a large role in the interpretation of the haiku. They also both discuss the importance of not rushing into writing/reading haiku. Although the poems themselves are short, they must be written with careful attention to little details, special relationships, and word choice. The same must be done in reading. The scene has to soak in for the full effect to hit the reader. When it comes to the composition of writing haiku, Sher obviously has a lot more to say on the subject. She divides the successful haiku into three tiers: the surface, the underneath, and the enlightenment. Although Peggy may not have classified haiku in this way, I think that she would agree in the fact that the aesthetic of*

a haiku is one thing, but the meaning and emotion it brings to the reader is another powerful thing as well. Overall, I think both of these readings gave me a better understanding of what haiku can be and what it should consist of, as well as how it should allow the reader to feel. *Alissa Kanturek, Fall 2018*

I found that both passages contained the same message in terms of the goals of haiku—that there should be a "jump" that the reader has to make in order to fully connect and experience the haiku in their own way—but that they have different ideas about how to achieve it. Sher, quite literally, lists how she accomplishes this, as well as how haiku should be written on three different levels. Most of these steps include an example so she can demonstrate her point more fully. It is a more specific description of haiku than Peggy Lyles' foreword because Lyles, while she mentions the same elements as Sher, does not explain it as in-depth. However, it is just as vivid because she describes the effect that these elements create, rather than how to craft that feeling. Her foreword is also more about the brevity of haiku, and how that creates a need for ultra-specific diction. Sher also discusses the shortness of haiku but chooses to focus on what kind of words should be used instead. Peggy Lyles' foreword is also written more like a piece of art, using words that evoke emotions in the reader, creating sentences that flow with beauty. Sher's, while well written, is more of a handbook or checklist on writing haiku than a comment on an artform. *Daria Koon, Fall 2018*

Kukai – Matching Contests

In kukai, students pick out favorites, share their imagined responses to these with the entire class, and celebrate the author for writing the haiku. However, in matching contests I have selected quality haiku and placed them in anonymous matched pairs. Each pair is carefully read out loud and imagined before the class votes on their favorite of the two haiku in that "match". The winning haiku continues on to be matched with another winning haiku in tournament style until there is a single "grand champion" of the matching contest. Matching contests are often based on certain topics or writing prompts. Sometimes the matched element between the two haiku is a simple word or image, but other times it is subtler—an intuition or similar atmosphere. Here are some examples of matched pairs and student responses from various matching contests.

father and daughter
floating in a canoe
the lake listens

Catherine Hixson, Spring 2012

sparkling shoes
daddy daughter
date night

Courtney Gerk, Spring 2012

I really loved these haiku because they both have to do with a very special and strong relationship. But they are about different stages of this relationship. The father and daughter haiku makes me think that the daughter is older, perhaps this is their last summer together before she goes off to college. They spend their last summer together canoeing on a lake and instead of getting caught up in actually canoeing, they spend the privacy on the lake to just be in each other's company. This emotion is so personal with so little action, there isn't that much going on or being said but it's in the silence that the true meaning is felt. The sparkling shoes is clearly about a father and his little girl going out for a fun night together, and since it's such a "special occasion" she gets to wear her special sparkly shoes. It's such a cute scene and that's what makes it special because it reminds us all about how cute we were with our daddy's before we grew up. This was definitely a hard decision to choose between these two haiku, but it comes down to each reader's personal opinion on which memory they value or enjoy more. It does not come down to which haiku is better but which memory the reader likes more. Stefanie Davis, Spring 2012

    dragonfly
    I have become the master
    of Wii Fit yoga

        Nicholas Sanders, Spring 2015

    hard day's work
    letting loose
    at the barre

        Eve Greenwell, Spring 2015

This was a hard match-up for me decide between, because both of these haiku had similar qualities that were presented well. Both haiku have some sort of comedic relief, which made them enjoyable to read. The "dragonfly" haiku started out serious, but the last line gives the reader a little chuckle, as the serious mastery has turned out to only be of a workout interactive video game. The "hard day's work" haiku had a play on words at the end. Some people after a hard, long day of work go to a bar to drink and let go of some stress. In this case, the bar spelled barre was referring to a ballet barre, which also makes sense because exercising and dancing can release tension and stress. I like the surprise of the first haiku, but I enjoy the pun and double meaning of the second haiku a little better. Ultimately, a "hard day's work" haiku came up on top, since the haiku was open for more than one interpretation, which makes it a diverse haiku for its audience to read and enjoy. Kendall Kott, Spring 2015

    old war medals
    the boy asks grandpa
    what they mean

        Blaine Buente, Spring 2014

    driving grandpa's truck
    by himself
    but never alone

        Aaron Fleming, Spring 2014

I picked both of these haiku because they are related but so different. I wrote this first haiku, but that is not why I like it better than the second one. I like the first one because it is more visual and takes more thinking. When I visualize it, I see a young boy sitting down to a story about the war. The young boy sees the violent side of the war, but the grandpa sees everything that went on during the war: the violence, brotherhood, exhaustion, etc. This makes for a very good story and this is why I like this haiku better than the second one. The second haiku is very straight forward. I see a man driving his deceased grandfather's truck and just knowing in the back of his mind that his grandfather's spirit is there with him. Maybe I don't understand this type of connection between man and grandfather, but I still believe that it is just too "easy" of a haiku. Not in a bad way, it just comes too easy to me, and I like a challenge. Blaine Buente, Spring 2014

old war medals
the boy asks grandpa
what they mean.

Blaine Buente, Spring 2014

braided pigtails
she chatters away
in grandpa's hat

Lexi DeSollar, Spring 2014

When I read these two haiku, I almost felt like two different authors had somehow written about the same grandfather. The two haiku connected so well and become part of one story to me. I imagined that the "old war medals" haiku happened first. Grandpa has gotten pretty old, but he still has enough strength to go upstairs and explain to his grandson, who is about 7 or 8, what all of the medals on his uniform mean. I imagine that maybe the boy's sister, who is a couple years younger, may have asked grandpa if one day she can have his hat from his uniform. Years later, you see her grown up a bit, more around the age that her brother was when grandpa explained the meaning of the medals, maybe a tad older. Grandpa died a few years ago, but she stills keeps him in her memory and in her heart by wearing his military hat, which he left in her possession as he had promised. Jackie Dumitrescu, Spring 2014

homeless man's bench
one stranger stops
just to say hello

Logan Bader, Fall 2018

at the drunk man's feet
the old hound
laps up spilled beer

Haley Vemmer, Fall 2018

I like the kindness behind these haiku. Both of the first lines begin with a location that transports me directly to an imagined scene in my head. The haiku each have a man who is down on his luck. I imagine a homeless man in tattered clothing with an unshaven face and a village drunk who drowns his problems in alcohol. Little moments of kindness like saying hello and making a new friend can brighten one's day, and I imagine that happening here. The two men start their days miserable and depressed, but their spirits are uplifted by a stranger and a dog. Emily Sullins, Fall 2018

I enjoyed this matched pair because they both involved an unexpected visitor that seems, in a way, to add a sort of softening comfort to each of the men. When I think of the companionship of a dog, I always think of how they always love humans the same, regardless of circumstance. They do not seem to propose bias to the sorts of humans that they enjoy being around. They trust all humans fully until they encounter a reason not to anymore. I think this is parallel with the stranger that stops to say hello to the homeless man in my own haiku. I think the homeless man did not expect to encounter companionship of the stranger that is different from him in terms of status, but the stranger is displaying affection to the homeless man, regardless of the external features of the homeless man. Like the dog, the stranger is only interested in providing pure companionship to someone who is alone. Logan Bader, Fall 2018

overflowing trash
dirty dishes
i'm not your mother

Andrea Burns, Spring 2017

smoke in the evening sky—
the first time i saw
my father cry

Emily Chudzik, Spring 2017

Both of these haiku elicited responses from me immediately. They each set up unpleasant images: the overflowing trash and the smoke in the evening sky. It is easy to get a harsh feeling right away. The one about the dishes continues with unpleasant images, and it is definitely something that I can relate to. However, this haiku then uses the unpleasant images to come in and make a joke. The other haiku brings a more nostalgic image to mind. It may have still been unpleasant, but it is relatable as well. I vividly remember the first time that I saw my father cry, and it is still a moment that I analyze today. I think that both haiku were related in their unpleasant imagery, but they took different turns at the end. They even relate to mothers and fathers. Mothers are always picking after the children, and it can be unpleasant. I like in the father haiku that the smoke is covering or masking the pretty evening sky. This could be the author having a cloudy image of their father because of his tears. The story could go many ways. Jordan Oelze, Spring 2017

stuffy classroom
daydreaming . . .
of the world outside

Stacey Orr, Spring 2003

stuffy library
a blonde's tanned legs
s t r e t c h e d

Ryan Jones, Spring 2003

When comparing these two, I find the second one more effective. The first poem certainly creates a nice juxtaposition between the feeling of a stuffy classroom and the world outside that the person can only long for. However, the one thing that I wish were more defined is exactly what the person in the haiku is longing for . . . what is it about the outer world that he or she longs for? The second poem also creates a nice juxtaposition between the feeling of being trapped indoors and a girl freely stretching her legs. This second poem is set apart by the clarity of the second image and its unique use of form that allows the reader to feel the stretch of the girl's legs. Bri Hill, Spring 2003

Both of these haiku do a good job of conveying a sense of heat. In the first haiku, the line "stuffy classroom," and "the world outside" give the setting of spring or late summer. The pause after daydreaming works really well, because you stop to think of what it is the person is dreaming about. This is effective when the last line is finally read, and the haiku comes together. The second haiku is also very effective in the same matter. "A blonde's tanned legs" reveals that a girl is wearing shorts or a skirt that would usually be worn in the spring or summer. The second is the winner because the imagery is much more developed, especially with the letters of the word "stretched" being stretched out. Jared Stahl, Spring 2003

dark road
sparks from a cigarette
bounce behind a car

Julia Shaver, Spring 2004

4th of July . . .
a crowd assembles
to a flaming car

Ben Kress, Spring 2004

I like this pair because of the series of images presented. In both we are first given a sense of time and place, "dark road" and "4th of July" (here I am assuming somewhere on Main Street, USA). This is followed by another image of the event in the sparking cigarette and gathering crowd which transitions into the third lines by a form of movement. The way these haiku transition make them a great pair (not to mention they both have the break on the first line). I think the way these images transition is important to note because of how they reflect the image of the bouncing cigarette sparks and the flaming car—movement of images and words. I really like the color in the "dark road" haiku. The darkness of the night is broken for a moment by two bright headlights and then when our point of view is passed, we get the residual remains of the color in the form of the cigarette sparks, a nice red-orange color that flickers for a moment. It is a nice combination of the cigarette sparks bouncing and the car driving off into the distance. The use of color and movement makes this the strongest haiku in my opinion. Travis Meisenheimer, Spring 2004

Chapter 6

Reading Selected Haiku of George Swede

The Hero's Dark Side

George Swede's collection, *Almost Unseen: Selected Haiku of George Swede*, is an excellent book of haiku and senryu for students to read after reading work by Peggy Lyles and Wally Swist. Although Swede does not discuss his approach in the introduction to his book, the students immediately recognize that his haiku are coming from a different emphasis. Students describe his haiku as more "realistic" and often humorous. His haiku deal with "darker" topics of human anxiety and struggles. Some seem political or focused on issues of social justice. We briefly discuss the senryu tradition of Japanese poetry, which often satirizes people and society. When I point out that he writes about events and perspectives he has never personally experienced, they realize that many of his haiku may be fictional or based on observations and knowledge of other's situations. They often make connections to his academic area—he is a professor of psychology. They enjoy reading his haiku and notice the wide range of topics he addresses that other haiku writers are less likely to address.

In her essay on George Swede's haiku, one student summarized his approach: "With the uncanny ability to make readers laugh as well as cry in the space of three short lines (or less), George Swede is a Canadian haiku poet who wears his heart bleeding on his sleeve. That is, before he rips your heart out and throws it on the ground. Swede's haiku is rife with clever observations about the human experience, every word chosen with meticulous care, even if it may not seem like it. Wry and witty, Swede does not cringe away from tough topics as lesser poets might. Abortion, divorce, death. All of these things and more can be found in Swede's work. Not only does he write effective haiku, he writes effective stories within them." Alexa Duncan, June 2016

Another student wrote: "When we first read a handful of haiku poet George Swede's work as a class, I was pleasantly surprised. Most of the haiku we'd read thus far had been lovely but had focused mainly on imagery. A lot of class discussions had been geared towards talking about how each haiku played on our senses. I was ready for something new, and George Swede offered that. While his haiku still tactically provoke the senses, they also uniquely address human behavior and the human struggle. His haiku is often observational, depicting the outside world, rather than reflecting on the internal. This approach allows him to analyze and make sense of complicated human experiences in a brief and artistic manner." Morgan Oliver, Fall 2013

Here are student responses to favorite haiku by George Swede:

first warm spring day
   I take my shadow
      for a walk

    George Swede, *Almost Unseen*, p. 17

I can feel the sunshine on my face on that first warm Spring day. I picture a small rural town where everyone is out in their yards, neighbors talking over the fence or on the walking track enjoying the end of winter. I can imagine my shadow being our lab dog who follows us everywhere in the house and who is anxious to get out of the house and enjoy a good walk or game of fetch. I can smell the fresh air after being cooped up in the house all winter. Kimberly Dial, January 2018

My favorite part about this haiku is the way the narrator talks about his shadow. It reminds me of Peter Pan. There is a whimsical feeling associated with life-like shadows. I imagine the narrator was probably feeling cooped up all winter. Once the first warm day came along, he went outside for a walk and took his shadow with for some time out of the house. It's light, playful, and easy to picture. Emily Chudzik, Spring 2017

I love the imagery of this haiku. The idea of venturing out after a long winter to bask in the sunshine and enjoy new life is intoxicating to me. Through the dark days of winter, my shadow would have faded into the background. Now, I am enjoying the first day of spring. There is something about the first occurrence after a long period without. I think you appreciate or savor it more than those that follow. The warmth of the new season soaks into my bones. The bright sunshine makes my shadow all the more pronounced. What a perfect companion to join me for a walk. Jennifer Yeakley, July 2017

empty baseball field
a dandelion seed floats through
the strike zone

    George Swede, *Almost Unseen*, p. 19

This haiku has a very bittersweet meaning for me. It makes me think of an old, run down baseball field that has not been used in years. The dirt infield is covered with grass and weeds, and the outfield is dotted with dandelions. A rusted chain-link backstop is still standing, although the fencing is dented in many places. Old wooden bleachers, worn and faded after spending years outside, are behind it. I have seen lots of fields just like this one in small towns throughout Illinois. Once shining examples of America's Pastime, now seemingly forgotten forever. Owen Pulver, Fall 2016

I enjoyed this haiku because it reminded me of all the years that I played softball and how much it saddens me for it to be over. I often drive past the softball field I played on for so many years of my life and think about all of the good times I had with my teammates playing the game I loved. This poem especially stood out to me because, when I played, I was a pitcher. I can imagine walking out to the circle on my empty field, and instead of seeing my catcher, all I see is dandelion tufts floating through the air. Whitney Gray, Spring 2016

the beetle I righted
flies straight into
a cobweb

George Swede, *Almost Unseen*, p. 24

This haiku just makes me laugh. Not a "it's funny" laugh, but an exasperated and short puff of air kind of laugh that says "of course, of course that happened." Although I cannot remember an exact time that this has happened to me, it feels really familiar. It seems to be describing a time that everyone has experienced; maybe it wasn't a beetle they righted, but everyone has had a time when something seems to be getting back on track and suddenly it's not anymore. Taryn Pepping, Spring 2016

Occasionally we have seasons of life that seem like everything that can go wrong does go wrong. This haiku makes me think of those times. You make something right, which is within your control. Then something completely out of your control ruins it. The truth is, there's nothing you can do about it. At least we made the effort to make something right in the first place. Brittani Allen, November 2014

Reading this really makes me look at my lifestyle. I've always been the "hero" type. When I see any of my friends struggling, I always do my best to help them. But most of the time they end up reverting back to their old ways or finding new trouble. One of my best friends from high school I no longer speak with because of this. His sophomore year, I helped him quit drinking. His senior year, he began smoking marijuana, and a LOT of it. I tried to get him to stop, but right after homecoming he got caught and sent to the "safe" school. I've tried continuously to get him to stop, but he is only getting worse. He is nervous, paranoid, and nauseous most of the time, and claims it helps him feel better. I know it's only making his anxiety worse. Time after time I have dropped everything in my life to help him right his life. He keeps finding new trouble. It took me six years to realize . . . I can't save everyone. There comes a point that people simply have to put in the effort and save themselves for once. Aundrea Marsh, Fall 2015

city park
the stone hero's dark side
hides a drug deal

George Swede, *Almost Unseen*, p. 24

This haiku really struck me when I read it the first time. I feel like this statue was of someone that was held highly in the opinions of the people in the town. If they put in the effort to make a statue of him, he must have done something pretty good. But the drug deal behind the "dark side" of the hero literally means the shadow of the statue, but it can also stand for the dark side of the hero. The drug dealer is hiding in the shadow of the hero to do his dirty work, but this may represent a dark side of the hero. Even though he did good things to help the city, there were some not-so honorable things he did behind the scenes as well. I think everyone sort of has a dark side; no one is perfect. Lauren Bartel, Fall 2015

My immediate thought from this haiku was of Batman. Batman is my favorite super hero and in nearly every movie it talks about his dark side and how many people view his actions as bad rather than good. Even though the haiku is referring to a shadow of either light or a blind spot from a camera, I take it to mean that every hero has a dark side. Every person that has a statue of them has done something bad at some point in their lives, but still made a hero out of themselves. This haiku is very easy for me to imagine in my head as two shady characters make this deal behind the statue to avoid being seen by police and the irony of it being a hero's statue that they use as a cover is fantastic. Michael Barber, Spring 2016

> stepping on
> sidewalk ants   the boy
> everyone bullies

      George Swede, *Almost Unseen*, p. 28

Swede brings out the honest truth of bullying in this haiku. Once someone is bullied, they feel the need to bully someone else. Because this boy has been bullied by everyone he knows, he feels the need to show power in another way, by crushing the helpless ants beneath his feet. This haiku brings out the worst of everyone involved. We see this helpless, victimized boy turn and cause pain to other helpless beings as though he has not experienced that same pain. The last line "everyone bullies" especially stops me in my tracks because it is true. Everyone bullies in some way or another: maybe it is to people, maybe to ants or animals. Where do I bully and how? Swede invites you to reflect on your own life experiences and treatment of others. Alyssa Becker, Fall 2016

This haiku reached in and grabbed my heart. I remember being bullied as a middle-schooler. I was smaller than the kids next to me, less athletic, and (here's the worse part) a good student. I remember coming home and feeling so powerless to stop the giants who were tormenting me. Kids can be so mean, without thinking of the lasting effects that bullying has. I can relate to the boy in this haiku. He's probably walking home from school, in his outside shoes with the worn soles, and wishing he had the power to stop the bullies. He's probably wondering what he did to make this happen. And maybe it started by accident—shuffling along, he kicks over an ant hill. But then he discovers that for once he's bigger than something. While he may be powerless to stop the bullies, the ants are powerless against him. We can only hope that the bullying stops before the kid becomes a sadist. Marah Kittelson, Spring 2016

> sunrise
> I forget my side
> of the argument

      George Swede, *Almost Unseen*, p. 44

This one made me laugh because I have had this exact experience. I know I am most moody at night before I go to bed. I become upset and angry at things more than any other time of the day. Most of the arguments I have with people are at night, but by the time I wake up in the morning I often forget why I was so upset. Many times, I also realize the next morning how ridiculous I was being and I laugh at myself. This haiku helped me do that all over again. Lauren Montesano, Spring 2016

This haiku portrays the common yet complicated struggle of the strains we face in our human relationships. In this case, the strain is an argument, which could easily be applied to any relationship: friend, romantic, family or other. Often times, when we are knee-deep in a falling out with someone, we cannot see a solution or end to the problem. This haiku allows the reader "to imagine a positive outcome," by suggesting that with a new day, a new "sunrise," with the passage of time, an argument can come to rest. Morgan Oliver, Fall 2013

after the abortion
   she weeds
the garden

George Swede, *Almost Unseen*, p. 54

This haiku left a really powerful impact on me when I first read it. Swede never tells us how we should feel about this abortion. Instead he filters it through the point of view of the woman who's had the abortion. Ridding the garden of weeds, she doesn't want is a bit like ridding her womb of the fetus she can't take care of. Either way, it's a feeling of release. And immense frustration. Alexa Duncan, June 2016

I feel like "she weeds" isn't only referring to the garden, but also to the abortion itself. When you weed a garden, you are getting rid of the bad plants you don't want. For the woman in this poem she was "weeding" by getting rid of the baby she didn't want. Somehow the awkward spacing emphasizes that even more for me. It seems like she really didn't make the abortion a big deal because she simply moved on and went back to normal life and started weeding her garden. It doesn't say "long after" or "a week after" or even "the day after" it simply says "after," which makes me think it was relatively soon. She didn't need time to recuperate or recover, she just went right out and started pulling out more weeds. Eve Greenwell, Spring 2015

What I love about this haiku is that the picture it paints is such a normal scene of a woman working in a garden, but it leaves so many questions open ended about her past, her reasons, the father, her coping process, and her current feelings. It leaves the reader with so many blanks to fill in it's almost overwhelming, and combined with the normalcy of the other lines, these emotions parallel the possible emotions of the woman. This haiku also does not start with one of the typical "snowflakes," "spring morning" or "warm sunset" lines to set a scene, leaving even more questions open-ended. Natalie Smith, Spring 2016

   under the dirty,
   one-eyed hen   a perfect
   white egg

George Swede, *Almost Unseen*, p. 65

Swede uses great imagery and contrast in this haiku. The description of the hen, "one-eyed" and "dirty", created an image of matted feathers, an ugly one-eyed face, and overall rough tattered hen. The contrast of this image and a perfect white egg is almost miraculous. I can place myself in the chicken house picking up eggs, waiting (with the use of the space) and expecting the egg underneath to be just as poor as the hen covering it. To my surprise I end up finding a beautiful egg and thinking "How does this perfect egg come from such a mangy farm animal?" I love how this brute imagery of a hen and her egg is almost in-your-face and forces you to reflect on how you view the world. Do we see people in the same way as this hen, stereotyping that nothing good or beautiful can come from the rough homeless man? Through this haiku, Swede reminds me that beautiful can come from anywhere or anyone. Alyssa Becker, Fall 2016

This haiku touches my life daily. As a Human Services major, I have to shut off my judgmental side that everyone is guilty of and dig deep to find the pearl in everyone. No matter what the person looks like or has done, they are still a human being and should always be treated like one. I have a vivid story in my mind when I was in junior high, I would always get called "preppy" by other girls in my class because I wore name-brand clothes and always looked my best. Some people wouldn't look beyond that and they judged me as if I was this stuck-up girl who lived with a "snobby" family and wasn't nice to anyone. That was not me at all; I was the most kind-hearted person to every-one who got to know me. Now, some of those girls are my good friends and we keep in contact up to this day. Even though this haiku talked about a "dirty one-eyed hen" I could still relate because I was being judged just like the hen. Because I am going to be working with people of all walks of life, we need to remember to never judge by looks or how the person comes off to you. We need to find that person and their strengths and build within those variables. Alex Dorchinecz, January 2015

leaving my loneliness   inside her

George Swede, *Almost Unseen*, p. 79

Wow . . . after I read this haiku, I couldn't do anything for a few minutes afterwards. It says so much in only five words. I love that the author put both phrases on a single line; it seems to indicate how connected they are. I wonder if leaving the loneliness means he won't be lonely anymore, or if she will share the loneliness. I just thought this was an exquisitely painful view on the union of a man and a woman. Katie Colletta, Fall 2010

This poem really stood out to me because of its simplicity but also because of the weight it held. The first image I got from this poem is of the typical tool guy who walks around like he is the shit, being disrespectful left and right. But in reality, he is lonely, unhappy, and unloved. With every girl that he disrespects and hurts, it gives him power and allows him to feel loved for at least the night. But he never lets her get too close for fear of being vulnerable and hurt. It's a defense mechanism; using and abusing woman that actually care about him. Brittany Falardeau, Fall 2010

This haiku, I feel, sounds very pleasant to hear. The flow of the words, and the sound of the L's are just really pleasing to me. However, I do not think this has a very pleasing meaning. I see this in two ways with the first reading being an emotional connection. I think of it being that she is his significant other, but outside of her company, he is very lonely. Therefore, he takes all of his loneliness and loses it because of her. However, an-other reading of this makes it more intriguing. I think of this as being about sex between a couple that no longer has emotions behind their relationship. They either lost touch, or this relationship never formed any nurturing emotions. Her company does not comfort him. Their sex is just the actions. There is no physical intimacy. There is no close con-nection. There is only the two people. My friend read this, and said this haiku was dirty. I do not believe that sex is dirty. It is a natural thing that involves intimacy and vulner-ability between two people. I do not think of it as dirty, but in this haiku, it feels dirty because of the loneliness. With this loneliness, the idea of intimacy and vulnerability are absent, therefore, all we are left with is the act of sex. The narrator knows that these are absent, that is why he leaves loneliness behind. He leaves part of himself inside her, as he literally leaves part of himself inside of her. Nicholas Sanders, Spring 2015

in one corner
of the mental patient's eye
I exist

George Swede, *Almost Unseen*, p. 82

No one likes to talk about mental illness. As a society, we've gotten a little bit better at destigmatizing things like anxiety and depression, but we still have a long way to go and this haiku shows that struggle in a deceptively simple way. Those of us who struggle with mental illness tend to "hide" in one corner of ourselves, like the speaker does in this haiku. I imagine a man, freshly out of his stint at a mental health facility, going back to that facility now that he's out. He sees another patient there and he sees himself in that patient. It's a vicious cycle. Alexa Duncan, June 2016

In this haiku, it is unclear who "I" may be to the mental patient in question. Could "I" be the nurse, the doctor, a family member, or simply another patient in the facility? This is where personal experience and bias would come into play and each person would relate to the haiku differently. For instance, if the "I" were to be a family member visiting the patient, this haiku could almost be sentimental. The family member could be visiting the mental patient, hoping that the patient would recognize him/her this time—it's almost as if the haiku is a plea for the patient to snap out of his/her condition. However, the haiku could also be interpreted from inside the head of the mental patient. In this case, "I" would be a figment of the patient's imagination—leading the reader down the thought path of a schizophrenic. Elise Scannell, Spring 2012

This haiku appeals to me because it is not literal. The idea of existing only in a mental patient's eye is not something that is physically possible (or at least possible to prove), but the image is a strong one even though it is not an experience that you can feel physically. This haiku represents a fantastical loneliness. The lonely feeling may not be sad, rather it is magical. This person exists only for one person, in one person's imagination. This mental patient can rant and rave about someone existing, but no one will believe them. If the mental patient didn't continue, this one person would not exist, and yet the mental patient can see them. The last line "I exist" seems a declaration of victory to me, as if to say I may only be in this one corner, but I'm still here and I matter to someone, no matter who they are. Beth Ann Melnick, Fall 2010

alone at last
I wonder where
everyone is

George Swede, *Almost Unseen*, p. 87

On campus, I live in a house with seven girls. It is very hard to ever find a time where you are at home by yourself. This haiku makes me think of finals week last semester. It was starting to wind down but studying so much had exhausted me. When I get exhausted, I get crabby. At the end of the week, I wanted nothing more than to just go home and relax and not deal with anyone. After a semester of living in the house, I had figured out that it was unlikely to be at home by yourself, but when I got home that afternoon, no one was there. It made me wonder where everyone was, but I really was not too upset about it because I finally got the peace and quiet that I was hoping for. Allyson Isenhower, Spring 2018

I am happily married with four teenagers. A moment of solitude is a rare treasure in this season of my life. Just the other day, I arrived home before everyone else. I had a few minutes of perfect quiet and calm. Did I take the time to savor it? Absolutely . . . but only for a moment. Within a few minutes, I am watching my phone for text messages. I scan my son's work schedule posted on the refrigerator to make sure that I remember our conversation correctly from earlier in the day. I send up a quick prayer for safe travels and begin watching the driveway for the first signs that my daughter will pull in the drive. As much as I long for a moment of aloneness, I just don't quite know what to do with it. Jennifer Yeakley, July 2017

I find this haiku very powerful. I am an introvert, and I find that I need to be alone for some time each day so that I am able to "recharge" and have time to myself to think and reflect on things in quiet. However, that being said, I also struggle with depression. As a result, I tend to isolate myself much more than I should. I find that I want to be alone, but at the same time, I want to be in the presence of others. I go to much greater lengths than I probably should to find alone time, but when I am finally alone, I find that I am lonely and that I long to be around others. It is a paradox—a very confusing one that I am still not quite sure how to handle. There are days when I force myself to go out and be around others, and I feel much happier, but then there are also days when I really do need to be alone or else I begin to feel surrounded and stressed and panicky. I just liked this haiku because it made me realize that maybe I am not alone in experiencing these conflicting feelings. Mackenzie Peck, Fall 2014

> at the height
> of the argument   the old couple
> pour each other tea

> George Swede, *Almost Unseen*, p. 109

If something is broken you fix it, you do not throw it out and get something new. Just like this couple, who even know that they disagree, know it is fixable. They go on with their loving task, simple things as pouring tea even though they were arguing. A life time of memories is not worth the few inconveniences of misunderstandings. This haiku makes my heart smile. Michelle Holsapple, July 2016

I found this one extremely warm hearted and it just made me happy, despite the fact that this old couple is arguing. They have been married for so long, I assume, that they know basically everything about each other, so they argue, just like anyone else, but their love for each other still shines bright as you can tell when they pour each other tea. Although they do not agree about something, they know that their love still holds true and that they will continue to love each other, but honestly, who agrees on absolutely every-thing? And if they do, how boring would that be? They have come to understand each other enough to know that people do not always agree but that their love will endure, and they will still respect each other, enough to still be courteous and caring to pour each other tea, even in the heat of an argument. I picture this old couple either sitting in the dining room of their house, which is in front of a large window that people passing by can see in, or even sitting in a little café that is not very crowded. Sydney Brangen-berg, January 2017

This haiku is everything a relationship seems to strive for. The old couple, beyond the state of physical attraction and in a new stage of their relationship, are still challeng-ing each other. They haven't resigned passion. They still delve into new topics (unless this is an old argument). They respect each other enough to still pour each other tea in the heat of battle. Unfortunately, I haven't met this mythical couple, this promise of the perfect marriage. I only imagine that someday I could have this. To find someone who would continue to challenge me for years to come seems a dream, and this haiku offers a glimpse into a dream. Bill Ryan, Spring 2009

on the bus
the teenager pulls out a mirror
and adjusts her pout

George Swede, *Almost Unseen*, p. 19

I found this haiku very cute because it reminds me of my high school days. I was a total fashion freak and I loved taking selfies all the time. I would literally take selfies everywhere—in the bathroom, at the mall, during some classes in school, at the bus stop and even on the school bus. And taking a pout-selfie was my favorite. Also, I would get bored on the bus because I had no friends to talk with. All of my best friends were on a different bus, so I would just take a bunch of selfies to pass away my boredom. Jesal Sheth, Spring 2018

As someone who just graduated from high school a year ago, this poem is relatable and cracks me up because it takes me back to 9th or 10th grade me. The "adjusts her pout" line is so accurate but also so ridiculous at the same time that it's hysterical. I remember at that age always having something to complain about at any given moment, and in all reality, that "pout" or negative attitude really was a part of my everyday persona. I either had to get up too early, or I was hungry, or I had a bad hair day. This poem captures that memory and allows me to laugh at who I used to be. It also is somewhat encouraging because it allows me to see how much I've grown up between freshman year of high school and now. Morgan Oliver, Fall 2013

This one reminds me of Saturday's in high school. I was on the speech team, and we had to be up very early. Most of the guys wore their suits but the girls didn't, and even when they did, they would wait until we were close to do their makeup. I loved watching them, because the process was so interesting, I guess. Most of the guys watched; it was rather strange. All the work that went into them "putting on their faces" just seemed ridiculous to most of us, but like a necessity to them. I can just see all the little gadgets and tools that went into it. This haiku focuses on the lips, however for me still paints a clear image of those Saturday morning speech team bus rides. Philip Koberlein, Spring 2007

Kukai - Favorite Haiku or Senyru on Coming of Age

Several of Swede's haiku, such as the "adjusts her pout" mentioned above, focus on human transitions such as coming of age. This is a topic that appealed to college students who are adults, for the most part.

quiet girl
walks away from her past
in hot pink pumps

Melanie Mclay, Spring 2006

I think this one was my favorite of all. First of all, the image I get from "quiet girl" is my best friend. We are complete opposites; I'm the loud one and she's the quiet, reserved one. She's gorgeous, but she doesn't really have confidence in herself. The next line, "walks away from her past", I literally see my friend leaving our town going to college. She goes to Western Illinois, and she has blossomed there: she has confidence and she's more outgoing now. She really came into her own. "Hot pink pumps" is an awesome image. Pink is all about girl power to me and so are the pumps. The girl in this haiku is forgetting everything she used to be and starting over being whoever she wants in these stellar pumps! Rachel Cook, Spring 2006

It seems to me that this haiku was written to have emphasis on the first two lines, with the third being a lead-in to her new life. I read it the first few times that way, but suddenly a different approach occurred to me. I read it again with emphasis on the first line and saw the second and third lines as a reference to the past. This is particularly meaningful to me because while I used to be crazy and wild, college has had a different effect on me. I've settled down. Even though I got excellent grades in high school, I've really begun to concentrate on my studies, working towards an early graduation. With my best friend thirty miles away and my boyfriend seventy miles away, I've become more of a homebody and less of a going-out girl. Some people might see this as a bad thing, but I LOVE it. I'm more focused and organized and I've caught up on my reading. I still have fun with my friends, but I've put away the hot pink pumps (or, in my case, hot-pink-knee-high-boots) for now. Sarah Corso, Spring 2006

12th birthday party
squeals as she opens
her first miniskirt

Jenesi Moore, Fall 2018

This haiku captures a moment that I feel like every girl goes through. Whether it is a miniskirt, a bra, makeup etc. we have all had that coming-of-age moment, when not only us, but the other people in our lives are coming to recognize our adolescence and womanhood. As this girl is opening her gift, she is very excited for her future, to feel pretty, wanted and accepted with her other friends and classmates. Her family members that are watching her are probably smiling and rolling their eyes, both excited for and dreading what will come next. Melanie Wilson, Fall 2018

grade school playground—
the boys help me look
for my earring

Aubrie Cox, Fall 2008

I like the image in this one—an adult woman searching on her hands and knees around a playground with the aid of a group of male children. Boys of this age would not be helping unless they really wanted to, and it's the eagerness of the boys that really shines through. The narrator may not have even asked them to help out; they may have just done it of their own accord, and there is just a simple humor about this poem that I really respond to. It's very hometown. Mark Beanblossom, Fall 2008

This one is just too cute to pass up. I can see a group of grade school boys helping out their teacher? She lost an earring and the boys think they are so helpful by helping her try to find it. The children will probably talk about their teacher's missing earring for the rest of the day, because it is so important to them that they were trying to help. Very cute. Brandy Bockewitz, Fall 2008

after school
kissing the girl
I used to kind of sort of like a little bit

Brian Rhode, *Millikin University Haiku Anthology*, 37

I love this haiku because it has a whimsical, middle school-ish vibe. I see a junior high boy and little girl passing secret notes to each other during the course of the day. Each time they read the other's message, they giggle lightly, knowing they aren't supposed to be passing notes during class. Then, one letter the girl writes to the boy asks if he likes her. He replies yes, and they meet after school in the empty gym. They kiss and run their separate ways, maintaining the naiveté of young schoolchildren. Eddie Pluhar, Fall 2010

I thought this one was one of the cutest haiku in the anthology because it deals with both young and old relationships. At first, you think of this haiku as depicting young children after school due to the language of the last line. However, after thinking more about this, I pictured the couple as one in college, kissing after class. The reason he includes that type of language in his last line is to show that they met when they were very young, before they were willing to admit overtly that they liked each other. But now they are still dating in college and are able to tell each other they love each other every day. Lauren Montesano, Spring 2016

I really like the sense of innocence I get from reading this haiku. I picture two young kids, probably no older than junior high age. I can see the boy walking home the girl that he obviously has had a major crush on for some time now. I get the feeling that she hasn't returned the feelings until this kiss. The last line makes me laugh because it's as if the boy is pretending to act all tough, like it's no big deal to him. In reality, though, he is on cloud nine kissing that girl . . . but that wouldn't be cool to admit. The wording of the last line sounds exactly how a kid that age would talk, too, which adds to the effect. Liz Ciaccio, Spring 2006

under the covers
midnight conversation
on the phone

Jessica Golden, Fall 2010

This haiku just is really true with what it is saying. I really like that when I was younger, I so remember trying to sneak conversations when I first got my cell phone. I definitely was the girl who would be on the phone, late at night, talking to her boyfriend. The worst part was always when my dad would walk in and he could always see the light from my phone through the covers. It was never good to get in trouble with dad. My dad was very protective and did not like his little girls talking to boys, especially after being in bed for 3 hours. Allyson Staudenmaier, Fall 2010

I like this one because it brought back a lot of memories. I remember thinking that if I hid under my blankets to talk on the phone that my mom would not hear me and I would get away with it, however, most of the time I did not. I like how the haiku mentions that its "midnight" because when you are younger being up until midnight seems so cool and you want to get away with it so that you can tell everyone that you were up so late. I feel like this haiku also represents times when I was even younger, before I had a phone, and I used to use a flashlight under the covers so that I could stay up reading past my bedtime. Samantha Miles, Fall 2010

polka-dot dress
fixing my lipstick
for the third time

Isabella Loutfi, Fall 2018

This haiku reminded me of the excitement and nerves before a dance. I'm not sure why it was that and not a date, but the polka dots reminded me of the crazy prints one can find at high school proms or homecoming. I was only asked to one dance during high school, but I made sure that my makeup was on point an hour before my date came to pick me up. Just reading the haiku, I felt the nervous jitters that cause pacing and looking out front windows, as well as the excitement to be seen in public all dressed up and on display with someone equally as dressed up and excited. Daria Koon, Fall 2018

valentine's dance
I only go
for the cupcakes

Brianne Marsel, Spring 2002

This is my favorite in the kukai. I love the hopeful opening against the dismal end. I enjoy how the girl goes merely for the food—I can almost see her stuffing her face in despair at the dance, as the boy she likes dances with another girl. I just love the sassy and sarcastic, yet not utterly depressing, tone of the poem. Instead of giving just an idea of why the dance is sad (like "I go dateless"), the poem provides a concrete image of why the person IS going. I think it's incredibly clever. Meg Schleppenbach, Spring 2002

slow dance
back of his shirt
damp with sweat

Alyson Ludek, *Millikin University Haiku Anthology*, p. 17

Middle school dances are perhaps the epitome of awkwardness. Pimple-faced teenagers dress up and stand around a sweaty gym waiting for someone to ask them to dance during "Just the Way You Are" by Bruno Mars. I remember getting to dance with a pretty girl once and the whole time I was sweating because I was so nervous Also, I had been jumping around a lot and there were a lot of kids in that hot gym. It was awkward then and coming home afterward and taking off my shirt to see how sweaty it had gotten was the nail in the coffin. Nicholas Scarpinato, Fall 2015

When I read this haiku, I got a clear mental picture of a high school dance. Everyone was in the gym, which was covered in decorations. There were tables with punch off to the side, and the basketball court was covered with groups and couples dancing. I could picture myself dancing with my date, surrounded by our friends. The next song that comes on is a slow song, so we all pair up. The boys are all sweaty from dancing so much. It's unfortunate that they have to wear long sleeves and long pants. So, as we danced, I could feel the sweat on his back that had soaked through his shirt. It is such a sweet moment, yet kind of touched by reality because of the sweaty shirt. Lauren Bartel, Fall 2015

first funeral
hand-me-down suit
two sizes too big

Jennifer Godwin, Spring 2009

This haiku brings a sad moment and a funny vision of a child in a suit that is way too big. Many people don't understand death and funerals when they are younger. I didn't really know the man that died at my first funeral. I remember feeling weird because everyone was sad, and looking at this man that was unmoving, but looked like a person. I think that a first funeral is a scary and memorable experience. I like how this haiku has a little comedic vision inside this otherwise scary experience. Lizzy Kelly, Spring 2009

underage cleavage
I let her order
another drink

Susie Wirthlin, Fall 2010

The first line really makes this haiku. "Underage cleavage" is perfect. Cleavage has such an immature connotation with it. It paints the picture of who the drink is being ordered for, the attitude of the person ordering drinks, and thus the circumstances of the haiku, very well. You can almost hear the annoyed sigh from the person ordering drinks when they see the smile plastered on the underage girl's face when the drink comes, like she just got a great treat. Jackson Lewis, Fall 2010

This senryu is not only shocking but has a number of layers and key word choices that make this an excellent senryu. The way that the author focuses on the cleavage, rather than the girl, emphasizes that someone who would participate in such actions typically is focused on body parts rather than the person as a whole. The second line leaves just enough to the reader's imagination—is the "I" the bartender or is the "I" someone buying the drinks for her. "Another" also implies that this is a reoccurring thing, despite knowing the girl is underage. It has a good balance of telling and leaving it to the reader's imagination; it has the best qualities of a senryu. Aubrie Cox, Fall 2010

she hides her blemish
and her baby bump
graduation day

Francesca Rios, Spring 2015

I liked this one a lot because of the irony. It reminds me of my high school. There was a girl a grade ahead of me who was pregnant on graduation day. She kept posting on social media that she was more worried about the massive pimple on her forehead rather than hiding the 5-month baby bump. I think it kind of relates to what girls prioritize in their lives. A lot of young girls don't understand the risks they take, and they're more worried about materialism. I thought that the irony was funny, which is why I liked it. Katelyn Rumph, Spring 2015

I like this haiku because it reminds me of a small town where a girl has not told anyone that she is pregnant yet. I think the contrast between her blemish and a baby bump is funny because it shows you how young the girl actually is. I imagine the graduation being a high school graduation and the girl not wanting to tell her parents because she does not want to ruin this positive time. The baby bump seems small, so it is recent news. Austyn Krueger, Spring 2015

quick grocery store trip
wearing no makeup. . .
class reunion

Heather Dolye, January 2016

The haiku is light hearted. Someone makes a quick decision to run to the store hoping to not see anyone they know. Wearing no makeup expresses their vulnerability. The last line really tied the haiku together, revealing numerous run-ins with acquaintances. Kailey Hurst, January 2016

This haiku made me laugh because of how typical this situation is. I pictured myself, needing something small, only one thing, from the grocery store to complete my meal for the night, and I run into a big group of people from my class in high school. It is a very awkward situation, seeing as I haven't talked to them or seen them for several years. I can relate to the part about not wearing any makeup, and how it isn't necessarily embarrassing but I haven't seen them in a while and now I look different than I would if I got ready that day. I like the ellipses after the second line, making me pause and think about what could happen next at the grocery store. At first, I thought maybe this person will meet someone they like and fall in love with later, but no, they are seeing people from the past, not the future. Emily Mihalkanin, January 2016

lying on the
trampoline
mapping out our future

Emily Chudzik, Spring 2017

This haiku describes a very important part of my childhood. Growing up, all of my friends had trampolines and after a significant amount of convincing, my parents bought me one for Christmas one year. So much time was spent on these trampolines. We would jump all day and go crazy, playing different games and attempting different tricks. However, at night we'd just lay there and look up at the stars. We would talk about crushes and funny memories. Those were the times when we were at peace with the world. There is such an innocence about this piece that I really appreciate. Brittany Walsh, Spring 2017

This haiku drew me in because it has a loose sense of childhood and a keen sense of growing up. I could imagine myself lying on a trampoline with a good friend, sister, or crush and talking about The Future. Often times as a child, I would bring up my big dreams just so I could live through the hope in them for a night, you know? Also, the trampoline adds a subtle movement to the haiku; I imagined undulating in a wave of black net below me. I noticed that the word choice is "our future" instead of "our futures", so that made me feel protected and connected to the person I was lying with in my head. Kala Keller, Spring 2017

coming home
with new experiences
my friends still having the same ones

Rob Spurling, Fall 2012

This haiku is somewhat sad and happy at the same time. Coming from a place where not everyone goes to college, it's a bit weird how you can go from one place to the next and come back to where you were from originally and noticing that sometimes nothing changes. This is a sad realization in some cases because to me it feels like the people you're around will never fully live up to their potential. Others seem to keep repeating the same things they were doing a year ago. And at the same time, it gives me hope for my future that makes me feel as though I'm going somewhere in life and moving on toward a better tomorrow. Christopher Potter, Fall 2012

This haiku was very relatable for me. Out of my entire group of high school friends, I was the only one who went away to college. There is a small community college in my town, and all my other friends stayed home and went to school there. Luckily, more of them are leaving now so they will not be stuck in a rut. But when I would go home last year, it was really weird to me because none of my friends really knew what I was talking about whenever I would talk about college. It was either that or they would complain about not being somewhere else. It just made things awkward for me sometimes. Most of those people who I was friends with before are not close friends with me anymore. Maybe it's just differences, but I can really relate to this haiku. Morgan Ewald, Fall 2012

speechless at her news
his gaze drops
to her navel

Megan Klein, *Millikin University Haiku Anthology*, p. 129

This one just made me happy when I imagined the look of the guy when he gets this news. I saw him being speechless because he's so happy at this news, and when he looks at her stomach, he is imagining what their child will look like and its future as well. He is probably thinking about everything that he wants to do with this child, what sex he hopes it is, possible names, what it will look like. I just think that this is a really special moment for a couple, especially if this is their first child. For this one, I had a break after the first line, making the reader wonder what this news is, is it good or bad news? Sydney Brangenberg, January 2017

The best thing about this haiku is that the reader can interpret it however they want. While it gives a clear image of a woman telling a man that she is pregnant, it doesn't give any real sense of emotion. The story is set and then it gives each person the opportunity to imagine the story in their own way and to make their own connections. I imagined it as a young couple, who hasn't been dating for long, getting pregnant on accident. She isn't sure how he is going to react, and she isn't even sure how she feels about it yet, so she doesn't tell him until after she has gone to the doctor on her own to confirm the pregnancy. When she tells him, he is shocked and scared, but they are both actually very excited. Mackenzie Larrick, June 2016

My daughter was born 4 years ago when I was 20. It was not a planned pregnancy and my husband and I were trying to finish college and start careers. I can remember the day

I told him and him doing the exact same thing as described in this haiku. He was completely speechless and looked at my stomach. Although she is a complete blessing now, when I first broke the news I could relate to the girl's pain at his speechlessness and his fear at what to do. This could also be a woman telling her husband of her pregnancy and her husband being so excited he is speechless. Maybe this is something they have wanted for a long time. Lindsey Wright, November 2012

neighborly chat
a young woman serving tea
in a mason jar

Jennifer Yeakley, July 2017

My grandparents were farmers. Their house was full of mason jars. To me, this glass container exemplifies a lifestyle full of simple pleasures, hard work, community, and hospitality. My grandparents worked hard planting, weeding, and harvesting their crops. In the late summer, they would store away fruits and vegetables after sharing their abundance with family and friends. My grandmother would often crack open a jar when company came over. In my mind, my haiku features a young woman who has set-up house recently and has assumed the role of hostess to a neighbor she is getting to know. It speaks to the refreshment of sun tea and the enjoyment found in good conversation. Jennifer Yeakley, July 2017

Kukai - Haiku on Human Struggles & Social Justice

she takes off her shoes
and her belt . . .
airport security

Emily D'Ambrose, Spring 2013

I absolutely love this haiku based on the sudden change of tone from the first two lines to the last line. A great example of comic relief in haiku, this poem creates a mysteriously sexual mood only to slap the reader into a new world of airport security. For reading purposes, the ellipsis used is also a great choice, as the pause between the second and third line allows the imagination to explore what might happen next before the "punch line". Therese O'Shaughnessy, Spring 2013

licking his face
the once small puppy
tastes Iraq

Morgan Oliver, Fall 2013

This haiku has so many emotions. There is the emotion of leaving, growing up, missing someone, returning home, etc. I don't personally know anyone that has left for war well enough that I have had to experience these emotions in this way, but they are not difficult to sympathize with. I especially love the use of the puppy because I understand the bond between a dog and their owner and have seen videos of dogs showing unbelievable joy when seeing their masters return home from war and without a doubt, they have brought tears to my eyes. Ramey Sola, Fall 2013

This haiku is very meaningful and full of emotion. Both individuals who have family members in the military and those that don't can understand the meaning of this poem and feel the emotions expressed in this haiku. A soldier can only take memories with him as he leaves for service. While he is gone many things change in his life at home. When the soldier returns, it seems like a lifetime has passed because he has missed some important and some not so important changes that have occurred. At the same time, the man's family experiences these same emotions because the man who is in front of them is a completely different person than who he was when he left. Codi Gramlich, Fall 2013

lighting candles
don't ask
don't tell

Caroline Lodovisi, Fall 2016

I imagine this haiku taking place at a military funeral of some sort. Since the phrase "don't ask don't tell" is associated with being homosexual in the army, I immediately thought of a funeral for a gay service man or woman. Perhaps the fallen soldier's significant other is at the funeral and everyone is wondering if they were in a relationship or not, but obviously the setting is not correct for such a question. The people that gather at funerals are often strangers to each other to some degree, leaving everyone wondering what the connection is. Savannah Riestenberg, Fall 2016

crisis hotline
she pops her gum
in between my words

Jenesi Moore, Fall 2018

This is one of my "darku". It refers to dark times. While I never myself have called a crisis hotline, I have a friend who did, and the person who answered the phone seemed to be more annoyed by my friend's pleas for help than receptive to them. She said that she kept making a noise that sounded like she was clicking her tongue when she would say certain things. I felt bad for my friend. The "annoyance" reminded me of how annoyed I get when people pop their gum or look away when I am trying to communicate with them. Hence, I wrote this haiku. Jenesi Moore, Fall 2018

in your rainstorm
I open
my own umbrella

Mikaela Vuglar, Spring 2019

I like this haiku because it reminds me of one of my best friends. When I close my eyes, I see my friend, who always seems to have a rain cloud over her. There is thunder, lightning, and torrential rainfall pouring onto her head. I imagine myself trying to give her an umbrella, but she pushes it back towards me as she stomps away. I simply open my umbrella and step into the rainstorm with her. Some days, I can push the rainstorm away and the sun will come out. Other days, the rainstorm only grows, and I find myself choking on the copious amounts of rain that come with her storm. It is cold, the sky is dark, and everything is wet. The storm grows like a poison, and I would love to save myself, but only if I can save her first. Amanda Bivens, Spring 2019

I enjoyed this haiku because of how deep and emotional it got me. It made me see multiple scenarios when I said it over and over. I pictured a single cloud over someone, and it is just pouring down on them, until someone else comes along and opens their umbrella. Another version I saw was actually one without the rain but more so seeing someone upset and another person going to spend time with that person in order to cheer them up and get them out of their storm for a while. Kevin Miller, Spring 2019

long line at the soup kitchen
mother-daughter
lunchtime

Susie Wirthlin, Spring 2010

I can imagine it is a summer day at noon, and the soup kitchen is filling with customers. A woman and her teenage daughter stand patiently in line, waiting for their meal. This lunchtime ritual has been theirs for quite a while, because they are suffering financially. I can imagine the silence between them as they eat their meal. Although they do not talk much, they still value their relationship, because it is all they have left. Jade Anderson, Spring 2010

chopping onions
mom asks
about Democrats

Nicole Zabrinas, Spring 2008

This makes me think of something I could see happening with some of my relatives (who were convinced I was going to be brainwashed in university and high school and middle school). It also reminds me of something a classmate said last semester when he had been talking to his grandfather who asked if he had turned into a commie liberal now (which I'm convinced is an oxymoron). It's another one of those poems that involve small talks during menial tasks. Aubrie Cox, Spring 2008

singing freedom's song
hush child
or they will hear you

Jessica Joyner, June 2018

I chose this haiku as one of my top five because the history behind the haiku is powerful. Black slaves were known for creating songs that had hidden messages, but they had to be careful while singing on their way north because someone may hear them. This haiku is like one of those songs with a hidden message, and it has become one of my favorites. Jessica Joyner, June 2018

shot after shot after shot
the room starts spinning
someone please save me

Naomi Klingbeil, Fall 2018

I found two different interpretations of this haiku. One reading of "shots" is like a shot of alcohol. I imagine that the author is at a party, has had too much to drink, and is starting to lose their bearings. Another interpretation, and my initial reaction, was that the shots are gunshots, which makes this very sad. I pictured a mass shooting, and that this was the narration of someone who is caught in the middle of it. Melanie Wilson, Fall 2018

Kukai - Favorite Haiku on Feminist and Gender Issues

fish out of water
i wear a dress
to please him

Brittney Gillespie, Spring 2007

Conforming to the patriarchy! Argh, I get so angry when I think about how girls waste so much time trying to dress in something that will please a man. It's very silly and in the end, no one ever benefits because you're uncomfortable, and that translates into your carriage. Just wear what you want, and if he doesn't like it, kick him in the shins, hard. Deirdre Fields, Spring 2007

I like this haiku because it reminds me of the phrase, there are plenty of fish in the sea. Meaning don't worry there are other men/women in the dating pool. This reminds me of the situation I am in now. Not knowing whether to settle down or to keep fishing, I keep dressing cute to catch my own. Lorin Glazer, Spring 2007

dumb, fat, lazy . . .
I look in the mirror
believing his lies

Jacquelyn Manicki, January 2009

This haiku can be interpreted in so many ways. I take it as a woman being hard on herself, thinking she is an idiot because she keeps believing a man that she knows is lying to her. She lets him get away with it because she thinks she is fat, and lazy, so she hangs on to this liar thinking she cannot do any better. Julie Trimble, January 2009

This haiku makes me think of a lady looking in the mirror having a bad day. Maybe she has PMS, which happens with women. She is trying on all kinds of clothes for the day and can't decide what to wear. She looks in the mirror and thinks to herself; I am fat, dumb, and lazy, I hate myself. As she is thinking, her husband or boyfriend tells her that she looks good. After he tells her that she looks good, she thinks to herself; he is such a liar. Amanda Cole, January 2009

as we slowly kiss
i wonder if he'd love me
if i was pretty

Courtney Burress, Spring 2013

One has to imagine this goes through the heads of many people when they are in a relationship with someone. It's so difficult to determine what role physical attraction should play in romance. As humans, we tend to be most interested in people we find physically attractive, but then it's easy to wonder if we are invested in the relationship for partially faulty reasons. I enjoy this haiku because it bluntly points out one of the most common thoughts humans have: am I loved for me, or the things I possess? Darien Sloat, Spring 2013

I like this haiku because even in such a tender moment, when someone is kissing you softly, you can still feel self-doubts. She is having self-confidence issues despite the fact that she is receiving soft loving kisses. I can understand where she is coming from becáuse I find myself doing that occasionally too. But what I've learned is that it is important to just cherish moments while they are happening, and not try to analyze them, because you will never get it right. Emily Crutchfield, Spring 2013

his honeyed words
stuck to my skin
hours of scrubbing

Alexsenia Ralat, Fall 2016

When I read this haiku, I picture heartbreak. This is relatable for anyone that has ever been led on by someone that they really liked. Even when you realize that the person is not good for you, it is still hard to accept. It takes a long time to lose the feelings that you once had for them. Even long after they are gone, they still sometimes cross your mind and that old hurting feeling comes back. This haiku gives a message that anyone who has ever loved and lost can understand. Owen Pulver, Fall 2016

I really like this haiku because of the use of the term honey. Honey in itself is something that is sweet and desirable, even innocent. Yet the author compares the lover's voice to honey, and the love betrayed has left the author scrubbing away the residue. I just think it's a very powerful piece that many of us can relate to. Jordan Comish, Fall 2016

dancing with a
Buffalo
the overcrowded bar

Emily Chudzik, Spring 2017

In this haiku, I can imagine a distinctly overcrowded bar that has people stepping all over each other. I imagine a very popular bar that has a promotion going on or that it's spring break. I find it ironic that the author uses the word "Buffalo" because this animal is enormous. To place a buffalo in an overcrowded place makes the scene even more uncomfortable, which is why I like this haiku. The buffalo becomes a human equivalent in size that is dancing with a person. They both might feel awkward because there is no room or just because the guy is the size of a buffalo. I liked the words used in this haiku that made it funny and interesting. Kate Gebultowicz, Spring 2017

lunch with a client
she smiles through
the sexist jokes

Lane Caspar, Fall 2017

This was my favorite haiku because it's a very relatable situation for most women. I imagine a successful business woman meeting with an important client, at a table in a coffee shop. He makes sexist jokes and she is offended but has to pretend everything is alright, so she doesn't lose the deal. I can imagine the frustration she is going through, because I've been through the same thing. She is also uncomfortable but is forced to hide it because of her job. Overall, I loved the topic and flow of this haiku. Georgia Martindale, Fall 2017

red lipstick
smudged at corners
Venus shines dull

Hannah Ottenfield, Fall 2018

While reading this haiku, I imagined a girl who hasn't had a very good night. Maybe stood up by an important date. This date was very special for some reason. Perhaps she was going to tell her date she loved them? They didn't show, and it broke her heart. She's been crying and upset all night, and her makeup is smudged with sadness. Venus, the goddess of love, has failed her. Sophie Kibiger, Fall 2018

halloween night
afraid of guys
not ghosts

Isabella Loutfi, Fall 2018

This haiku captures the very real fears women have beyond Halloween night. While going to parties, women must be wary of men following them and watch their drinks at parties. Halloween is just another night where their fears for themselves trump their fears of ghosts or monsters. I appreciate the alliteration of the words "guy" and "ghost" because it is a nice connection between the two things. Rachel Pevehouse, Fall 2018

New York subway
a hand on my ass
that doesn't belong

Sophie Kibiger, Fall 2018

I like how the first line and last two connect—the image of a New York subway implies lots of people, which is where the random hand on her ass comes from. I appreciate how the language is simple and not flowery because it doesn't distract from the reality of the situation. It captures a specific moment that many women can relate to, even if it's not this situation exactly, and the simplicity allows various women to insert their own unique experiences with harassment. Rachel Pevehouse, Fall 2018

Chapter 7

Reading Masajo Suzuki's Love Haiku

A Season of Fireflies

Masajo Suzuki is one of the Japanese haiku authors that my students read in depth. They read her book of selected haiku: *Love Haiku: Masajo Suzuki's Lifetime of Love* with translations by Lee Gurga and Emiko Miyashita. Both Gurga and Miyashita are accomplished contemporary haiku authors, plus Emiko was a lifelong friend of Masajo Suzuki. Their translations are authentic and read well as English haiku. Suzuki's haiku are selected from her published books, arranged in chronological order. Students enjoy her honest haiku about relationships written in her bold, independent woman's voice.

In an essay on Suzuki's haiku, one student wrote:

> *"What was amazing to me about Masajo Suzuki's haiku was that in post-war Japan one special woman overcame her hurdle against society's expectations of her and delved into the art of haiku. Suzuki stepped onto a path of independence to live her life the way she wanted and was open about her affair with a married man. Masajo defined her art as an extension of her own heart because that was her own way to celebrate her independence to choose whom she could love and what path she could take, even though sadness sometimes leapt from her haiku. She used her art of haiku to express her views on her culture as well as the restrictions that Japanese women experience since their virtue is tied to their ability to follow the cultural expectations. Therefore, Suzuki's style of haiku was like an autobiographical narrative of moments in her life that she felt were worth experiencing, even though many of the memories brought her sadness. Her belief in the wonderous feeling of being in love and living life fully made her haiku exceptional."* Alya Saqar, Spring 2007

Reader responses:

a moth dances into the flame . . .
the nape of the man's neck
draws me in

Masajo Suzuki, *Love Haiku*, p. 25

Suzuki's haiku is a refreshing break from some of the other haiku that we have read. Her words are extremely passionate, and I appreciate the fact that she's not afraid to reference sexual things in her haiku. If every haiku about love, or really any subject, was pure and innocent it would be an unrealistic representation of life itself, but this poem is red hot with passion. The flame paralleled with that particular spot of someone's neck is a beautiful image and one that I am sure many people can relate to. Considering this poem was so early in Suzuki's collection, I knew I was going to love her work immediately. Sam Miller, Spring 2017

I like this haiku because of the comparison of the author and a moth. The image in the first line of a moth dancing in the flame is very visual and something I can really picture. The image recalls night for me, and moths circling the lamp outside of my house. The moth is drawn to a light which creates a sense of danger for the moth, but still they go to it. This is mirrored in the relationship between the man and the author. The man (specifically his neck) draws her in like the flame draws in the moth. He is dangerous, but she is still drawn to him. This haiku takes a cliché phrase and puts a fresh spin on it. The ellipses after the first line create a lingering effect. It makes the reader pause at this spot, just as a moth would pause at a flame. Beth Ann Melnick, Fall 2010

> that one time
> my heart so merciless:
> I burned a hairy caterpillar

>   Masajo Suzuki, *Love Haiku*, p. 27

I really like this poem because it shows, to an extent, that everyone goes through rough times. "My heart so merciless," makes me think that a girl has just gone through a breakup with someone and is heartbroken. She then does something that she knows later she probably shouldn't have. I think everyone at some point in their lives goes through a tough time, whether it be from a breakup or from losing a loved one. It is really difficult to adjust to such a big change that makes our hearts sad. It might throw us off the loop for a while, to where we just aren't normal. It's like there's a piece missing from the heart that has molded to you for such a long time that it's so hard to let go. Emily Holthaus, June 2016

I just love this haiku, it is definitely my favorite one from this book. It is so sensory and filled with emotion. I feel like it was born out of guilt as someone looks back to a time when they were hurting and because of that they were able to do something horrid. In this haiku they admitted and confessed their regret and understood that they have come far from there. I also got some serious sensory images with the last line alone. The rest of it is more of an idea but that last line brings in a scent of burning hair and the image of the caterpillar writhing in pain. It is so powerful even though it is a very small image. Great last line. Jessica Brooks, January 2015

> in these three worlds
> a woman is never at home;
> snow on snow on snow

>   Masajo Suzuki, *Love Haiku*, p. 28

This haiku is my life. It makes me think of the saying that a women's work is never done. As a wife and mother my job is never finished. From waking up early getting my son ready, doing the dishes, doing homework, cooking dinner, you never get a break, which is why the author said snow on snow on snow. Marshaya Sangster, July 2016

This haiku speaks very strongly to the gender inequality in Japan and the rest of the world historically (and in some places, currently). A woman is always considered an attachment to some man, whether it be her father, her husband, or her son. The wording of never being at home just really captured the feeling that these women had, unable to make their own decisions or forge their independent lives. It also is important to see that this occurrence is not strictly history—Suzuki felt this same sensation in the 20th century. I also like the way that the weight of the snow piling up on top of itself, repeated 3 times to match the 3 male homemakers, reflects the weight of being aware that no matter your situation, you have no control over your life, and letting that slowly sink in. Cori Grzenia, Spring 2016

> your letter concealed
> in my kimono's breast pocket—
> basking in winter sun

> Masajo Suzuki, *Love Haiku*, p. 28

I really enjoy the concept of winter sun. There is the cold dead feeling of winter along with the distant warmth of the sun. I enjoy how this relates to the topic of letters from a lover. Like the sun the lover is far away but still able to give warmth to the reader. Perhaps she keeps it in her pocket so it is close to her and giving that warmth. However, the winter suggests that the love may not be what it always was and that something has caused it to grow stale. Maybe the letter is even from a while ago and just kept as a reminder of the good times. Savannah Riestenberg, Fall 2016

I really like the way Masajo Suzuki uses the seasons in her haiku. I think the use of the season furthers the image, particularly in this haiku. I can imagine this letter, which is probably concealed because it is a love letter that she doesn't want someone else to see because it is forbidden or because she wants to keep it private. The letter is concealed in her breast pocket, which means it is close to her heart. I love the way she writes about the warm winter sun. I can imagine the cold that comes with winter, which is contrasted by the sun. This also implies that she is warmed by the words of the letter. I can imagine her walking and thinking about the beautiful love letter in her pocket and I can imagine her feeling the warmth of the winter sun even more because she is warmed by the words of her letter. Emily D'Ambrose, Spring 2013

> a glass of beer—
> I serve it to a man
> I will never love

> Masajo Suzuki, *Love Haiku*, p. 34

I loved this one. I see it as a lady bartender or a waitress. She is strong. There is this roughness to a lady bartender. I don't mean to swear but I believe the term is "hard ass bitch." I see this as her poem. There is a silence to the poem though. She might like him, but she is stronger. In all I just loved the vibe of this poem. Definitely on my top ten list so far! Amy Hofstetter, Spring 2007

This haiku describes a disinterested woman in a pub. She pours a glass of beer for the man over at that table. He's been making eyes at her all night, but she's just not interested in him at all. She has to pretend to like talking to him, though, because that's what her job requires of her. This man isn't the man she loves, the man she longs to be with. She pours his beer because she has to and that's it. No emotional connection there, even if he wants it. She doesn't care. It's a bold haiku for a Japanese woman of that time to write. Alexa Duncan, June 2016

This haiku made me sad, point blank. But I feel like this is truly the case with so many people today. We, as humans, will stay with someone we don't love just because we don't want to be alone. I know I have done it. I've obviously never served a beer to this person, but I have tricked myself into looking at only the bright side of a horrible situation. I wonder if the author is with this person or not. I automatically assumed that she is in a relationship with this person, however, it could be that this man loves her, and they are just friends and she feels guilty that she will never love him the way that he loves her. Courtney Burress, Spring 2013

autumn wind—
he pretends not to see me
as he passes

Masajo Suzuki, *Love Haiku*, p. 35

This haiku appeals to me because within seconds, I can feel a rush of cold air slapping my face as "he" passes by. Autumn wind is cold and crispy, and frequently calls for a thicker sweater. I can feel the faux warmth of the narrator's sweater as she remembers the warmth he once gave her. There is a moment of hope and communion from the narrator, but instead of it being recognized, it is responded to with disengagement and indifference. An autumn has commenced after a sunny and fruitful summer—a silent coldness seeps into something that used to breathe. In a way, I read this haiku and imagine the skin worn by the narrator . . . possibly seeing some fading tan lines underneath her sweater . . . and definitely documenting stiffness in silence and cold skin. Kala Keller, Spring 2017

I liked this haiku because I can not only relate to it, but the words chosen were very clever. By adding "autumn wind," it made the haiku seem even more painful. I imagine that you are passing by an ex-lover whom you once had so much comfort and pleasure in being with, and now you cannot even get a glance as you pass. If Suzuki had not added the first line, it would've just made the encounter awkward, but by adding "autumn wind," the reader can actually feel the hatred or coldness that remains between the two. Whitney Gray, Spring 2016

without regret . . .
is such a life possible?
beer foam overflowing

Masajo Suzuki, *Love Haiku*, p. 70

This haiku is probably my favorite haiku I have read. I can picture a man sitting in a dimly lit bar staring into his beer and contemplating life. He thinks about his past and all of his regrets. Thinking about it, he realizes that having regrets is a part of life and everyone has them. The three periods at the end of the first line allows for a long pause and for the reader to think. At that point, I started to think about all of the regrets that I have in my life, just as I assume other readers do. Also, the question the speaker asks himself makes the reader answer the question in their own minds. Michael Barber, Spring 2016

I don't think a person can live a full life without regret. I think we learn from our regrets and our mistakes. They help us grow as people. I really like the last line because it makes me think that the person in the haiku is wishing for a life with no regrets, but he is drinking away his regrets right now. I think he is pondering the decisions he has made in his past and wondering how things could have be different. Trying to find the answer

in the bottom of the bottle. Drinking away his feelings that he no longer wishes to feel.
Megan McGurr, January 2016

> April Fool—
> I do my hair and go
> nowhere

Masajo Suzuki, *Love Haiku*, p. 46

I loved this poem because it has a playfulness to it in the "April Fool" line on the surface, but also a deeper loneliness within its meaning. I have done this, done up my hair
and make-up just to feel pretty and had nowhere to go, and more importantly, no one to
be with. I like while it does not mention being alone, it still implies loneliness in the last
line. I also particularly like the "April Fool" line because I think of how as people, we
tend to make jokes to cover up our deeper emotions. I get a sense of that in this poem.
I also think that this poem is more geared towards women because of the imagery of
doing up your hair, which men don't really do as often and may not relate to as well.
Morgan Oliver, Fall 2013

This haiku immediately hit home with me. I love to look pretty and do up my hair and
go out, but in high school I often would end up sitting in my room, waiting for a boy to
call or text me back. This especially happened a lot with my ex-boyfriend. He would
promise to call me back, take me out, come over . . . and then never follow through.
While he was doing who-knows-what, I was sitting at home alone on the day I had
left free for our plans. The "April Fool" was especially fitting in this haiku: she was so
excited to go out and see her lover, but in the end, it was like he had called and said,
"Just kidding!" I can feel that disappointment weighing down on her as she looks at her
done-up hair and face, alone. Susie Wirthlin, Spring 2010

We've all been there, haven't we? All dressed up with nowhere to go and the April
fool's joke turns back on you. I love the honesty in Masajo's haiku. She doesn't put on
a façade or bother with formalities. She writes from her heart and this is one instance
where it really shines through. The woman in the haiku does her hair all nice and pretty,
but she's not even being stood up at a bar or something. She literally has nowhere to go.
I like to think she found some entertainment for herself at her house, though. Maybe she
wrote some haiku. Alexa Duncan, June 2016

> washing at night—
> all the laundry
> is my own

Masajo Suzuki, *Love Haiku*, p. 55

This haiku is very simple but conveys the overwhelming sense of loneliness so well. I
love how it is also specific that the washing takes place at night. This gives a dark feel
to the haiku. It also conveys that the narrator has been putting off the laundry because
it reminds her of her loneliness. Doing just your own laundry after doing yours and
someone else's feels strange and heartbreaking, and Masajo Suzuki conveys that feeling
so well and so simply. Rachel Humphrey, Spring 2018

This haiku feels so lonely to me, and I think it captures the feeling perfectly. The line "all
the laundry is my own" seems to me that the laundry used to include others as well. This
shift in learning to be by yourself and all alone can be a difficult one. I think that setting

this haiku at night also adds to the feeling of isolation in this haiku. However, I also think that this haiku could be taken another way, and that it could be the first description of her freedom and independence from her past relationships. She is only responsible for herself and she no longer has any obligations to other people. She is finally free from her previous burdens/relationships. Anna Harmon, Fall 2016

> for a woman
> unable to pray . . .
> a falling star

> Masajo Suzuki, *Love Haiku*, p. 105

I love this haiku. As someone who is not religious, I often wonder how to do the equivalent of praying. There are some desires that are just too strong to simply think about; it seems like some greater power must be contacted. I enjoy that the author equates wishing on a star to prayer. Although it seems foolish to wish on a star, it gives the wisher a sense of action that they have done something about their desire. The falling star shows that there is something bigger and aware of our desires, but only we can do something about them. Savannah Riestenberg, Fall 2016

For this haiku, I imagine a woman kneeling trying to pray but finding herself unworthy, uninspired, and unable to. As a sign of comfort, a shooting star appears, and the woman feels more at peace. I found myself really relating to Masajo's haiku. This is a bit backwards from the haiku, but I have a very vivid memory from my time in London. My friend and I were sitting outside in the back garden of our flat, looking up at the stars. We were listening to the song "Stars" from Les Misérables, and all of a sudden, a shooting star shot across the sky. It was one of the most magical things I've ever experienced. It also came at a really needed time, because I was starting to miss my family, and it felt like a sign of comfort. Emily Chudzik, Spring 2017

I chose this haiku because of the sheer beauty of the mental picture I formed while reading it. While it does not directly relate to a life experience for me, I can relate similar experiences. While reading it I pictured a caregiver praying for and/or with a woman that was no longer able to do something so dear to her. I could see myself in the place of the caregiver and taking the time during a work shift to offer a prayer for a patient who no longer could. I depict the falling star portion as a person who used to be very vigilant to their faith, but age could be preventing them from it in the time this haiku is set. While I can see various people having different responses to this haiku, I believe I formed this mental picture based on one of the things in life I hold most dear, caring for the elderly. I love the wording in this haiku and will think about it frequently when I say my evening prayers. Sara Siegfried, Fall 2014

Kukai - Favorite Haiku on Love and Relationships

first date
not sure
where to put my hands

    Cliff Ault, Spring 2004

I really enjoyed this senryu's ability to capture the awkwardness of a first date. This poem embodies the initial giddiness of a first date that is the conglomeration of nervousness and excitement and anticipation, all combined with the inadequacy of wondering what is to come. Almost all of us have been on a first date and questioned what to do with ourselves. I envision a young high school couple on their first date to the movies. The boy wants to hold her hand, but just doesn't know if she's ready for that. He doesn't want to seem too pushy. The entire time she thinks to herself, "why doesn't he hold my hand already?" Sneakily, she rests her hand loosely on the armrest hoping he'll finally get the hint. Alida Duff, Spring 2004

This is a great image. I think this is one of the most awkward things about a first date. It's the time when you are testing the limits to see what is acceptable. You may want to hold the girl's hand, but you're not sure if it is ok yet. Then you think she sends you a sign, but maybe it's not and then you tell yourself to stop over-analyzing everything. But it's too late and your hands gently meet, but not on purpose. So, instinctively you back your hand away, but then try to go back because it was about to happen, but now it's too late. So, it's a confusing thing. Colby Hanik, Spring 2004

he whispers . . .
   I love you
rain
   on the windshield

    Jennifer Griebel, Spring 2003

This haiku is one of my favorites from our Valentine kukai. I think that part of the reason it is so powerful is because of how the author uses space. I like the back-and-forth motion that the lines create. To me, it accentuates the rain on the windshield. The unsteady starting point of each line is comparable to the unpredictable fall of raindrops. The pitter-patter of the rain on the windshield is not only heard but felt through the use of space and pauses within the haiku. It helps set the mood and the moment. The hesitation it creates as you read it seems to reflect the nervous uncertainty of the man in the haiku. The space before the actual words, "I love you", show the reader that perhaps he hesitates before he says it aloud. And then quickly after he says it, "rain". Again, the reader can feel the silence after he says it. No one speaks, only rain is heard. I think that without the excellent use of space in this poem, it would lack atmosphere and feeling. Michele LaBrose, Spring 2003

I really like the form in this haiku. The three dots (ellipsis) are more punctuation than form, but I like what they add to the haiku. It starts off and gets you almost ready to listen to a story and then there is a pause until the "I love you." I like the suspense created there. As for the form, I feel the overall form sort of symbolizes and brings the rain to life. The phrases are all scattered around just as raindrops would be on the windshield. Courtney Ruffner, Spring 2003

someone to confide in
this sudden gust
of wind

Laura Podeschi, Spring 2005

This made me think of when I met a person, got to know them quickly and then we
went our separate ways. Usually it takes a long time to get to know a person and be able
to confide in them. Sometimes you meet a person, you click, and the entire lifespan
of the friendship is put into hyper-speed. This haiku made me imagine what it is like to
have a person come into your life and confide in them soon after meeting them, and
then having the relationship disintegrate. You can almost sense some wistfulness about
the loss of someone in this haiku. Rachel Walker, Spring 2005

barefoot
in the grass
we talk about everything

Erin Knott, Spring 2008

I like this haiku because it reminds me of the night I started dating my high school
boyfriend. It was July 5, 2005, and I called him to stop by and say hello before I slept
over at my girlfriend's house. I was wearing a yellow t-shirt and gray sweatpants, and
the night air was slightly chilly. He came outside for what we thought was a quick hello,
and we sat down in the grass to talk. What was supposed to be ten minutes turned into
three hours. The sky was pitch black with sparkling silver stars. At one point during the
evening, I was telling him something and he kissed me midsentence. It was the perfect
end to a perfect evening spent with my best friend-turned-boyfriend. I ended up staying
there a little longer until my girlfriend called me and was worried about where I was.
This haiku really captures the essence of two people who care about each other care-
lessly passing the time. Lindsay Scully, Spring 2008

pebbles on my window
I look
for you

Nicole Zabrinas, Spring 2008

With this haiku, I imagined a college dorm. There is a girl and a boy, and they have
crushes on each other, but they're not quite dating yet. One day, the girl comes back to
her dorm room later than she had expected to because she had some sort of meeting
and she notices that there are pebbles sitting on her windowsill. She wonders if he had
been looking for her earlier. She knows that the pebbles weren't there before she left
for classes that day. At that moment, he comes into her view carrying a bouquet of red
roses. Erin Knott, Spring 2008

he mirrors my movements
a good sign
according to Cosmo

Sierra Shaw, Spring 2009

I like this haiku for a couple of reasons. Aside from being comical, it is a great expression of a first date. It shows the thoughts of one person in the situation, although they are probably not far off from the other person's thoughts. She is paying close attention to his movements and seeing how he reacts to her. Is he into me? Is he not? Is he giving me a sign? Am I into him? These are all things I see her asking herself, while thrust deep into conversation, and it is something that we all do in this type of situation. Furthermore, the fact that she is referring her observations back to what she remembers from Cosmo is an excellent representation of the modern woman in our society. Bill Ryan, Spring 2009

my twelve-page confession
you say
thanks

Kale Ewing, Fall 2010

When I first read this poem, I was reminded of the episode of *Friends* where Rachel writes Ross a 24-page letter, front and back, talking about why they broke up and how she felt and everything. But personally, although I've never written a letter like this, I've had a conversation like this. The moment when you have poured your soul out before another person while you wait for their response is agony. On a technical perspective, I love the construction of this haiku with "thanks" all on its own, and the decreasing syllabic pattern. Katie Colletta, Fall 2010

There is definitely a certain unspoken code when it comes to writing notes, and now texting. It's so incredibly obnoxious when you type up a bunch of stuff and then all you get back is a 'k'. It's ten times worse when they throw in a period at the end. I also loved how all the girls in class ganged up on the guys about the curt reply then it turns out that Kale wrote this haiku. It's always assumed that guys are the ones that always deny the girls, when in reality it probably happens just as much to them. Laura Scoville, Fall 2010

watching the stars
somewhere
someone loves me

Mikayla Shaw, Fall 2014

This haiku is so perfect. I am a dreamer and a wonderer, and I often think of what the future holds for me. It is so strange to think that there is someone out there that will love me one day, and who I will love as well, and we may not even know each other yet. I could drive myself crazy trying to figure out what will happen in the future, and who I will end up with, but there is no point because things will happen as they are meant to happen. Life will lead me where I am meant to go, and until then, I'll just have to sit back and enjoy the ride. Mackenzie Peck, Fall 2014

I like this haiku because of the emotions it conveys. I love to look at the stars and be amazed by their beauty. I imagined myself at home in my driveway looking up at the night sky. The idea of thinking "somewhere someone loves me" would be something that I would think because I get so inspired by the sky. When I feel alone, I can look at the sky and see that everything is so much bigger than just me and that there are people out there that feel the same and people that I will meet later in life and connect with very well. Erin O'Brien, Fall 2014

Orion's Belt
a path that leads
me to you

Daria Koon, Fall 2018

This haiku is just so sweet. It personally reminds me of how my boyfriend and I always look for Orion in the sky. It is something little that connects us and reminds us of small, beautiful things. I think it is also interesting because people would find and tell stories in the stars and this person is creating their own story in this constellation. It also reminds me of how people used to navigate with stars and this constellation helps the author navigate her feelings and relationships. Rachel Pevehouse, Fall 2018

I like the reference to an actual celestial body. This just gives me a really beautiful image of a long-distance couple. They are so far apart and yet they see the same stars and the same planets and the same moon. Also, the fact that they likely have to fly to each other gives the space imagery another layer. I think it's a really beautiful and well written haiku. Hannah Ottenfield, Fall 2018

boy friend
the small space
that is the friend zone

Francesca Rios, Spring 2015

I like this one because it has a pun and play on words with the phrase "boy friend". Boyfriend as one word means a guy in a relationship, but this boy is just a friend who is stuck in the friend zone. It is funny because the small space between the two words is what separates his title from being her lover, but he is not. The haiku is well written to give it the meaning of that funny pun. It also is just entertaining to read because I feel like that is relatable for a lot of people. Being in the friend zone is an awkward feeling and position to be in, and often people don't know where their relationship stands. The small space the poem refers to is almost like a reference to walking that thin line on the border between "friends" and "something more". Kendall Kott, Spring 2015

Valentine's card
no match
for a lighter

Breana Bagley, Spring 2019

This haiku brings in a pleasant moment of surprise. At first reading this, I was hesitant to keep reading because I thought it was going to be another "forever alone" Valentine's Day haiku. But, the addition of the final line brings in a different story on this Valentine's Day. I am curious if the Valentine's Day card came from someone who the narrator didn't want to get one from—like an ex or mother? Whoever it came from, the author of this haiku was not happy about it. Connor Mendenhall, Spring 2019

let go of my
spaghetti,
tramp

Emily Mihalkanin, January 2016

I thought that this haiku was funny. I immediately look at the haiku and get two different meanings. First, I think of the movie "The Lady and the Tramp". I think of Lady looking at the dog pulling on the other end of her piece of spaghetti and insisting that he back off. The other way that I looked at this haiku is from the eyes of a woman angry with another woman. She looks at the woman and calls her a tramp before making sure that she doesn't touch what is hers. Samantha Bies, January 2016

coffee brews—
you tell me you
need more time

Emily Chudzik, Spring 2017

I loved starting out with an image and almost a topic that the couple is fixated on. This is the reason they are together right now, the coffee, but it isn't what they're talking about. The coffee stands as a distraction should they need it, but they really need to discuss their relationship. I also like the multiple "you's" for their sound, and they also give a feeling of despair and confusion with them. It's not a nervous energy, it's an absorbing action that takes a second to work through. Andrea Burns, Spring 2017

yellow dandelion
I ask him
if he's happy

Laura E. Podeschi, *Millikin University Haiku Anthology*, p. 113

This haiku reminded me of running into an ex-boyfriend. Yellow dandelion suggests something outdoors, something plain and ordinary, commonly overlooked, but seen, even if only momentarily, as beautiful to someone (perhaps like the relationship they had). Now, however, it is just a weed. I see it as the guy left the girl for someone else, and the relationship ended in a whole mess of heartache for the two. When they run into each other, the girl is hoping that he will admit how his life is in shambles and how karma has succeeded again, however she finds him loving life and where he needs to be, and only further realizing she hasn't fully recovered. Brittany Falardeau, Fall 2010

the family calls her
his fiancé
at his funeral

Lane Caspar, Fall 2017

I love this haiku. It's so heartbreaking. I imagine that the man was planning to propose to her, and he told his family about it, but he died before he ever got the chance to ask her to marry him. If she didn't know about this until the funeral, that makes it even more devastating. It's so sad to think of what could have been for the two of them. They could have gotten married, had kids, and grown old together, but their time together was cut unexpectedly short. It's so unfair. Maya Dougherty, Fall 2017

This haiku pops out to because of the surprise at the end. The first two lines create a nice little intro to the story that seems all sweet and dandy. The third line totally swerves the haiku in the polar opposite direction. It makes me take a deep breath and collect myself every time I read that line! When looking at the haiku I imagined a man that has just asked his girlfriend to marry him, and that they were in the beginning stages of planning their wedding. However, he died a sudden death before they could get married so during the funeral, instead of referring to her as his almost wife, they keep her title to him in the present time and still call her his fiancé even though there is no possible way for them to get married now. But another person could interpret it as the man was about to ask the woman for her hand in marriage before he passed, and she had no idea, but the family did, which would be absolutely devastating for the woman to find out that way. So many ways of interpreting such a tragic yet beautiful haiku. Maria Klek, Fall 2017

spring sun
quiet conversation
in the grass

Jared Stahl, Spring 2003

barefoot in the rain
we confess
those unspoken feelings

Chrissy Hulse, Spring 2003

I chose this matched pair of love haiku because I think they are both very well written. The first one paints this beautiful image of the grass and the sun. This, by default, makes us feel warm, thus making the conversation that is being had a warm and gentle conversation. This is a great image. Then we get the second poem. In this one we start in a much different way, with the rain. Maybe it is just me, but rain helps to symbolize passion. Think about love scenes in Hollywood, the "best" ones are under a waterfall or such, therefore showing the passion of rain. So, when we get the rain setting the scene instead of the sun, a totally different image is poised. Then we get this great word "those". If we were to confess unspoken feelings it would not be the same, but when we confess "those" unspoken feelings, this poem takes on a deep meaning and the passion of the rain carries through. Christopher Bronke, Spring 2003

The first haiku gives a feeling of peacefulness and warmth. You can feel the warm spring sun on your shoulders and the soft grass on your feet. Quiet conversation creates a romantic feeling and also includes the sense of hearing. The second haiku also captures the feel of spring with the cool splashing of rain on bare feet. The sense of hearing is also included in this one with unspoken feelings. Both these haiku are a bit romantic and both are peaceful. Jennifer Griebel, Spring 2003

late late night
my t-shirt smells a bit
like your deodorant

Alissa Kanturek, Fall 2018

This haiku makes me so happy because there's nothing better than new love filled with constant romance. The smell of someone you like on your clothes doesn't just give you butterflies, but it fills your whole heart and makes you smile from ear to ear. I can't help but be happy when I read this, and I just want to read it over and over again to be continually filled with contentment and happiness. I picture a girl in a baggy t-shirt smelling the front of her shirt with the slight smell of her partner from possibly spending a very late night with him and with the sniff of her shirt, she's reminded of the memories which were created the night before. Hannah Haedike, Fall 2018

the french fries
are cold—
     we gossip

Tina Horve, January 2019

As a 21-year-old girl I was immediately drawn to this haiku. I picture a circle of girls that went to high school together coming back from college to share the year of memories together. They ordered their food and anxiously sat down to begin conversing. The girls hardly noticed when the food was brought to them, too captivated with every story. As they gossip about the friendships and loves they created and that were broken, their fries get cold. However, the girls could care less because they are just happy to be together. I loved the pause after cold, a tragedy at first but all is well because there is a feeling of togetherness. Maggie Comerford, January 2019

my mug is empty
you smile
and fill it full

Isabella Loutfi, Fall 2018

I loved this poem instantly because it gave me such a warm feeling. I love the metaphor of the empty mug representing a heart or a soul. I find it sweet that something as simple as a smile fills that person's "mug", which shows that this person makes the author extremely happy. I also appreciate the universality of the haiku because anyone could relate this to a friend, family member, or significant other. Rachel Pevehouse, Fall 2018

When I read "my mug", I automatically think of having a cup of coffee in the morning and the sadness that comes with seeing the emptiness in the cup when all of my coffee is gone. The next line of "you smile", makes me literally think of all of my loved ones and anyone that has ever made me happy and I just picture them all smiling at me and the joy their happiness brings me. This haiku is just so genuine and sweet and shows that with a few simple words one can be filled with contentment and happiness. Hannah Haedike, Fall 2018

peanut butter lid
on the counter—
no longer newlyweds

Joanne Weise, *Millikin University Haiku Anthology*, p. 83

I loved this haiku because of the intimacy that it brought to mind. It seems to me that when people get married, they still try to keep up a type of façade during their first months of marriage. They still sneak out of bed to brush their teeth before their significant other wakes up, they fold their clothes, wash their dishes, and just generally present themselves as a more put together human being as a whole. This idea of leaving the peanut butter lid on the counter makes me think that this person has found the comfort of marriage, and is in some way presenting a more truthful, if not as perfect, version of themselves. I love the emotional intimacy in a relationship that that requires, and I think it lends sweetness and depth to the poem. Molly McCullough, Spring 2013

I think this one is adorable. When you first get into a relationship with someone, everything is somewhat on edge. You're careful about what you say, what you wear, and how you act. Then if all goes well, it gets to a point where you stop caring so much and finally let go. You're able to let the other person see all sides of you, including the crazy bed head, smeared make up, morning breath, and messy apartment. I think when you find someone that you're comfortable enough around to be completely yourself, then you're incredibly lucky. It takes time, commitment, and love to be able to let someone else completely into your world. Laura Scoville, Fall 2010

> face to face
> with an old friend
> only beers between us

> Ryan McDonald, Spring 2018

I loved this very simple haiku which is how I want to shape my next batch of haiku. But this is a very relaxing haiku—good friends just sitting and drinking a beer. Not only enjoying the beer, but the moment with the old friend. Deion Corley, Spring 2018

I liked this haiku because I could easily see myself in this situation. Sitting down at a table in a bar. Talking. Drinking. It just seems so simple and easy in this haiku. To me, this haiku ends positively, me and my friend are overjoyed to see each other. Conversation flows naturally and the only thing on the table is literally cans of beer. Andrew Cliatt, Spring 2018

> in your eyes
> a thousand mysteries from
> before you were mine

> Haley Vemmer, Fall 2018

This haiku brought me to a sad place. It made me think of someone that you've just met. This person is so perfect, almost as if they were meant for you. You're blinded by all the things you are finding perfect about them without even knowing their past. Not knowing that they grew up in a terrible household or not knowing that their mother died when they were young. And maybe they've had some behavior that may allude to these mysteries that they have yet to tell you about. Maybe you want them to tell you all of these things without pressing them. Rather than pushing them to tell you, you just wait patiently. You listen and appreciate all the perfection that you see in them. Naomi Klingbeil, Fall 2018

I think this haiku is very beautiful but also very sad. I imagine a couple lying next to each other, under the stars, and they want to know everything about each other. They never want to leave that moment and just keep talking into the night. But they're both jaded, they have some scars that haven't healed yet and the relationship is still new so they both don't want to scare the other off with their baggage, but all they know is that they want to be together. Hannah Ottenfield, Fall 2018

Chapter 8

Reading Contemporary Haiku Anthologies

The Many Voices & Silences of Haiku

The students in Global Haiku Traditions read anthologies of contemporary haiku in order to learn more about the diversity of contemporary voices and approaches to writing. We begin by reading *The Haiku Anthology: Haiku and Senryu in English*, third edition, edited by Cor van den Huevel. We also read a recent *Red Moon Haiku Anthology of English-Language Haiku* edited by Jim Kacian and an editorial board. The annual Red Moon anthologies feature selected best haiku and related haikai arts published in the previous year. The third anthology, *Haiku: The Art of the Short Poem*, edited by Tazuo Yamaguchi and me, includes a DVD video featuring interviews and readings of haiku by haiku poets at the 2007 Haiku North America (HNA) Conference in Winston-Salem, North Carolina. These anthologies and video provide students with a glimpse of the broader contemporary English haiku community.

Here are a few reactions of students to reading these anthologies and watching the DVD video:

The English-language haiku community struck me as very collaborative. I noticed that at the conference, there was never just one particular style of haiku. It ranged from jazz haiku, to nature haiku, to musical reflection haiku, to all other forms. I personally thought that the American style of haiku was very contemporary as compared to the traditional Japanese. This really supported the claim at the beginning of the video, that stated that the development of American haiku is a completely different path, that branched from the original Japanese traditional haiku. Logan Bader, Fall 2018

Listening to the various English-language haiku authors speak, I understood that the community is very accepting. They accept that haiku can come from any language, culture, perspective, or country. Many of the authors also discussed how haiku connects them to the world and their feelings. Haiku opens readers and authors to a clearer and more accepting view of themselves and their surroundings. One poet that especially intrigued me was Sonia Sanchez. Rachel Pevehouse, Fall 2018

I learned that the English-language haiku poetry community is extremely dedicated to their craft. They read and listen to all of the haiku they possibly can, and they often get together with each other to read their haiku. They appreciate Japanese haiku and take inspiration from it, even though the English-language style can be very different from the Japanese style. It was cool to see how excited everyone got about haiku when they were all together, sharing their writing. Sophie Kibiger, Fall 2018

From my years of participation in the haiku community as a writer, editor, and teacher, I would say that the most fundamental misunderstanding about haiku is related to conceptions of form in poetry. The essence of the haiku as a global genre of literature is related to form, but not as a characteristic of the structure of haiku. As students encounter a wide range of haiku from the anthologies, they often raise the question about form and the structure of haiku on the printed page. The DVD anthology from HNA 2007 also includes extensive discussion about the form of haiku, so this becomes a key question at this time in the Global Haiku Traditions course.

Early in the semester my students realize that their conception of haiku as taught in the schools or based on the usual dictionary definition (a 5-7-5 syllable poem about nature) is limited or as students say, "it's wrong." After reading some haiku, inevitably, one of them asks, "Dr. Brooks, if haiku is not five-seven-five syllables in three lines, then what IS the form of haiku?" I tell them this is a good question, and one that they already intuitively know based on their reading experiences. I suggest we can find the answer by listening to haiku that we read out loud. We read several haiku out loud and I ask them "Did you hear the form of haiku?" They puzzle over it for a little while, and if necessary, I say, "Okay, let's read a sentence or two and compare the sound of a sentence to haiku." They listen to both sentences and haiku and hear that a sentence almost always has another sentence before it and after it, and that they don't give the reader much room to get into the thoughts or words of the sentence unless you really slow them down with artificial pauses. I ask the students to consider how the form of haiku guides their inner thoughts and reactions as they read a haiku out loud and think about them.

My students offer, "Ah, so form in haiku is about the silence!" And I answer yes, it is about the quiet space before and after the haiku, and usually the pause somewhere inside the haiku. Form is something that is heard, and in haiku the essential form is about the silence or the pauses crafted by the writer to invite the reader into the haiku's space. The Japanese refer to this as the "haiku cut". Form is a means of providing the writer and reader with a movement of consciousness—something that occurs in readers' minds and hearts as they take up the phrases and silences around and within the haiku. Haiku is not about a haiku moment, though most are written in the present tense, as if we are jumping into the middle of things happening. Haiku are shared consciousness.

My students and I discuss haiku form as a psychological process of (1) noticing, then (2) thinking deeply about what we are noticing. The writer draws the reader's attention to notice something, then invites the reader to join in the process of meditating or contemplating the deeper significance of the thing being noticed. The noticing is up front and often explicit, but the contemplation portion is left open to the reader as a process of felt imagination, interpretation, association, and/or cultural memory. The form of haiku is to say, notice this! Then the haiku implicitly asks, what do you think of that?

Haiku is not a closed form of verse with three lines of five-seven-five syllables, self-contained and finished by the author. Haiku is an open form of poetry in which the silences before, within and after the haiku resonate with surplus meaning. Basho called this surplus of meaning "yojô". These unfinished silences are deliberately left open to the reader, so that the reader can enter into the imagined space of the haiku as a co-creator with the author to discover the feelings, thoughts, insights, and overall significance of the haiku. This surplus meaning is shared by the writer and reader, with a playful variety of unpredictable responses. In my opinion, this is the primary joy of haiku—the writer has crafted a haiku as a creative response to nature, reality, dreams, art, imagination, or to other haiku, and the reader gets to enter into that playful haiku with his or her own creative response and imagination.

Students also ask about the visual structure of haiku on the printed page. They have observed the variety of lines and appearances of haiku in our readings, so they want to know what I think about English haiku structure. I note that language usage is closely tied to cultural conventions, so we find a wide variety of structural approaches to haiku across different languages. Japanese haiku are typically printed in a single vertical line and read from top to bottom. English haiku are typically printed in three lines, often with short-long-short phrasing. However, as my students have seen from their extensive readings, some English haiku are printed in a single horizontal line, in two lines, and sometimes in vertical lines of one word or less per line. Some are miniature concrete poems often referred to as "eyeku". We celebrate this diversity of playful creativity by haiku writers seeking to deliberately shape and precisely control the structural presentation of their haiku. The structure of the haiku on the printed page helps guide the reading process, and as noted before, we place a high value on reading each haiku slowly and out loud as an aural experience. I especially enjoy asking students to read Marlene Mountain's famous "f   r   o   g   frog" haiku out loud. The structure of haiku on the printed page varies widely depending on cultural conventions and deliberate preferences of editors and haiku writers. However, haiku form as a psychological process of noticing and contemplating remains fairly consistent across cultures and language structure conventions.

Reader responses from *Haiku: The Art of the Short Poem*

rooster crowing
two old soldiers
at the bar

Lee Gurga, *Haiku: The Art of the Short Poem*, p. 15

I enjoyed this haiku. If and when I decide to go to a bar for a few drinks, I prefer to go to the "hole in the wall" establishments. I'd rather sit next to a few old veterans and listen to them talk about the old days, instead of the high-energy type bars. I like to listen to their stories on how things were simpler in their times. It makes me realize that even though people pretty much have everything they want, having everything doesn't provide happiness. When you have everything, you want more. That's when greed sets in. I have sat with many old-time vets and spoke with them about different views of life. Norman Mears, July 2017

I love this haiku because I am not sure how to interpret it. It says two old soldiers and I wonder if they are in fact veterans or if they are a group of high-ranking officers. I think these two soldiers went out partying at some bar because of a promotion or some sort of war victory. They spent all night at the bar because they became so intoxicated. The rooster crows to signal morning. These two men are probably late for formation. The military likes to meet the sun and they have failed to do so. Hannah Mahr, January 2016

class reunion
everybody loves
my wife

John Stevenson, *Haiku: The Art of the Short Poem*, p. 25

This haiku made me laugh. I laughed because I imagine a person in high school who wasn't the most popular kid bringing to his reunion his wife, who is a model or in the fashion industry and no one can believe how that guy ended up with such a hot wife. It also may be inferred to mean that a husband was unsure if his old high school friends would enjoy spending time with his wife. However, in the end everyone at the reunion loves his wife which is a great relief to the husband. Alex Cardascio, Spring 2015

in a smoky blues bar
your fingers slide
on the neck of my spine

Juice Lee, *Haiku: The Art of the Short Poem*, p. 28

I love everything about this haiku. The first line is just so incredibly descriptive. Five words and I feel like I'm there. You can see the smoke rolling off cigarettes, and you can hear the music, and see the atmosphere. While reading it, I thought the narrator was watching someone, perhaps a lover, cheat on her. But then I read the last line and now I think she's just trying to get over someone. You have to wonder why she's in the bar, and I immediately think something bad happened. Furthermore, I think she's with a stranger. At the second line I thought she knew the person, but at the end I think she doesn't. I really like the twist. It threw me for a ringer and I just love it. Francesca Rios, Spring 2015

This is one of my favorites because it reminds me of a scene in a movie I love. "Love Jones" was about Black love, and the movie is a classic in the Black community. In many of the scenes they were in the club doing poetry or dancing to blues music. It also conveys Black love to me. Blues started in the Black community and when I picture a smoky blues bar, I picture an intimate scene with not too many people and those there know each other. I also picture a man having his woman close and doing just what the poem says, sliding his fingers down his date's neck. I can even smell the bar; I've been in a bar like this with someone I love. I can relate. Yunek Moore, Spring 2017

I really like this haiku because of its play on words. Given that the setting is in a blues bar, I expected the fingers to be sliding on an instrument. Then when I read the last line, I could almost feel the fingers on my neck and was almost a little creeped out. The way that the setting is given in the first line of the haiku, it is very easy to develop the image that is trying to be portrayed through the imagery. The word choice of "my" instead of her or his, or some other pronoun, involves the reader directly into the haiku. Michael Barber, Spring 2016

jampackedelevatoreverybuttonpushed

John Stevenson, *Haiku: The Art of the Short Poem*, p. 34

I thought this haiku was really interesting, particularly because of the structure and its content. The author pushes all the words together, so they are "jam-packed" just like the people in the elevator. It really contributes to the squeezed and claustrophobic atmosphere of the haiku. I thought it was interesting how the author included the idea of every button being pushed in the elevator. This is probably because so many people are in the elevator that they accidentally pushed someone against all of the buttons. Either that or there are so many people in the elevator that they are all going to different floors. It's also interesting to think that the elevator will probably be full for a long time because they will have to go to every floor. Trey DeLuna, Fall 2017

I chose this haiku as a favorite because I usually do not like one-line haiku that do not have any spaces. Personally, I have a hard time picking apart each word and figuring out what the haiku is saying. I also feel like this type of haiku feels extremely cramped and uncomfortable to look at. Even by just looking at the words, I feel overwhelmed and tense. However, the negative feelings that these haiku usually bring out in me is exactly why I like this haiku so much. Being in an overcrowded elevator is cramped, uncomfortable, overwhelming and tense, which is exactly what this unique spacing shows. Looking at these letters smushed and jumbled together reminds me of an elevator full of too many people, with elbows touching and purses and coats filling all the empty spaces. Anna Harmon, Fall 2016

> official death count
> excludes so called looters, shot
> on sight of their skin

> Kalamu ya Salaam, *Haiku: The Art of the Short Poem*, p. 30

This haiku is like a punch to the gut. It is so real, so raw, and it makes me so angry. Really what this makes me think of is the events last August in Ferguson, Missouri, and other occurrences of racist police brutality. This haiku highlights that problem in alarming clarity. It calls out the inherent racism in society that allows white men to carry guns in stores without a blink of an eye and leads to young people of color being shot and killed for crimes that they have not committed, for protesting peacefully, or wearing hoodies. Natalie Zelman, Fall 2014

> my daughter's eyes
> when I refuse
> the beggar

> Carlos Colón, *Haiku: The Art of the Short Poem*, p. 36

This haiku is so telling of a truth many adults like to ignore—children see everything. I think we ignore it because there is much more guilt in showing a child a flaw than actually having one ourselves. This word choice may have been unintentional, but I think in some ways it is written from the perspective of a child. "Beggar" isn't a word we usually use in conversation, but we find it in fairy tales like the beggar in Snow White or Beauty and the Beast. Instead of just a homeless person sitting on the street passively, the word beggar implies that the person was actively asking the parent for help, and "refuse" implies that the parent actively turned them down when they most likely just passed by a person on the street. Whether the parent really turned down a beggar or ignored a homeless person is irrelevant, because the way the haiku is worded is how a child sees it either way. Natalie Smith, Spring 2016

This haiku struck a chord with me. I really like the vulnerability and innocence that is described perfectly in only a few words. It made me remember when I was a child, and how in my childhood innocence I believed everyone was good, and that every human should help another human. In reality, life is complicated, and sometimes people who appear to be in need of help do not have pure intentions. Adults sometimes need to make these hard decisions, and it comes across as cruel to young children. Lane Caspar, Fall 2017

> all grown up
> and buying myself
> a night light

John Stevenson, *Haiku: The Art of the Short Poem*, p. 43

I love the innocence and realness of this poem, as it hits on one of the main points of growing up. Even though you age and experience more in life by becoming older, there are things in life that scare you. It is different for each person, but fear will never flee. Growing up doesn't mean you don't get scared. I think we feel the need to hide it as adults. Alyssa Becker, Fall 2016

I imagine the subject of this haiku driving back home from the store really late at night after buying the night light. His face is only periodically illuminated by the hanging streetlights above him, and when he gets to his house, he turns on the lights to redis-cover that he lives alone. I hear the whir of the small fan in his bedroom as he plugs the newly purchased nightlight into the nearest wall socket, and I can feel the warmth of the covers he slips under when the light finally gives him the security he needed with its soft glow. I also think that this haiku is a perfect metaphor for growing up and having to leave everything you know behind, yet somehow managing to retain something that reminds you of those younger days for comfort. Nicholas Scarpinato, Fall 2015

> I think if I catch your breath
> and take it inside me
> you will stay

Sonia Sanchez, *Haiku: The Art of the Short Poem*, p. 51

I think this haiku is so beautiful, but also a little heartbreaking. I think the wording is in-teresting. You always hear the expression "catch my breath," but I've never heard anyone say, "if I catch your breath." Any haiku about hoping someone will stay automatically makes me a little sad. The fact that she is trying to get him to stay by keeping his breath inside her just seems so desperate, because that isn't even something she could realisti-cally do. I love this haiku. Maya Dougherty, Fall 2017

This haiku hit me on a personal level because this weekend I had to meet with my boyfriend of two years to discuss our decision to break up. There were moments in our conversation where neither of us would be talking and I was trying to think of something to say in order to get a reaction out of him. I could tell he did not want to be in the car with me and that he wanted to leave. In order to make him stay, I would think of any-thing (including something as abstract as "catching his breath") I could do to continue the conversation. Lauren Montesano, Spring 2016

Blues Haiku

Is there a rent sign
on my butt? You got no
territorial rights here

Sonia Sanchez, *Haiku: The Art of the Short Poem*, p. 49

I really liked "Blues Haiku" because of its tone and attitude. When I read this haiku, I think of a man mistreating a woman. I imagine it being the summer time and this woman is wearing pretty short shorts. A man is trying to get a woman's attention by hollering at her from a car window like she's a dog. He whistles at her to try to get her attention, which works, however, just not in his favor. She didn't appreciate his disrespect, so she turns around and tells him off. Alyssa Rodriguez, Spring 2018

This poem speaks to me for so many reasons. As a woman seeing other women objectified because they are considered the weaker sex is a reality. The audacity of sexual harassers is unbelievable. I have encountered chauvinists that perceive a woman not wanting to be sexualized as her being overly sensitive. More directly I have had to fight to maintain my physical boundaries. More than once I have found myself in positions where I had to defend my value. This haiku is so much more real to me it's not about nature or the love of others or about kids that I don't have. It's about a real encounter, it's about an attitude that some men have. It sheds light on a real problem. Christa Hunt, June 2016

This haiku is quite different than almost every other haiku I have read so far. It uses capitalization and punctuation. This haiku is two sentences with a pause in the middle. Yet, it works so well, or maybe I just really like the concept behind this haiku. It's humorous and edgy at the same time. The pause gives you a moment to process what you have just read. Many haiku are small, gentle and peaceful. This haiku is almost aggressive with its use of punctuation and tone. Trista Smith, Fall 2014

custody hearing
seeing his arms cross
I uncross mine

Roberta Beary, *Haiku: The Art of the Short Poem*, p. 54

I liked this haiku because it shows the pettiness of custody battles. The mother and father may not be in love anymore and the child has to go back and forth between parents, but the parents are still showing remorse towards each other. Whether or not they are divorced or just not together, one is still being petty and thinking about the other. So, it also shows me that they are not completely over each other yet. Ryan McDonald, Spring 2018

The theme of this haiku shows the contrast between feuding parents who, in the moment, aren't even thinking about their child, but about the bitterness between them. You can feel their animosity in their actions, causing me to think that perhaps neither parent is the best for their child—though I can relate to this hatred. Wanting nothing to do with a person, even if it means crossing or uncrossing our arms to appear different than them, is something we all might do. Rory Arnold, Spring 2018

dandelions
old ladies
under hairdryers

Johnette Downing, *Haiku: The Art of the Short Poem*, p. 62

I chose this haiku as one of my favorites for multiple reasons: one, I love the elderly, and two I love how the author tied flowers into the idea of a beauty shop. At home it is a tradition that each week the older ladies head to the beauty shop to have their hair washed and fixed. At Garden Place, where I work, we have our own beauty shop. I love to go downstairs and visit the ladies while they get their hair done. I think it is adorable when they try to talk while under the hairdryer dome. The author of this haiku did a fabulous job of working the beauty of this routine into her writing. I love how she used dandelions, which are bright and cheery while they are in full bloom and tied it into something so precious and beautiful. I love this haiku and chose it for the beauty it creates in my mind. Sara Siegfried, Fall 2014

I pictured a group of old ladies sitting under hairdryers like they do every week gossiping. They've been friends for as long as they can remember. Their husbands served together and made a pact to stay together forever, and with that, their wives stood together forever too. It's a good thing that they all get along. But every week, without fail, they go and get their hair done. It reminds them of being young and when they first met. It's also the perfect time to catch up and gossip. You wouldn't believe the rumors that pass through those ladies' lips! Corrin Littlefield, Spring 2016

beaten to death
for candy
Piñata

Johnette Downing, *Haiku: The Art of the Short Poem*, p. 65

This haiku is very heavy on the dark humor. Reading the first line, I couldn't imagine what could possibly come after that wouldn't make me instantly sad or sick. But then the next two lines came, and I laughed out loud. Part of the reason why it's so funny is because of the dark set up. Downing totally makes a 180 and incorporates some lighthearted material which ended up enhancing the poem overall. I also like how the word "piñata" is capitalized, as if to make it a living character within the context of the haiku. This adds yet another layer of brutal images in the readers' heads. Nicholas Scarpinato, Fall 2015

This one is just hilarious. I've beaten a lot of piñatas, but I never looked at it this way. I don't think I'm going to be able to beat one open again. Actually, I know I will, because I definitely have an insatiable sweet tooth and a broke college budget. BREAK OUT THE PIÑATAS. TIME TO SPILL THEIR GUTS AND FEAST. Okay, maybe that's a bit much. I definitely need candy now. I'm still giggling about this. Aundrea Marsh, Fall 2015

granddaughter wiggles and flops
in my hands
hooked — I can't throw this one back

Bob Moyer, *Haiku: The Art of the Short Poem*, p. 67

I really enjoy the humor in this haiku. I think of it as a man comparing his granddaughter to a hobby he loves: fishing. She is probably still very young and energetic learning to interact in the world, so his description compares her to a fish out of water. Little kids are often bouncy and flopping all over the place, much like fish when they are pulled from their natural habitat. Mackenzie Larrick, June 2016

This haiku has such a warm feeling to it. The poet, presumably a new grandfather, is so in love with his new granddaughter that he instantly falls in love with her. I like the juxtaposition between fishing and parenting in that its floppy and messy, but sometimes you can't throw it back. However, it makes me wonder about how he was as a parent since he says he can't throw "this one" back. I wonder if he had a rough relationship with his children and now realizes what it means to be a good role model. Savannah Riestenberg, Fall 2016

kids throwing rocks
I play grown up
sternly

David Lanoue, *Haiku: The Art of the Short Poem*, p. 79

I really like this haiku. It reminds me of when you reach the age where you aren't really a little kid anymore, so you try to act super mature so that nobody will treat you like one. I remember being around that age, and my younger cousins would ask if I wanted to go play pretend. I would say no, and instead of playing with them I would sit with the adults and listen to their conversations. I also really like the fact that it says, "play grown up," because you know that you're only acting like a grown up, but you aren't actually a grown up. Maya Dougherty, Fall 2017

I am not a real teacher yet, but I am already very familiar with the idea of playing grown up. Most of my friends here probably think playing grown up means pretending to have their lives together when in reality they drink juice boxes and don't know what a 401K is (fun trivia: I don't know what that is either). I think it's very different. I think it's when you know you have to be the adult in a group of kids, even though you think whatever the kids are doing was pretty awesome and you don't want to break it up. Teaching elementary practicum and observing middle school classes have given me a lot of time to play grown up. I would rather laugh at the sassy seventh grader's comeback than calmly tell them that it wasn't appropriate, and I was always tempted to let the one disruptive third grader keep making frog noises during work time because I thought they were funny. But instead I had to play make believe that I was a mature, stern person and get my act together. I've never read a haiku about that feeling before and I enjoyed knowing I'm not alone in that feeling. Natalie Smith, Spring 2016

Kukai - Favorite Haiku Experimenting with Voices & Approaches

pi x radius squared —
the area inside
a wedding band

Amy Van Rheeden, *Millikin University Haiku Anthology*, p. 21

I love math and geometry and I really liked this pi haiku. The circumference of the love can be found in the ring by using geometry. I haven't read of any haiku before that incorporated math and logic. The idea that a wedding ring is this simple thing you put on your finger to symbolize that you are taken, and how big pi is in the math world, shows how big marriage is. The ring is way more than showing that you are taken, but the fact that you are committed forever. Bayleigh Tabor, January 2017

This haiku is a combination of two of my favorite things: math and romance. I really like how this haiku connects these two ideas in a cute way. I can just imagine a bride holding her ring and twirling it between her fingers and admiring the beauty of it. It's like the joint connection of something so exact and black and white with something that is so magical and unpredictable. I love how it links these two things in a simple, elegant way. This also reminds me of my high school sweetheart because we used to do our math homework together and this is a cute reminder of those days. Samantha Miles, Fall 2010

           a   heart
     on   my   sticky
        note   it's
           the   little
               things

Daria Koon, Fall 2018

This haiku is so sweet. Sometimes, when you're having a stressful day, it's extra appreciated when someone does even the smallest thing to make your day better, such as writing a little note on your sticky notes. I also like this haiku because it's written in the shape of a heart, and I think the shaped haiku are fun. Haley Vemmer, Fall 2018

I loved how this one was in the shape of a heart. I also enjoyed the subject matter because I love when people do small things for me. It is an easy way to show someone you care about them, but it can go a long way. Zachary McReynolds, Fall 2018

two fish
to infinity . . . and
beyond

Amanda Lee, Spring 2013

I like this haiku because it sounds cute. It makes me think of the saying, "plenty of fish in the sea," that you tell someone after they have had a rough time in the dating field. This sounds like these two "fish" have found each other and know that they will be together forever. Randi Mehrmann, Spring 2013

```
        re
  a
           rrang
      ing           my life
   for you
   Winter's indifference
```

Travis Meisenheimer, *Millikin University Haiku Anthology*, p. 174

The form in the haiku is so effective! I think that in life today, many couples are forced to readjust themselves to learn how to get along with their significant other. Learning to co-exist with someone is not something that happens overnight, it is a growth process; a time when a man and a woman learn about each other and learn how to "deal" with the other person's habits and oddities. In this haiku I see a woman who is slightly frustrated at the rearranging and adjusting she has had to do. She even claims that she is becoming indifferent about change; is she beginning to stop caring about her true identity as she attempts to adjust her life to co-exist with her significant other. I definitely sense anger and resentment in this haiku; but the form is what makes it! Maureen Coady, Spring 2004

The display of the word "rearranging" is just brilliant and shows just how much the narrator has compromised his life for this person, a person who clearly doesn't share his feelings. In fact, like Winter, this person is indifferent to the narrator's efforts at accommodating her. The visual aspect of this haiku is at least as important, if not more so, than the actual words. The word "rearranging" is like a puzzle that has been taken apart—you can still tell how it is supposed to go together, but since you've already begun the process of taking it apart, there's really no point in trying to put it back together quite yet. Jenny Schultz, Spring 2004

    scalding water
    are you the potato
    or the egg

        Christa Hunt, June 2016

I love this haiku. It relays such a deep message in so few words; it's excellent! I thought about the different effect scalding water has on a potato versus an egg. When cooking, you would use boiling water to soften the potatoes before mashing or cutting them. With eggs, you use boiling water to harden them and completely change the consistency. So, this haiku is asking, in a serious situation with the power to change you, do you become harder and stronger like the egg, or do you become softer and weaker like the potato. Mackenzie Larrick, June 2016

    Fine then!
    I will be a dandelion,
    weed in name alone.

        Kaia Ball, Fall 2016

I absolutely love Kaia's haiku. It's so defiant and sassy and strong. You can just feel the determination within those lines. It's as if she's saying fine, call me what you want, make your own assumption, but I know who I am. I will not change because you say so. I will not bend to become the thing that you think I am. "I will be a dandelion/weed in name alone." Knowing Kaia personally, I know that this haiku is personal, and I admire her for being able to write what she's feeling in a way that is healthy and beautiful. Alexsenia Ralat, Fall 2016

skipping stones only one completes its journey

Benjamin Woodcock, Spring 2019

I know we are not to interpret every haiku as metaphor, but this one is spewing in metaphor to me. The stones being a group of siblings. The sibling that completes the journey is the star sibling. I do not know why my mind went to siblings and turned this into metaphor, but I think it works. It is always sad to see a group of people trying to succeed but almost all fail. I mean, you could say that speaks true for all humans. Everyone is going to fight to be the best, but only a handful can be the best. But, who's to say who that is. Connor Mendenhall, Spring 2019

I thought of a boy, alone, skipping rocks across a lake while the sun sets on it. I felt the loneliness he was feeling and the willingness to keep skipping rocks in hope of getting one to finally skip for a long distance. I think when he finally got one, he felt accomplished and excited to see what he had just accomplished. It made me happy to see his excitement and the loneliness leave him for the brief moment. It was a cool scene and it was very well written. I just imagined the boy that was bored and lonely, finally getting to skip the rock across the lake and into the sun. Evan Chastain, Spring 2019

apocalypse
of cauliflower heads
her jean hips

Randy Brooks, Spring 2017

I loved this haiku. I'm hoping that I interpreted it correctly, but I felt immediate 70s vibes from it. Apocalypse?! The first line describes the literal end of the world, and a new era of sorts, which incites danger and excitement. The first line, coupled with "of cauliflower heads," really put the image into my brain. . . I imagined the millennial youth of the 70s, bonded together in a rough huddle, crowned heads in flowers and clad bodies in genuine hope. But the last line was the true kicker—"her jean hips". I really liked that the adjective for her hips was something that does not typically describe hips (like wide, soft, smooth, etc.). I felt sunshine and love in the air, but it is still a little off-white, you know? Kala Keller, Spring 2017

orange fish, blue fish, new fish
she does not look the same in person
catfish

Yunek Moore, Spring 2017

I liked this one a lot because it's super relevant in today's technological society. Everyone seems to have hundreds of social media platforms, but the way we act and behave online is often different than who we are in real life. It's so easy for someone to save a few pictures from anywhere on the internet and slap them onto a fake Facebook profile, and it can be dangerous too sometimes. Jacob Melssen, Spring 2017

I thought this was a very funny haiku. It starts out by using a Dr. Seuss reference, which I really appreciate as literacy is my sorority's philanthropy and I'm always on the lookout for different Dr. Seuss quotes. I think it's also funny because it brings in the idea of a relationship forming and the idea of fish in the sea. But it's quite comical because it ends up talking about the idea of catfish, a new term used for someone who fakes an identity on Facebook or a dating app. Paige Dorsel, Spring 2017

two fish in a tank
does either know
how to drive it

Benjamin Maynard, Fall 2017

I thought this haiku was really clever. Obviously, the biggest reason I decided to write about the haiku was because of the double meaning of the word "tank." The author writes in the first line that there are two fish in a tank, which is normal enough. However, the next two lines suggest that the fish aren't in a fish tank, but possibly an army tank. It asks us if the fish know how to drive this tank and how to operate it. I imagine two goldfish sitting in seats within this big camouflage tank. There are flopping around on the seat. I liked this haiku because it is so different and creates a completely weird, yet interesting image within my head. I would have never thought to compare a fish tank to an army tank, but this haiku puts that image in my head. Trey DeLuna, Fall 2017

This haiku made me laugh very hard. I cannot deny that it took me a moment to understand the joke, because I was not expecting for someone to expertly craft a joke into a haiku like that. But once I understood the joke, I found it to be hilarious. I think the haiku is well written, as well; the joke is perfectly paced to surprise the reader, but not completely blindside and confuse the reader. I really appreciate the punny "dad joke" nature of the humor. Lane Caspar, Fall 2017

silent novel
the things people
don't say

Kaitlyn Foster, Spring 2018

This is one of my favorite haiku because I think this would be a very interesting novel to read. I picture this novel filled with awful thoughts on each page. I think it includes all the things that people say in their mind but don't say out loud because it would cause a problem. I think everyone can relate to this because there are a lot of things that we don't say and if they were to be put into a novel, we would all shutter. Lexi Dross, Spring 2018

I love this because of the play on words. A silent novel? How is the novel silent? Is it a novel on what people want to say but don't? Is it a novel about a silent film? In my head, I think that it is a novel written on things that people are thinking but don't have the nerve to say. We live in a world where everyone is outspoken, but I think a lot of people are still holding back. Katherine Goethals, Spring 2018

Chapter 9

Reading *The Millikin University Haiku Anthology*

College Student Voices

Although I have already included some haiku and responses from the *Millikin University Haiku Anthology*, this chapter features responses on several topics and themes unique to this anthology of college haiku. This anthology features haiku written by Millikin University students from the first course in 1999 through Spring 2007. Students enjoy the voices of fellow students and subjects that are so easy to relate to. They also appreciate the depth of feelings, struggles and insights shared through these haiku. They enjoy the playful language of their peers. Here are a few of the reader responses to favorite haiku from that anthology.

Reader responses:

> small town
> traffic jam
> John Deere turns right

> Alida Duff, *Millikin University Haiku Anthology*, p. 15

I like this haiku because I find it very relatable. I have had the experience of growing up in a small town, and my father is a farmer. I can relate to the frustration of being in a hurry to get somewhere but getting stuck behind a tractor. The frustration is put to ease a little bit, because you know that your turn is only a half of a mile down the road. However, your frustration turns into an overload when the tractor makes the same turn as you. I can feel the frustration in this haiku, but I also find peace in it. Every time that I get frustrated about the tractor holding me up, I think about how I wouldn't have the comfortable life I live without farming. It is how my father "puts the bread on the table". I like this haiku because I feel like it gives a variety of emotions, depending on the background of the reader. Renee Sample, Fall 2016

I really like this haiku because it has a sense of home to it. Anyone that lives in a small town, or in the country, has dealt with this situation. It always seems like you get stuck behind a long line of traffic that is caused by a tractor when you are in a hurry or have things you need to be doing or getting to. Once the farmer finally turns off, it's like the whole line of cars gets back to the speed limit so quickly. It's almost as if that should be a life lesson the next time you get stuck behind a tractor. Take advantage of the time slowing down and embrace it because time flies by anyways so getting angry at the farmer trying to get where he's going to is not going to get you anywhere any faster. Emily Holthaus, June 2016

moonlight serenade
a gentle smile as you call
the police

Brian A. Blankenship, *Millikin University Haiku Anthology*, p. 36

When glancing through the pages, this haiku seems entirely harmless. Amid relatively blatant haiku, this poem caught me off-guard. I'm generally a sucker for well-timed turns of phrases, and this haiku does just that. That being said, unless there's a serious history of creepy offenses and refusals to leave the serenaded person alone, calling the police seems to be a bit brash for a simple song. I can't decide if during the last line the speaker is upset by or oblivious to the impending legal action. Either way, the poem is quite enjoyable. Darien Sloat, Spring 2013

This is a bitterly comedic haiku. I can just imagine a guy, likely drunk, stumbling under the window of a girl he met earlier in the night. Sloppily, he sings to her—many of the lyrics are probably inappropriate. Blushing, she smiles at him while dialing 911. Oblivious to the phone call and thinking of the smile as encouragement, the guy gets even more brash. When the police arrive and stand over his shoulder, he looks up in complete shock before passing out. The girl in the window waves as he is dragged away. Samantha Parks, Fall 2010

Kukai - Favorite Haiku on College Life

unable to cry
I sharpen a
stack of pencils

Nicole Silverman, Spring 2005

I could really relate to this haiku. Since it's the end of the school year and everyone seems to be under a lot of stress, crying turns into a regular event with my friends. However, there was a time in my life when I was really sad, and for some reason I could not cry. I would try anything else to release tension—I would play the guitar until my fingers were sore, run, or write in a journal until my hand cramped up. When I read this haiku, I was actually able to feel that frustrating feeling of built up emotions and the need to release them. I also imagine the pencil sharpener is an old metal one that you have to grind and grind to get the pencil sharpened. By the end of the haiku I can feel relaxed because I can imagine my arm getting tired and that tension being released, only after a whole stack is completely sharpened. Sarah Bassill, Spring 2005

I really like this haiku because I have felt this feeling many times. I have been in a position where I want to cry so bad and yet I don't want anyone to see me or think that I am weak. One time I can remember being in a class and the professor was so mean and we had just gotten our tests back. I was so disappointed in my grade and I thought I had done so much better. It seemed like when he gave me the graded test, he enjoyed it. I wanted to burst into tears and run out of the room but instead I just acted like it did not bother me and went on finding something else to do. Jill Guffey, Spring 2005

I ask him a question
he continues to read—
bronze man

Alyssa Thompson, Spring 2008

I'm still particularly fond of this one because of Pat's expansive backstory (in short, a drunk guy talking to the bronze man, getting angry and punching him). In general, though, I think this is something relatable to any Millikin student, or anyone that has been on Millikin's campus. Whenever you first see the bronze man, he startles the crap out of you. I think even the first three or four times he startled me—especially at night when I thought he was an actual person. However, I can also see this as someone who needs a person to talk to, so he or she sits down on the bench and just begins to talk to the statue. Aubrie Cox

I really like this haiku partly because of how easy it is to relate to it. I think that almost everyone has had a least one encounter with the bronze man, whether it be walking over to the bronze man to see if he's a real man or posing with him to take a picture. The bronze man is basically a famous part of the Millikin Campus. I also like this haiku because of the fact that if you did not know who the bronze man was you would probably be able to relate to this situation. It's almost as though the person asks someone a question that they are so uncomfortable answering. So, they freeze and, in this case, become bronze or they pretend like they didn't hear you and keep on reading. Amanda Aukerman, Spring 2008

two friends gossiping
past the bronze man—
he pretends to read

Julie Weightman, *Millikin University Haiku Anthology*, p. 89

I think that this one is cool because I always walk past the bronze man, talking to my friends. And you never really think about if the bronze man could actually talk or listen, all of the gossip that he would hear. He would know the stories from all over campus, and that would be really cool. I liked the personification. Morgan Vogels, Fall 2016

I loved the humor in this haiku. I got a clear image of two girls walking on Millikin's campus right past the bronze man. The girls were talking about their days, and what else was going on around campus. I could see them walk right in front of the bronze man's bench, where he didn't move. He just continued to read his book like he does every other day. It was funny to think of the bronze man actually listening to the girls' conversation. He would hear so much of what we all talk about, and probably just laugh at all the information he would gather from our conversations. Lauren Bartel, Fall 2015

returning to campus years later
the Bronze Man
still on the same page

Kyle Curry, *Millikin University Haiku Anthology*, p. 111

I enjoyed this haiku because of what the Bronze Man represents at Millikin. I remember on my first visit to campus, the tour guide stopped at the Bronze Man and talked about how important that statue was to the campus. I also enjoy this haiku because of the feeling that I got from reading it. The haiku reminded me of something my mom used to tell me when I was younger. She told me that no matter where I go in my life and no matter how much has changed, every time I come back home there's always going to be some things that stay the same. Alexander Pratt, Fall 2017

Although I can't identify with returning to Millikin as an alumnus, I can relate to going back to my high school or middle school. The feeling of memories washing over you while knowing that you do not inhabit these buildings anymore is really unique. It's a sense of knowing that you are not of that place anymore, but you carry part of it with you. It's interesting to think about. Very melancholy to me. There is a feeling of joy to be back, but these places also hold pain. The mix of past, present, pain, joy, and loss create a very strong feeling I can't really equate with anything else. I loved this haiku because it is simple, not artsy, but it says so much. Katie Colletta, Fall 2010

> home from college----
>   only one tattoo
> her parents can see

Kara Bohannan, *Millikin University Haiku Anthology*, p. 90

I see a young girl coming home for the first time from college. She walks in the front door and smells her mother's fried chicken and the aroma of green beans cooking with bacon and onions. She sits down at the table with her parents for supper. Forgetting the tattoo on her wrist, she rolls up her sleeves and her parents gasp as they see. Good thing they can't see the other two the young girl thinks. Amanda Ferguson, July 2016

I have several tattoos. For a long time, my parents did not know about any of them. Just recently I showed them to them. They didn't care that I had them, but they did care that I didn't tell them. This haiku reminds me of my parents being disappointed that I hid tattoos from them for so long. Just recently I got a tattoo in their honor and they love it. I am reminded of family and having people who care for you from reading this haiku. Tyler Trzcinski, Spring 2016

> tattoo!
> tattoo?
> tattoo

Patrick Steadman, *Millikin University Haiku Anthology*, p. 144

I really love how this haiku is so simple and yet portrays so many different emotions, specifically by use of punctuation. The first "tattoo" makes me think of the mother or father who are in shock after just discovering what their innocent daughter did while away on spring break. The next "tattoo" with the question mark is the parents wondering why and what the heck got into this girl's mind. The last "tattoo" and possibly my most favorite one just says 'well, there's a tattoo that we can't do anything about now' . . . it's just there. Liz Ciaccio, Spring 2006

I love that the use of just one word can bring about such a clear, humorous image in this haiku. This makes each punctuation mark that much more effective. The first line implies shock, the second uncertainty, and the third an unmoved response. This haiku could be taken from many perspectives. The perspective that I imagined was from that of the person getting the tattoo. One of her crazy, fun and trendy friends decides it is time for her to get a tattoo, so she is dragged into the tattoo parlor. She sits in the waiting room while her friend basically picks out the tattoo for her as she begins to panic and fear the needles. After it is over, however, the affair eventually loses its spark and she gets used to her tattoo and it is no longer a big deal. Faith Martin, Spring 2006

This piece caught my eye immediately. It's so simple, short and sweet. Only three words, yet punctuation is everything. I can appreciate it because I have tattoos. My very first one was when I was 18 years old. Of course, at the time, you think you won't regret it and you swear that you will love it forever. By the time you are 26 years old, you think you could've definitely done without it. The first line speaks of excitement of the tattoo, the second is unsure it was a great idea and the last states, "well, now I'm stuck with it." Heather Allen, Fall 2015

coming home
with new experiences
my friends still having the same ones

Rob Spurling, Fall 2012

This haiku was very relatable for me. Out of my entire group of high school friends, I was the only one who went away to school for my freshman year of college. There is a small community college in my town, and all my other friends stayed home and went to school there. Luckily, more of them are leaving now so they will not be stuck in a rut. But when I would go home last year, it was really weird to me because none of my friends really knew what I was talking about whenever I would talk about college. It was either that, or they would complain about not being somewhere else. It just made things awkward for me sometimes. Most of those people who I was friends with before are not close friends with me anymore. Maybe it's just differences, but I can really relate to this haiku. Morgan Ewald, Fall 2012

stuck in class
a Frisbee
hits the window

Brock Peoples, *Millikin University Haiku Anthology*, p. 40

This senryu just gives me the imagined feeling of all my friends playing outside, while I am in class. I don't mind going to class, but when everyone else isn't in class, it's kind of disheartening. The worst yet is when you can look out the windows of the classroom and see them playing outside. You see them playing Frisbee, and one of them throws it near the window. It hits the window, and a friend retrieves it, knowing full well the reason was to annoy me even further. Finally, I get out of class and can join them in the game. Andrew Kirchgesner, Spring 2002

This sounds like the highest form of boredom. Stuck in class, during a stagnant lecture and being able to see any form of movement outside the window makes you long for freedom. The mumbling of the teacher becomes so droning that you completely block it out and hear nothing but silence and the ticking of every waking second. SMACK! Suddenly, you are startled by a seeing a Frisbee hit the window and break the trance you were in. You begin to wipe your drool as you settle in for the next round of lecturing. Only five minutes has passed . . . dear God. Nathan Heppermann, January 2017

college lecture hall
my feet dangle
off my chair

Anna Harmon, Fall 2016

I think this haiku really captured the essence of a college student. Many students feel like and are treated like adults. However, most students still feel like children and are maybe not ready to approach life after graduation. This haiku encompasses the contrast in feeling like an adult in a large lecture hall, but also feeling like a child at heart at the same time. Caroline Lodovisi, Fall 2016

At first, I thought this was just an observation of a short person whose feet literally did not touch the ground from the desk and I thought it was humorous. But with closer inspection, I find a much deeper meaning within that actually connects with me personally. When I read this haiku, I am reminded of the fear that is always in the back of my mind that I am not ready for the next step in my life. Even though I am about to turn 20, I still feel like a child and I have no idea what I am doing or how I am supposed to make it through life on my own. The feet dangling off of the chair symbolizes still feeling youthful while in an adult setting, sans college lecture hall. Though at first glance this haiku could just be written off as a funny observation, it is up for a deeper and more meaningful interpretation. Savannah Reistenberg, Fall 2016

microwave dinner
still cold
two bites in

Rachel Humphrey, Spring 2018

This was one of my favorite haiku. I can clearly see that this person did everything right with this microwave dinner. They poked the holes in the top of the little plastic film and put it in for the right amount of time but when they took it out to eat it something just went wrong on the inside. As they cut into it and put the first bite in their mouth, they realize that the middle is cold. But they are so hungry that they don't care and just keep eating. Andrew Cliatt, Spring 2018

This poem has so much defeat and acceptance in it. We have all gotten to that point where there is nothing left to give to something and sometimes that manifests itself in small defeats such as this one. The thing to think about though is, hey, at least you have anything to eat at all! Elizabeth Pillow, Spring 2018

end of the semester
returning home
with half of myself

Sophie Kibiger, Fall 2018

This haiku is far too relatable. I read it in a few different ways—the first way being the most personal for myself. I tend to run my battery level near empty in a semester and by the time I head home I am completely drained of the happy lively girl I usually am. When you invest so much energy in everything you're doing, it drains you and takes part of you with it. But another way I interpreted this haiku is the simple fact that we play different roles at home than what we do at school. At home, I'm the youngest and will always be seen as the youngest whose input on conversations can't be beneficial because how could I ever know more than the people around me because of my age. When I'm at school, I'm respected and heard for what my opinion is and why I believe what I believe, so it's like I have to leave that part of me behind—the part of me that is an independent woman who does everything on her own. Plus, leaving your friends is never fun and they're a reflection of who you are! Hannah Haedike, Fall 2018

Something about this haiku really speaks to me. By the time we get to a break, I am always so drained. I feel like I am constantly going at 100 miles an hour and when I get to go home it feels like a full stop and it's draining. I also have so many close friends and different experiences at school and at home I feel like a different person. I've become acclimated to life at Millikin and forget how to let that go and reacclimate to home life, so in that sense it's like I'm shedding that skin and leaving it at school. Hannah Ottenfield, Fall 2018

> finally, a lazy day
> I slip into
> my running shoes

> Natalie Perfetti, Spring 2009

I'm not sure why I enjoyed this haiku as much as I did—a rare break in my normally objective reading. I don't connect to the image, either directly or indirectly. For some reason, I find the image beautiful, and written perfectly. The first line is perfect. The use of "finally" to open the haiku expresses the sense of being in the middle of things happening (in media res). The narrator seems to have been waiting for this moment. Once the moment arrives, he/she puts on his/her running shoes and gets to work. Ryan Murphy, Spring 2009

I love the attitude of this haiku because it sets up the scene of a lazy day, and ironically ends it with the author putting on their running shoes, a very anti-lazy day. There are words in the haiku that imply the feeling of laziness such as "slip" and "finally" which give the reader the feeling of hectic-ness is over. However, again the poet does the technique of placing the irony at the end of the poem. Will Frankenberger, Spring 2009

> thinking of how far
> we've come
> old running shoes

> Austin Taylor, Fall 2017

I enjoy this haiku because it is very simple and has a deeper meaning. I wrote this haiku while I was sitting in my room looking at my trashed running shoes. I thought about the number of miles I had put into them for the four years I wore them and all the experiences I had with them. Normally, people think of experiences with other people, but looking at my running shoes, I was able to recall a ton of things I did. I thought of vacations where we went hiking in the black hills or obstacle course races with my brother. This haiku brings back many good memories and I encourage people to look at shoes that they are about to throw away and think of the memories that they experienced with them. Austin Taylor, Fall 2017

the weight of the world
she tells herself
just keep swimming

Bethany Wetherholt, July 2016

It's been a long day, a long month, and a long year! Life hasn't been easy since her divorce and it got even worse after she lost her job and couldn't pay rent. She is a single mom who is now on welfare until she lands another job. Job hunting has been her full-time workload these past two months and with every rejection she feels more beat down. As she walks into a local church to visit the food pantry she reads on the wall, "Giving up is not an option". Instead of tears, she breaks into a smile, grabs food for her children, and walks out of the church with a new-found confidence. Tomorrow, she will find work because she will just keep swimming. Sonja Chargois, July 2016

I really like this haiku because it has two meanings to me. One being the funny one from *Finding Nemo* and the second meaning more inspirational. Life is full of obstacles and storms, but you have to remember that the storm does not last forever. You can get through anything if you remember to just keep pushing and striving for greatness. Which is where I get the just keep swimming part. Marshaya Sangster, July 2016

Chapter 10

Japanese Haiku & Aesthetics

Where Do Haiku Come From?

After reading several translations of Japanese haiku, my students read excerpts from *Haiku Guy* by the accomplished Issa translator, David Lanoue. This novel is a playful introduction to Japanese haiku poetics and related aesthetics. Let me provide a quick summary.

Traveling back and forth through time and space from New Orleans to old Japan, Buck-Teeth, the main character, is trying to become a haiku poet. While his primary teacher is "Cup-of-Tea" (a character based on Issa), there are several other haiku writers who try to teach him their secrets to inspiration and how to write high-quality haiku. The novel starts with Cup-of-Tea accepting Buck-teeth as his student. Cup-of-Tea teaches only by example and participation, inviting Buck-Teeth to engage in the activities that lead to being receptive to haiku. He learns how to write haiku by being with Cup-of-Tea and seeing how spontaneously his teacher writes haiku from everyday occurrences.

In contrast to the master from old Japan, the nuns from a Catholic school in Omaha, Nebraska were more direct with their lesson to "Stop, look, and listen, children!" (p. 7) before crossing the street. Our narrator explains that this was "my first lesson in the art of haiku" (p. 8). Hanging out with Cup-of-Tea, Buck-Teeth spends a great deal of time just observing—stopping, looking, and listening. This approach is what would eventually be known as the shasei approach to writing haiku in which the author simply observes closely and writes from significant details happening here and now.

The next lesson comes from Buck-Teeth witnessing an extended example of what not to do. Lord Kaga arrives in the novel's village and wants to become Cup-of-Tea's student. He is eager to learn how to write haiku so that he can win the heart of Lady Plum, whom he loves. Every day he mixes ink with his tears and writes another lovelorn haiku about how sad he is that Lady Plum has broken his heart. Each day the resulting poem is egotistical, self-centered, expressing only his disgusting self-pity. Lord Kaga presents the haiku to Cup-of-Tea who promptly sticks it into a fresh cow pie. This happens repeat-edly for 100 days. On the last day he "crept to his writing table, stepping gingerly over three nude concubines, asleep in the shadows—one, sucking her thumb like a child. Then mixing his ink with a few fresh tears, so easy to shed whenever he pictured in his mind his cruel mistress, Lady Plum . . . he dipped the horsehair tip of his bamboo brush into the black puddle and prayed for a miracle. None came. But ink was dripping, and so not to waste it, he dribbled out what was in his heart, not quite knowing what he was going to say till he watched it materialize on the page: the old fart / stacks the winter /

kindling" (p. 19). When presented to Cup-of-Tea, Lord Kaga is shocked that the master finally says, "Yes". Only when Lord Kaga breaks out of his usual poetics (write about your personal emotions and pray for inspiration) does he succeed at being spontaneous. By not trying to follow his concept of writing a love haiku, Lord Kaga finally writes a successful one about someone other than himself—with humor and empathy for others.

In the chapter "White Black Green", three haiku masters join Cup-of-Tea and Buck-Teeth for a moon viewing party. Each is a caricature for various Japanese haiku approaches or poetics. Shiro, the white poet, represents the extreme wordless approach of Zen poetics emphasizing moments of satori. He doesn't actually attempt to teach Buck-Teeth how to write haiku. Instead, he frequently demonstrates his wordless approach by merely thinking—deeply—silently—about things instead of writing them down as haiku. As our narrator explains, "A poem in its pure form exists as a nonverbal insight called a 'dibbit,' a flash of wordless perfection that words can never capture" (p. 48).

The other two haiku masters offer more direct advice to Buck-Teeth. Kuro, the black poet, "constantly dwelt on the shadow side of things: on death, loss, despair, and sorrow" (p. 43). He emphasizes that a haiku poet should always write with an expectation of loss and suffering—nothing lasts. This is more commonly known as the Japanese aesthetic concept of mono no aware, an awareness of the impermanence and incompleteness of all living things. The goal is to embrace this aesthetic as the primary truth in order to write effective, realistic haiku. Capture the beauty of the moment—cherry blossoms or dewdrops—because it will not last. By seeking Buddhist detachment, the haiku poet is free to express the reality of beauty despite suffering or lost hope. Seeing that Buck-Teeth was taken up by this "dark philosophy", Mido, the green poet, "took it upon himself to offer Buck-Teeth some unsolicited poetic advice" (p. 50) as an alternative to the Black poet. Mido's advice is to "go out of your mind" and just enjoy the playful, spontaneous approach "where haiku just happen" (p. 52). Buck-Teeth tried to follow Mido's advice for a while, but finally gave up and sought his own way.

I ask my students to read *Haiku Guy* as they are working on their contemporary haiku reader response essays. With these essays they are reading several books by a single author, or several authors on a specific topic or approach. I ask them to consider the "genesis of haiku"—where do the poet's haiku come from? Why do they write about these particular topics and what's unique about their language? What is their source of significance or insights—their poetic goals that guide their writing of haiku? I also ask my students to consider their own approach to writing haiku. Where do their very best haiku come from? Why do they notice, observe, feel, reflect or focus on certain things for immediate impact and lasting significance? These reflections often become the basis for introductions to their own final collections of haiku at the end of the semester.

I also ask my students to try writing haiku following the "Stop, Look, Listen" approach, the Kuro "nothing lasts" approach, and the Mido "get out of your right mind" approach. We have a matching contest with the students' original Kuro haiku versus Mido haiku. Here are some of their reflections about haiku poetics from these assignments.

Responses to Buck-Teeth's haiku teachers and writing assignments from *Haiku Guy*

Kuro is very pessimistic. He believes that everything is fleeting, and so essentially, nothing is important. You shouldn't get attached to anything, because you will inevitably lose it. I do like the idea that you shouldn't have any expectation that your work will make you be remembered forever, and that people from future generations will know you. I think it's true that haiku should focus on capturing life as fleeting moments. But I also think Kuro is overdramatic. Mido's theory interests me a bit more. His main idea is that you need to be a little out of your mind to create something worthwhile. If you're always just thinking about things so logically and "inside the box," your raw voice and uniqueness will never come through. I find truth in this, because the first time we had haiku homework, I just wrote blindly about the things that I felt, without really knowing what was good or right. In some ways, I feel like these early haiku captured my own essence better and were more spontaneous than some of mine are now that I know some of the rules. Alissa Kanturek, Fall 2018

Kuro's haiku are written to voice witness to the tragedies of life even though, in the end, no one will remember either us as human beings, or the haiku we write. They are temporary things, ultimately written to proclaim the sadness and horrors of our lives. However, we write because we must. Mido, on the other hand, believes in writing only what is raw and real. One must get out of the trap that is the mind, for nothing artistic is ever accomplished from staying in there. Mido believes that planning cannot be a part of haiku, for that interrupts the creative process. I am not quite sure who I agree with more. I am depressed by Kuro's philosophy, but agree that people write because they must. Writing is a creative outlet, without which, most people would live a truly tragic life. However, I also agree that some of the most beautiful pieces of art (especially coming from an actor's perspective) come when an individual directly reacts to seeing something/an experience. If I had to choose one, it would probably be Mido's advice because it is not quite so grim, and I, personally, tend to think too much so my best work comes when I let that thinking go. Daria Koon, Fall 2018

Mido and Kuro have very different viewpoints. Kuro sees haiku as an opportunity to display the pessimism of life. The darkest and saddest aspects of life are the best sources for haiku, according to Kuro. Life is short and temporary, so there is no reason for hope or love. For Mido, though, pessimism nor optimism are necessary. Rather, writing haiku entails the author to forget being right and concentrating too hard. One must forget everything in his mind and just let the haiku flow out. Mido uses alcohol to help himself write haiku. I think Kuro's advice is depressing, and I do not believe in treating life as he does. Though it is true that life is temporary, we should not just let the darkest parts consume us. Sorrow, grief, and anger will all be experienced, but there is no reason not to celebrate all of the beautiful moments of life. The fact that life is temporary only means that we should enjoy the beauty even more! Every little thing that brings happiness, joy, and love should be recognized and praised! Sure, we can notice the dark parts of life and even be grateful for the lessons that trials bring us, but we can also be thankful for the blessing of being able to do life at all. Emily Sullins, Fall 2018

Kuro is extremely dark and depressing. He doesn't believe in trying to see the good in anything because everything will eventually come to an end. Thus, Kuro believes trying to see the good or positive in anything is pointless and clouds your thought processes when trying to focus on the impending doom of everything. Mido, on the other hand, is happy. He believes that constricting your haiku to your "right mind" thinking is blocking your full haiku potential. Mido encourages Buck-Teeth to stray away from his "right mind" as it will constrict and limit Buck-Teeth's expression in the haiku form to only his sole thoughts. I definitely stray more towards the Mido side. I feel like his stance is more along the lines of the phrase "Let haiku come to you instead of searching for it." This phrase also aligns with the "stop, look, and listen" approach because you observe things that you usually, in your "right mind" wouldn't. The idea of just sitting and observing is not only refreshing and helps you escape the pressures of everyday life, but it also helps you realize things that you usually wouldn't. Jenesi Moore, Fall 2018

Kukai – Favorites from *Haiku Guy* Approaches

Stop, Look & Listen Approach Haibun

Living in a sorority house among 40 other women has its benefits. However, finding a quiet spot to have complete privacy is not one of these benefits. For this assignment, I did my best, because I was curious to see what I would observe in the Pi Phi house while stopping, looking, and listening. I was right in my assumption that I would be hard-pressed to find an area of the house that was completely quiet, but our Date Room was empty, so I set up camp there. I sat next to the windows, in a chair at the table where many girls do homework. I decided to observe the area of the house itself. I sat at the table in silence and did not allow anything to distract me. I noticed that as I listened, I was able to figure out, for the most part, which one of my sisters was speaking because of how well I know them. I smiled whenever I heard a laugh that I recognized resonate through the house. The constant chatter became almost hum-like after a while; instead of hearing the sounds individually, it became an underlying tone for the entire house. I shifted my focus slightly off of human noises to the house itself. I heard the familiar creaking of our old floorboards all above my head as my fellow sisters walked around their rooms. I heard the soothing tones of a running shower that sounded almost like rain. I heard doors opening and closing, and cars driving by outside. I felt the coldness of the air coming from the nearby window behind me. The overall experience was calming. I do not sit and simply observe very often—at least, not without some distractions. It was nice to take a step back and appreciate the place where I live, and all of the people who live with me.

shower running
the creak creak
of the floorboards

    Lane Caspar, Fall 2017

I chose to sit in my room and observe my roommate's chair. There is a blanket draped over her chair that I see every day, but I've never really stopped to look at it closely before. I noticed that the pattern is white rabbits in a garden. The main colors in the blanket are white/cream, shades of green, red, pink, and red. I had never noticed before that there is also purple and black on the pattern as well, it had blended in to the other colors. I also noticed that the fringe along the border of the blanket isn't consistent. It alternates between white and black, white and green, and white, red, and green.

hanging from the blanket
one piece of fringe
longer than the rest

    Maya Dougherty, Fall 2017

•

I decided to sit and practice the stop, look, and listen technique while on break from work. I work in the mall, so I observed a lot going on. There were many families walking around, some couples, and even some groups of children. Working in the public leads to some pretty entertaining things going on. It was kind of relaxing to sit on my break and just observe.

walking the mall
the aged couple chats
lap after lap

    Katherine Goethals, Spring 2018

•

A mess, a giant mess. An organized mess that is, my mess. My attic bedroom cold as ever hovering over the rest of the sleeping house. I never wear any of these clothes, yet they take up the majority of my room. I am always more relaxed when my room is clean, so maybe I should clean it, maybe tomorrow, maybe. The only thing calming about my room right now is the incense and my sleeping guinea pig and, surprisingly, the train in the near distance. I can't stop thinking about this mess. As I sit here in my shack, I reminisce on everything I should be thinking about during the day and not during the vulnerable night, but that's that.

sleeping
with my eyes open
   choo   choo

    Kyle McMahon, Spring 2017

•

Today I decided to stop and observe the cat that hangs out around my house.
We've named this cat Mr. Whiskers, even though further investigation revealed that
Mr. Whiskers is a female cat, and I am plotting to kidnap this cat and take her home
with me when I graduate. She wears a red collar that is frayed from prolonged
scratching and has no tags. My roommates and I speculate that she is not actually
owned by anyone but that the neighbors put a collar on her to keep her out of the
hands of animal control. She's extremely affectionate, playful, and remarkably well-
kept for a cat who spends a lot of her time outdoors. She is also always kneading,
no matter what surface her paws are sitting on.

she stares through
the glass door
my landlord says "No Pets"

    Sam Miller, Spring 2017

•

I observed the park from my back-yard porch. I sat on my patio looking at anything
that drove by, walked by, or flew by. I mostly payed attention to wildlife and pedes-
trians on runs. I saw squirrels digging for what I assume was their nuts that they had
buried earlier. Then running up and down the trees being chased by their squirrel
buddies. Fairview Park has a lot of middle to older adults that either run, walk, or
bike. I saw a lot of over-exaggerated strides. Some kids with backpacks walked by,
probably walking home from school that Friday. I also noticed an abundance of
people on roller-skates. The weather was super nice, and the sun was shining bright,
so everyone seemed to be happy about the change in pace from the cold windy
spring break.

neon hairband
skating through the park
smiling at the flowers

    Nicholas Kemp, Spring 2017

•

I sat at my apartment table and stared through the living room and past the window. Although there was only one other person in the room with me, it was amazing all of the different sounds I heard. There were faint birds singing outside, and
the wind continued to whistle outside. Inside, the clock ticked like a metronome,
my roommate typed and sighed, neighbors muttered and slammed cabinets, the
dishwasher complained, and the walls and windows creaked with the wind. What I
had perceived as silence was really a symphony.

second hand keeping time
her sigh
and the wind's song

    Taryn Pepping, Spring 2016

•

I sat and observed my roommate painting for her design class. She painted an octopus onto cardboard that was made out of different shades of gray and black. A part that really stuck out to me was when she would shade a part of the legs. She would blend a sharp line between gray and black paint into a shape that helped to define the legs of the octopus. It was interesting to "zoom in" on a small part that was being blended, and then look more at the big picture to see how it had changed. While the painting was obviously very visually interesting, I also liked to listen to the brush and how the sounds changed depending on how the brush was being used. At one point, I closed my eyes to try and see if I could tell when she changed directions. The sound that it made is very hard for me to describe, it was rough and scratchy but also was not an unpleasant sound. It was also interesting to observe my roommate and how focused and "in the zone" she got while painting.

new direction
paintbrush
changes its sound

Anna Harmon, Fall 2016

•

Kuro Approach Haiku

hair rising on my neck
the song
played at his funeral

Nicholas Sanders, Spring 2015

I really like this haiku. I don't think it's as sad as what most people initially would read this. I see someone who just lost someone they loved, and it's not extremely recent but a year or so and they're just out minding their own business and a song that was played at the funeral comes on. They stop and get goosebumps, whether from the memory or from some supernatural other stuff, it's up to your own interpretation. I think I liked this one so much because it had the perfect amount of surprise in it. Francesca Rios, Spring 2015

creased edges
of the picture
always in his wallet

Catrina LaDew, September 2015

This haiku is full of meaning to me. My dad has my mom's senior picture in his wallet. The edges are definitely creased and worn. It is always the first thing he sees when he opens his wallet. Kathy Housh, September 2015

This haiku makes me think of multiple things and that's why I love this. It reminds me of a father carrying a picture of his daughter or son, a husband carrying a picture of his wife, and even a grandfather carrying a picture of one of his grandchildren. Obviously, it's cherished because the creased edges symbolize that it's been in and out of the wallet as the man shows off pictures of the people he loves. Kasara Welch, September 2015

she slowly approaches
a small grave
flowers in hand

Cristine Lourash, July 2016

This haiku reminds me of someone who lost someone long ago and way too soon. I can see a young woman approaching the grave with tears in her eyes as she is there to visit the small child that was lost. I can see the heart shaped tombstone with the angel engraved in it. There are lots of teddy bears and old pickle jars because the young girl loved pickles. This is very clear for me as I do this a couple times a year when I go visit my niece's grave. Amanda Ferguson, July 2016

I imagine a woman, early 20's, who is trying to find her way in the world. Her mother has recently passed away and she feels lost in the world. She isn't sure how she will ever go on without her mother. Her mom was a single mom. She was strong, she did everything she could to provide a good life for her daughter. Her mother shaped who she is today. Her mother's mother also died when she was young, and the girl doesn't have any memories of her since she was just a baby when she died. One day, she decides to visit her grandmother's grave for the first time. She felt that she needed to go visit the woman who raised her mother. Walking through an old cemetery overtaken by weeds she searches through the headstones. Finally, she spots her last name. With yellow tulips (her mother's favorite) in her hand, she slowly bends down and wipes off the headstone. She stares for a few minutes and then begins to cry. Bethany Wetherholt, July 2016

best friends
an entire conversation
with a tombstone

Geoffrey Eggleston, Fall 2012

I find this poem, though about a very sad subject, to be brilliant. I imagine these friends were those who did everything together. Even with one of them passing, the other still goes to talk, just as they have always done. The last line really changes the haiku, but I also like the meaning in that last line. It gives me hope that the friend is still finding time for that relationship and healing at the same time. Hannah Gifford, Fall 2012

I liked this one because I imagine someone sitting next to the grave of his or her best friend in life. They are just sitting there having a normal conversation like they would if the friend were still alive. One friend is telling the other about what has been going on, whether it is school, work, relationships, or anything. It's just really cool that the person didn't forget even after the friend is dead. Morgan Ewald, Fall 2012

I stop and stare
at the dried-up leaves
fallen soldiers

Sydney Rudny, Fall 2018

I have a very large elm tree in my front yard that covers my lawn with brown, crunchy leaves every year. The tree is very old and there has been much debate about cutting it down through the years, but it still stands. This haiku reminded me of that tree, the leaves are like soldiers fighting for their home to stay, and the image of them covering the ground always reminds me of being home and comfortable. It's a very interesting image to think of the leaves as soldiers, but I really like it. Hannah Ottenfield, Fall 2018

> funeral day
> coffee and crumbs
> at the bottom of my cup

Melanie Wilson, Fall 2018

This poem brings me back to the services that I've had to attend for my family. Specifically, it brings me back to my grandfather's wake and funeral. When someone passes away, it is such a time of stress and mourning. There is so much to do to get the services in order, and there's no time to really think or adequately grieve over their death. The moment this haiku presents is very simple yet so sad. The person seems to just be sitting at a lunch or in the kitchen, zoning out due to lack of rest and emotional stress. In this case it's on something as simple as the coffee cup. Jordan Niebuhr, Fall 2018

This is my favorite haiku. It is one of the few really good haiku that I have written that was based entirely in truth and personal experience. Early this semester, my grandfather passed away. I went home to attend his funeral and kept an eye and ear out for moments that could be transformed into haiku. When I wrote this haiku, I was sitting in the reception area of the funeral home with my sister. We had been there for the entire day and were taking a break for coffee and some cookies that were laid out. I had been dipping my cookie into the coffee, and when I finished the cup, there was a mess of crumbs at the bottom. The haiku just popped into my head. Something about the lingering warmth of the empty cup, but the messiness of the crumbs was somehow the perfect image for the day. Melanie Wilson, Fall 2018

> belly laughs
> from the backyard
> this won't last forever

Naomi Klingbeil, Fall 2018

This haiku made me extremely nostalgic. While reading this, I remembered all the times that me and my friends from back home would sit in our back yards together around a fire and talk for hours; some of my fondest memories of them are from those nights. Whether it was one of our birthdays, after a school dance, or just another summer night, we would sit around the fire and talk about anything and everything until the fire burned out and we had each devoured about five s'mores. This haiku perfectly captures the feeling I get when I think back on those nights; a mixture of warmness and nostalgia. Isabella Spiritoso, Fall 2018

I love this one as it makes me think of a mother sitting out on her back porch on a warm summer evening. Her young children are playing in the yard, getting along for once, as they laugh and play. She can't help but watch them and only them as she appreciates their youth. It's nights like these that she will look back on when they're 13 and hate her. Or when she catches them sneaking out in the middle of the night. It's these summer nights that she will never forget, and she must stop to appreciate them as they won't stay this young and innocent forever. Naomi Klingbeil, Fall 2018

the wind—
a reminder that this too
shall pass

Jennifer Tohill, July 2016

This haiku is so true; that is why I enjoy it so much. It is such a big message in just three little lines. So many of us get caught up in a moment, bad or good, and do not realize that it is just one moment of the big picture of our lives. Unfortunately, I have had too many people take their lives due to this thinking. I try to encourage my friends and family to keep a blessing jar or journal so that in the midst of these bad times they are able to look back and remember that it is bigger than them. That where they are now will not be where they end up. Where they were a year ago was so different just like what the future holds. There are people and paths that they need to become a part of. This haiku is a reminder of those paths. Michelle Holsapple, July 2016

Christmas morning . . .
the snowman wears
my dead brother's gloves

Francesca Rios, Spring 2015

This is an awesome haiku because it hints at how life must go on for those who are still here on earth. Of course, it is alright to be sad, but we should never let the death of a loved one bring us down. This year has been a tough one for me in that respect, and I think that this is why this particular haiku hopped out at me first. I have learned through my first real experience with death that life must go on, and we must enjoy life always to the best of our abilities. Adam Peters, Spring 2015

I liked this haiku during the kukai because of the imagery it brought to my head. When I read this, I imagined a family who had made a snowman the day before Christmas, and their oldest son put his gloves on the snowman to make the smaller children happy. I imagined later that night that the brother got into a car accident by a drunk driver and died, and in the morning, instead of celebrating Christmas, they are mourning the death of their brother. The sensory imagery in this haiku was strong, and I believe that's why I liked it so much. Katelyn Rumph, Spring 2015

last year's hero
this year's
waterboy

Adam Peters, Spring 2015

wounded bird
like people he only
dreams to fly

Nicholas Sanders, Spring 2015

This match happened in the second round of the Kuro matching contest, and I think it was interesting because I believe the first haiku is about a struggle. I read it and I thought that the star athlete had an injury and is now restricted to the bench and forced to do a role that we've learned is basically at the bottom, but he still wants to contribute to the team. Then you have this bird who is also injured and just wants to be back where he was. Back in the sky in the top of his world, both literally and figuratively, but now he just has to sit back and watch as all the other birds get to fly and so he desperately wants the same thing. Francesca Rios, Spring 2015

This was my favorite matching pair haiku because they both deal with injury and the disadvantages of that. I like the first one because I get the sense that this person was the star of their high school team, and then they came to college and got an injury, and they have to sit out and watch other people take over their position. I also like the second one because the bird is dreaming just like humans dream of flying. If I could be any animal, I would be an eagle because I would want to soar and fly across the land without a care in the world. Nicole Koch, Spring 2015

a cold wind
dead child's horse
rocks by itself

George Swede, *Almost Unseen*, p. page 36

closed mental hospital
swings creaking
among windblown weeds

Wally Swist, *The Silence Between Us*, p. 107

I think these haiku match well because they both create the same feeling of uneasiness and tension. They both use the image of an inanimate object moving by itself due to the wind. They also both create a somewhat creepy and unsettling image through the use of elements that usually make us uncomfortable, such as death and our collective fear of mental institutions. It preys upon our fear in the best ways to create a strong and vivid picture that reminds me of the beginning of a horror movie. I also like both of these haiku because I feel as if they're a lot different from most of the haiku we have read in class. I also find it interesting that both haiku incorporate the wind, which is an element outside of our control, which is doing the action in both haiku. This wind makes me think of the end of fall, around Halloween, where everything is a little more spooky than it would normally be. Anna Harmon, Fall 2016

Mido Approach Haiku

summer sun
my road map
flies out the window

Christine Sandidge, *Millikin University Haiku Anthology*, p. 46

This is such a DELICIOUS haiku, the outer and inner nature mixing quite perfectly. The map flying out the window gives such a buoyant freedom to the image and message. It's like the author or protagonist has just graduated college or has otherwise gotten his or her first break in a long while. The map for her life has just gotten whipped out from underneath her, and she is embracing the unknown. Summer sun is just a genuinely, universally understood image of bliss. Here it captures the entirety of the image, sluicing down her back, the car, the map and its breeze. I had a similar experience this past Saturday when I drove with friends to Fairview Park to enjoy the unprecedented 60-degree weather. Genevieve Breitbach, Spring 2016

With the windows down and the radio up, a group of friends on the verge of 20 drive just over the speed limit to explore the country. Although they had plans and intentions in mind for their destination, the summer sun has encouraged them to veer into uncharted territory and follow to where they feel led. It doesn't even matter where they are going anymore—it's all about the adventure. I cannot count the times my friends and I have talked about doing this; what if we just took off, didn't tell anyone where we were going, and got away for the weekend? It was such a relatable haiku. Lexi DeSollar, Spring 2014

puzzle pieces
my head
your shoulder

Hannah Ottenfield, Fall 2018

I see this haiku in two different ways. One way in that her head fits perfectly in the dip of his shoulder as they are cuddling. Almost as if they were made for each other. But I also see this in a way that her head could fit in the dip of his shoulder if she just squeezes it in there to make it fit. Like when you're doing a puzzle and you're trying to make a piece fit. It sort of fits if you really press hard on the two pieces, but there is also a more fitting puzzle piece that you may encounter later on. Naomi Klingbeil, Fall 2018

This is another cute and warm haiku. I like the physical image of a person resting their head on someone's shoulder. This is a symbol of reliance, comfort and support. I also like the use of the phrase "puzzle pieces". It is a really sweet image and makes me believe that these two people are perfect for one another. Without words, they can connect and become one being, one image. I initially pictured a young couple, but I also like the idea that this is an old couple that has been together for years and years and is still fitting perfectly together. Melanie Wilson, Fall 2018

in our first home
we dance
on the bare floors

Olivia Gonzalez, Spring 2017

I love this poem because of the awesome image that I can picture in my head. I see
a huge living room with dark wooden floors. The floor is empty because no furniture
has been put in the room yet. The room is so big when it is empty, and the couple is so
excited about their new house that they do not care what is in the house or living room.
They are just glad to be together and to have a new house that they can call their own.
I, personally, cannot wait for the day that I can move into a house with my husband.
Caitlyn Latshaw, Spring 2017

I liked this haiku because it broadcasts a feeling of openness and playfulness. The image
of "our first home" speaks measures. In defining the "our," one could cover all op-
tions—lovers, families, roommates, even sorority sisters. The image of dancing brings
movement and life into the poem, and the added "bare floors" detail solidifies it. I can
imagine romping around barefoot on hardwood floors, in an empty room, with no
things surrounding me. Possibly the homeowners have not unpacked yet, or they do not
have enough things to fill the room. The floor is bare, but the people dance on. I really
appreciated the cast of hope and excitement throughout and could immediately create
the picture in my head. Kala Keller, Spring 2017

midnight swim
stirring the moon
with our fingers

Katherine Steimann, *Millikin University Haiku Anthology*, p. 99

One of my best friends in high school had a very nice in-ground pool. During the summer we would always have late parties or just swim the two of us. The water always
seemed so iridescent due to the moon's reflection. I would lay on my back and look up
at the stars, my ears filling with water, so only a buzzing sound was heard. The water
trickled and flowed over my body as I lightly paddled with my legs. I love the concept
of stirring the moon with my fingers. I think it's a beautiful image. I can just see the
reflection of the moon in the water, and my body creating ripples in it as I swim around.
Jordan Oelze, Spring 2017

This haiku makes me think of a young couple doing something illegal, or at least not socially accepted all the time (like maybe skinny dipping?). I imagine that this is a moment
where two teenagers have jumped a fence that surround a deserted beach at around
11:30. They have snuck out and they are just kids really that are looking to rebel but not
doing anything bad. They hop the fence and then run down to the beach laughing. They
strip down to underwear and jump into the lake. They are teenagers who are attracted to
each other, but didn't really notice until they were alone, in their underwear, in a lake
at midnight. It's a moment of discovery for the people involved, but nothing more than
a spark of interest as their hands touch in the water as they create ripples through the
moon. This haiku is very visual and is one of my favorites from this group because it creates a very clear image that is easy to imagine. Beth Ann Melnick, Fall 2010

falling star...
why we are
here

Rachel Morrison, Spring 2007

I really like this haiku because I think this is a question that we all ask at some point
in our lives. I often wonder about the world and how it works and everything that is
involved in it. I also can see this as a small child looking up at the stars and asking
their parents, "why are we here?" I think this is something all children ask and usually
all adults do not have a real answer for it, but it is something we all wonder. Whitney
Minor, Spring 2007

staring at the stars,
we make our own
constellations

Danny Delaney, Fall 2010

I like this haiku because of the imagery. I envision a wide-open field, which makes
me think of my grandparents' farm. I remember a night when I was ten or eleven and I
looked up at the sky on their farm. It was the clearest night I had ever seen, and I actually saw the Milky Way. I wasn't with a person and I wasn't making my own constellations, but I can remember staring at those stars searching for each constellation, just realizing how small my problems were compared to the universe. Eddie Pluhar, Fall 2010

I like this haiku a lot because I love the night. The stars are a mystery, and constellations
take away a little from that mystery, because they are organized and named. By putting
the "constellation making" back in the viewers' eyes, it opens up the mystery once more
and creates a space that can be filled in a lot of different ways by the viewer. Having
your own constellations is something special that you can share with someone. That is
emphasized even more by the word "we". It evokes a close relationship and something
that only these two share, whether it is a family member, a close friend, or a boyfriend/
girlfriend. For me, this haiku makes me think of an autumn or winter walk, when the air
is brisk, and the trees are bare enough to see through the branches. Walking with someone you really care about, you look up at the stars and make up constellations that only
you two will ever remember. Beth Ann Melnick, Fall 2010

Chapter 11

Reading Matsuo Basho

Seeking Sabi & Celebrating Karumi

After reading several translations of Japanese haiku, the students in Global Haiku Traditions read haiku by Matsuo Basho translated by Makoto Ueda in *The Master Haiku Poet Matsuo Basho*. They begin by selecting and writing about favorite haiku. I ask them to imagine their own reading responses first, without relying on the commentary provided by the translator. After sharing their imagined responses, we discuss Basho's biography and the cultural context of the haiku, as discussed in commentaries by Makoto Ueda. The students are pleasantly surprised that they relate to Basho's haiku the same as contemporary haiku, but they also recognize that there are cultural allusions and contexts that they simply do not understand or know. They are very interested in Basho's shift from being a court poet to independent wandering poet.

In chapter two, "The Haiku", Ueda categorizes Basho's development as a haiku poet into five phases: (1) Haiku as Pastime:1662-72; (2) Technique of Surprising Comparison 1673-80; (3) In Search of Identity 1681-85; (4) Manifestations of Sabi 1686-91; and (5) Last Phase 1692-94. In each of these phases Ueda discusses Basho's shift in haiku poetics—the aesthetics he sought in his best haiku attempts.

Here is a brief summary of these shifts in poetics.

(1) As a court poet, Basho sought to demonstrate a "refined wit", writing clever haiku that demonstrated his literary and artistic refinement as a rising young samurai.

(2) Renouncing his samurai status after the death of his friend, Basho moved to Edo to be part of the rising business class. There he started teaching haiku and gained several patrons, teaching them effective techniques for kukai competitions so that they could participate in renga writing parties. Ueda places Basho within the Danrin school of haikai which celebrated surprising language and "earthy humor" instead of elegance.

(3) Basho writes his "bare branch" crow haiku with simple intensity which leads to the development of his own approach and style. This approach emphasizes avoidance of linguistic flourish in favor of simple language and everyday subject matter, which Ueda characterizes as "descriptive, objective haiku" with implied, rather than overtly stated, emotion. He seeks aesthetics similar to the Chinese Taoist poets.

(4) Basho builds on the Buddhist Tao poets' approach with a unique emphasis on the aesthetic of sabi. Ueda writes, "He might borrow from Chinese verse, juxtapose two separate objects, create ambiguity of meaning, or rely on any number of other methods, and yet his poems always had something uniquely his own. This unique quality can be explained by applying the idea of sabi" (p. 51). Ueda provides extensive examples of haiku with sabi to expand understanding of this Zen aesthetic principle beyond mere

"loneliness" or "solitary" definitions. It is a mix of feelings of independence, aloneness, peacefulness, loneliness and related Buddhist recognition of impermanence and shared suffering.

(5) While many of the haiku from Basho's fourth phase emphasized nature, the last phase emphasizes living in the social world of man. While the range of emotions vary wildly as Basho writes about everyday life in Edo, this phase has several playful haiku that convey an aesthetic goal of "lightness" known as karumi. Students in my class especially enjoy Basho's haiku about the cherry blossoms on the picnic under the trees as an example of this aesthetic principle.

In addition to reader responses to Basho's haiku, students match English haiku with Basho's translations to consider how Japanese aesthetic principles are evident in English haiku as well. Students also attempt to write haiku based on sabi, wabi, and karumi. Here are samples of some of their attempts.

Kukai – Favorite Sabi Haiku

home from work
no dirty dishes
but my own

Debbie Myers, Fall 2008

This haiku reminds me of when I lived alone during the summer. I couldn't wait for my roommates to move out, but I found it difficult to come home after work, night after night, to no one but my empty house. It was nice because I was the only person making a mess in the house, and I didn't mind cleaning it up, but at times, it would have been nice to have someone else there to clean up after. This haiku does a great job of capturing the loneliness of the person in the haiku. There is also a sense of longing as well. The person just doesn't want to be alone anymore. Samantha Sinkhorn, Fall 2008

storm is brewing
I stand
and face the wind

Bailey Welch, January 2018

I like the defiance that is brought into the poem with the phrase "and face the wind". It is kind of like the phrase "face the music". Being able to bear the consequences or your fear of something is, to me, extremely brave and courageous. It wasn't until two years ago that I was able to own up to my mistakes and accept the effects of my actions. Danielle Morgan, January 2018

visible
even in the city
shooting star

Mackenzie Peck, Fall 2014

I thought that this haiku was very well written and formatted. I really enjoyed the fact that the shooting star, even in the midst of great buildings, could be seen. This gave me a great picture about how it would look and how the people in the city would see it. In big cities, there is a constant light, making it hard for anyone to even see stars. I can imagine a couple looking up at the night sky and seeing the shooting star pass by, extremely bright. They are filled with excitement because the act of physically seeing stars of any kind is rare in the city. It seems like a stroke of good luck to see this. Daniel Rausch, Fall 2014

    long shower
    I think
    where am I going?

        Christopher Potter, Fall 2012

For me the shower is where I do some of my deepest thinking about life other than before I go to sleep. I often think about current good things as well as bad things in my life, but other times I go further. I think about the future, and in doing so I feel lost from time to time. I have faith that things will work out, but at the same time, thinking about the future can be scary and overwhelming. I think the fact that this haiku is so simple but can trigger so many thoughts is remarkable. Seth Harshman, Fall 2012

    midnight confessional
    in the dark . . .
    she searches

        Jennifer Godwin, Spring 2009

This haiku gives me almost a sense of guilt because I have been in that position where you know you have to pray for something, but your conscious won't let you open your mind to the wrong doing. It's an unsettling feeling for someone who wants to confess but isn't able to. Hector Galvan, Spring 2009

    alone now . . .
    even this spring day
    her shades all drawn

        Anne LB Davidson, *Mayfly* 47, p. 6

    alone at last
    I wonder where
    everyone is

        George Swede, *Almost Unseen*, p. 87

Each of these haiku focuses on loneliness. Although part of each is the same, I feel that there are different approaches used. Davidson uses a "..." after stating the aloneness. This sets up an almost suspicious atmosphere. Swede, however, follows the aloneness with "at last." Instead of setting up suspicion, this implies a more satisfactory tone. It is as if the person is pleased to be alone. These very different ways of introducing the haiku sets the reader up for expectations of what is to come. Another difference is the pause or separation in the haiku. In Davidson's, each line is a distinct phrase. Swede sets the first one separate, but the second two are part of the same phrase. In Swede's, it makes the feeling stronger of being alone and then not wanting to be alone. It makes the irony and contrast very bold. It makes it seem like the person is relieved to be alone, but then feels lonely and wants people back. This person is isolating himself. Davidson's haiku, however, has a different flow to it. It seems as if the person wants to be part of the world, the spring is welcoming her, but she must close herself off. The difference in person is also clear, Davidson uses "her" while Swede uses "I," perhaps to evoke a different response and connectedness with the reader. Olivia Birkey, Spring 2010

Kukai – Favorite Wabi Haiku

swinging at our old park
my friend and
her daughters

Melanie McLay, Fall 2008

I am at the age where stuff like this is starting to happen. Classmates are starting to get married and have children, and classmates that had children earlier now have children big enough to be swinging. The sudden adulthood that sneaks up on people is definitely at the heart of this poem, as is a sense of loss of those old childhood days. The fact that the narrator points out that the park used to be theirs shows that the narrator perhaps wishes things hadn't changed as much as they have, or at least gone in the direction they did. Mark Beanblossom, Fall 2008

hand-me-down
my once favorite shirt
now my son's

Bill Fields, July 2016

sister's dress
how pretty she looked
now it's mine

Michelle Holsapple, July 2016

Both these haiku are bittersweet. In the first haiku I see my son wearing his father's clothes. My son's father passed away when he was 9 years old, so anything related to his father brings tears to my eyes. However, as he gets older, I see more and more of his dad in him and hope he appreciates everything his dad left him. Even when his father was alive our son was the light of his life and left him so much. One day I see my son going out on a date in one of his dad's dress shirts or even wearing one of his ties to work. The second haiku makes me think of when I was growing up. I have a sister 3 years younger than me and she followed me everywhere I went and did everything I did. I remember at Christmas we were Mom's perfect Facebook picture. My mom would dress us alike, earrings and all. My sister would love it, but I despised it. We even have pictures of my having a ticked-off look on my face and my sister with a huge smile! However, at the age we are at now I realize how special that was to her. I now teach my kids that if someone younger wants to follow them and idolize them, then let them. You never know what that could mean to them. Both haiku talk about passing things down and appreciating their value. Jennifer Tohill, July 2016

crack a smile
your crooked teeth
perfection

Courtney Gallup, Spring 2012

missing teeth
the old woman's
brush

Catherine Hixson, Spring 2012

This is my favorite haiku matching pair because they both relate to teeth and smiling. The first one means to me that no matter how imperfect your smile is, it still can be perfection to someone. Or someone could think that your smile is perfection and fall in love with it. It is a reminder to always smile because you never know who could fall in love with it. The second one is that an old woman's smile can still be perfect as she looks in the mirror and brushes her hair with her old brush. I like how they both relate to the beauty of a smile and the way that even if they're broken or chipped, they can still be loved. Kathryn McDaniel, Spring 2012

grandfather's old boots
    I take them
for a walk

George Swede, *Almost Unseen*, p. 62

attic sun
from Grandmother's gown
a grain of rice

Peggy Lyles, *To Hear the Rain*, p. 69

I found these two haiku to be an interesting "matched pair". One thing these two poems have in common is that they both have a similar message. In Swede's poem, he paints an image of a little boy trying on his grandfather's old boots in a reminiscent way. In Peggy Lyles' poem, she paints an image of a granddaughter or daughter stumbling across their grandmother's gown and a grain of rice indicating the gown could have possibly came from her wedding. They both share a reminiscent message and have a common attitude and tone. They're both pretty calm and enlightening. They're not reminiscent in a negative tone at all, but more so in a positive light. Alyssa Rodriguez, Spring 2018

Kukai – Favorite Karumi Haiku

in their multitude
lighting up the night sky
stars

Kendall Kott, Spring 2015

I liked this haiku because it brought out a lot of sensory images for me. When I think of watching the stars, I think of late summer nights with my best friends and my sister. We would sit in the backyard, on our trampoline when we had one, and stare at the stars while we talked until the sunrise in the morning. I could feel the slightly cool air on my skin, as well as I could feel the material of the trampoline rub against the backs of my arms as I laid down. I could smell the summer air, which was warm and inviting, and I could hear crickets and the occasional airplane, since I lived by the airport in Saint Louis. This haiku made me excited for summer. Katelyn Rumph, Spring 2015

impromptu road trip
we find a new
favorite restaurant

Nicholas Sanders, Spring 2015

I liked this haiku because I love road trips, no matter how long. This haiku is interesting to me though because I am never brave enough to drop into any random restaurant and just try it out, I always go to some place I have been or at least heard of. This haiku kind of challenges me to be a little braver next time and try out the unknown, maybe I will find a new favorite restaurant or something else interesting. Also, I love the word "impromptu" in this haiku, it makes it so much more fun. The reader can sense that caught up in the moment feeling and excitement when you decide to just follow your impulses and have fun enjoying life. Eve Greenwell, Spring 2015

fortune teller
she warms up
the farmer's coffee

Randy Brooks, Fall 2012

I can just feel the weathered, honest love in this haiku. A farmer, insinuating hard labor and difficult times, means that this couple has been through it all. Yet, his wife kindly prepares his coffee. Maybe he is just now getting done with an early morning shift out in the fields. Knowing that he has done so much, she graciously completes this little gesture in thanks for his work. Ryan Fraedrich, Fall 2012

no one home
she sings out loud
dances in the kitchen

Christine Lourash, July 2016

This haiku makes me laugh because I can completely relate. All I can see is a mom with a messy house in her robe. She gets up in the morning on the kids' first day of school and she is making coffee and breakfast. She is making sure the kids are dressed, and their book bags are ready. The minute the bus picks up the kids and drives away she feels free! She turns on her iTunes and dances all through the kitchen singing at the top of her lungs. I can relate, not on the first day of school, but on the feeling of being alone. Being alone does bother me but there have been times when the kids are gone, and I turn up the music and enjoy the freedom of an empty house. It's funny though if I've dance around with my headphones and my music turned all the way up, then my kids walk in and look at me like I'm crazy. Jennifer Tohill, July 2016

> weeds sprouting
> purples and blues
> let them grow

>> Renee Sample, Fall 2016

> a spider
> watches from the corner
> my bubble bath

>> Savannah Riestenberg, Fall 2016

I love this matching pair for their differences. This first haiku was my favorite. It resonated with me in a way that I wish I had written it. I like how the third line is a command. It could have easily been "letting them grow" or something similar but making this last line a command gave it a new meaning. It was as if someone wanted to hack away these weeds (representative of something that had flaws) and another tells them to let them grow, because these flaws were not something to attempt to crush, but to embrace. This second haiku was more fun. I thought about times when I have been in the bath or shower or really anywhere and have spotted a spider. There are a few minutes where you both just stay still, staring at each other, almost daring the other to move. Shannon Netemeyer, Fall 2016

> extravagant party
> nobody
> knows the host

>> Olivia Cuff, Fall 2014

I am a sucker for anything that reminds me of F. Scott Fitzgerald's book, The Great Gatsby. Beyond that initial interest, however, I find myself drawn to the subtle social commentary of the haiku and the original novel. How superficial are we as a people that we will attend parties and praise a host that we cannot even pick out from a crowd? I'm guilty of it. It's just so interesting that being seen and present at a party is of more value than knowing who to thank. Olivia did a really swell job with this haiku. It is so sly that someone who does not pick out intimations of Fitzgerald could enjoy it. For those who pick up on the attachment, it is an added bonus. Taylor Hagerdorn, Fall 2014

> houselights flickering
> like birthday candles . . .
> the winding road ahead

>> Natalie Perfetti, Spring 2009

When I drive home to see my family, every turn becomes more and more automatic. Every stoplight, business, bridge is like a road sign leading me home. Birthday candles are a treat and a milestone, and so is the opportunity for me to go home. I think this metaphor is very successful not only because of its accuracy, but because of its universality. "the winding road ahead" could lead anywhere, and therefore anyone can relate to it. Sierra Shaw, Spring 2009

cool morning of dew—
cutting radishes
for my wife's lunch

Wally Swist, *Silence Between Us*, p. 28

Saturday
he whistles as he turns
the children's pancakes

Peggy Lyles, *To Hear the Rain*, p. 56

I believe these haiku could be considered a good "matched pair." Both are three lines and are simple to read. The word choice is pleasant and easy to understand. Both haiku describe simple actions dealing with food. Swist describes the simple action of cutting radishes for his wife's lunch and Peggy Lyles describes the simple action of turning a pancake for children. Along with the simplicity of the haiku, both have a relaxed vibe to them. Swist uses the words "cool morning" and "wife's lunch" and Peggy Lyles uses "Saturday" and "whistles." All of these words seem very relaxing and calming. Neither haiku is gloomy or negative. Both are positive and give the reader a happy attitude that most likely brings back good memories. Both haiku have close to the same arrangement. In the first line the authors begin with the day or weather, in the second line, a verb tells the reader what is going on in, which is followed by saying who the food is meant for in the third line. Austin Taylor, Fall 2017

long twilight
at the woman's ear
a small pearl glows

Peggy Lyles, *To Hear the Rain*, p. 50

ocean sunset
he whispers something
and her earrings glow

George Swede, *Almost Unseen*, p. 51

In the first line both authors describe the time of day in two words. Swede's beginning line with the sunset paints the reader's mind with a brighter more vibrant array of colors. Meanwhile, Peggy Lyles uses darker colors to set the mood and tone. These darker colors bring about a sort of mysteriousness. With the last two lines, I feel like Swede is trying to add a more romantic tone. He has set the reader at the ocean and now directs their focus to the couple. The setting isn't dark and mysterious, but the phrase or words whispered in the woman's ear is a mystery. In Peggy Lyles last two lines, our focus is directed to the woman's ears and the pearl earrings she is wearing. In this poem we are left thinking about what the woman may be doing dressed so elegantly at night, instead of pondering about the words whispered in the other woman's ears. Both haiku talk about a glowing pair of earrings, but in a different way. In Swede's the earrings almost come to life and are in touch with the emotion the woman is experiencing after the man has whispered in her ears. The woman may be blushing, or excited, and the earrings seem to take on the aura of the woman. In Peggy Lyles's poem, the earrings serve only as an object. They are used to provide the reader with an image of how the twilight moon or stars makes the woman's earrings glow. The earrings do not seem to have a double meaning like the earrings Swede writes about. Hannah Mahr, January 2016

children's day at the zoo
I find myself watching
the children

George Swede, *Almost Unseen*, p. 101

lunch at the zoo
even among gorillas
some who sit apart

Peggy Lyles, *To Hear the Rain*, p. 59

I chose to compare these two haiku, as they both talk about being at a zoo. Both are similar in length and format. The one by Swede has a happier feeling than the haiku by Peggy Lyles. Her haiku seems sad and lonely as opposed to Swede's haiku. Swede points out how when we get older, we aren't amused by the animals as much as the children at the zoo. Seeing their excitement and happiness is more pleasing for us than seeing the animals at the zoo. It gets me excited to take both of my nieces to the zoo when they get a little older. I can see myself watching them more than the animals. Peggy Lyles seems very distant in her haiku. She compares gorillas sitting apart to the actions of humans. I see someone sitting alone at the zoo. Chase Smith, Spring 2017

Chapter 12

Collaborative Linked Verse

Sharing the Creative Process

In order to fully understand the origins of haiku, Global Haiku Traditions students read and enjoy writing linked verse. The Japanese tradition refers to all variety of linked verses as "renku". To get started, my students read two renku (both kasen renga) translated in chapter three of Makoto Ueda's book, *The Master Haiku Poet Matsuo Basho*. First the students read just the renku without commentary, responding to a favorite pair of links. Then after sharing responses, they go back and read the entire chapter, which provides an introduction to the renku-writing gathering of poets. Ueda also provides commentary on each link in the translations of "A Winter Shower" and "Summer Moon". The students are surprised by the quick shifts and changes evident throughout these examples of 36-link kasen renga. They also enjoy how a link can change the meaning or feeling of the previous link. To fully gain understanding, the students write three or four types of linked verse, starting with tan-renga.

Kukai – Tan-renga

Tan-renga is a linked verse with two links. To jump-start the linking process, I ask students to find a favorite haiku from a previous kukai and add two more lines to make a tan-renga. Sometimes several students or teams of students write a possible second link (capping verse) to the same starting haiku (the hokku). Then we have a "mini-kukai" and select the best link for the new tan-renga. After doing several of these, I ask the students to describe what they think makes for the best link in a tan-renga. They point out that the best ones have some element of surprise and don't simply continue or repeat the thoughts or feelings of the haiku. I explain the idea of link and shift as a key strategy for all linked verse. Each verse should have some link or connection to the previous verse, but it should shift away and offer something new as well. Here are some examples of favorite tan-renga by the students.

> walking slow
> he waits for her
> to catch up
>
> splashing in puddles
> to waste time

Susie Wirthlin & Hollie Logsdon, Spring 2012

The shift in this tan-renga grabbed my attention. From the hokku, I imagined an elderly couple, or a young man helping his grandmother along. She can't walk that fast, so he has to make sure not to get too far ahead of her. But once I read the cap, the ages reversed. I think of a father waiting on his daughter, whose legs are so much shorter, but to top it off, she's not in too much of a hurry. Rather, she's splashing in every puddle they come across. The cap successfully continues the hokku by not only adding to the image but morphing it into something new. Aubrie Cox, Spring 2012

I really like this because it could be interpreted in many ways. When I first read it, I assumed it was talking about two young kids walking together, but then reading it a second time I saw a grandmother walking with her grandson and he's jumping in puddles to pass time while she catches up to him. Tara Goheen, Spring 2012

> midnight snow
> it's like you
> were never here
>
> the empty
> sock drawer

> Aubrie Cox, Spring 2012

I chose this solo tan-renga because it has a lot of emotion. I see a lot of imagery here . . . maybe it's about a husband or a wife who all of a sudden left and the other one is still in denial that they've left. Tara Goheen, Spring 2012

I really like this one. Through the words, I can feel the sadness of the narrator, and I can just imagine somebody standing in his or her room at midnight, while snow is visibly falling outside the window, and the person is staring at his or her lover's empty sock drawer. It's just so sad, and I love the imagery and emotion that this tan-renga evokes in me. Kate Eagler, Spring 2012

> a beautiful garden
> lies behind
> a brick wall
>
> piece by piece
> she lets him in

> Rachel Pevehouse & Haley Vemmer, Fall 2018

I love this tan-renga because it details an experience that I have gone through. I envision the beautiful garden being all of the wonderful and sensitive and creative and cherished things about a woman. But she hides all of this behind a brick wall and has a hard time letting anyone really get to know her because of negative experiences from a bad breakup. It broke her heart, so she hides her true self behind a brick wall for protection. With the added link, we see that she has found someone who she may be able to trust. And slowly, very slowly, she removes some of the bricks from the wall. She is being cautious, but beginning to be free to love again. Jenesi Moore, Fall 2018

I loved this tan-renga because it created such beautiful imagery. I could imagine someone taking down the wall brick by brick, slowly letting this new person into their life. I also really liked the addition to the original haiku because I never would have thought of adding in the element of a relationship. I thought the idea was very clever, and it worked out to make a gorgeous tan-renga. Sophie Kibiger, Fall 2018

> this rain
> pulling me down
> as it falls
>
> I turn over
> and go back to sleep
>
> Doug Sherrill & Matthew Vangunten, Fall 2016

I like this tan-renga because it changed my attitude towards the first part for the better. The original haiku gave me a dreary impression, with a negative and dark connotation presented by the rain and being pulled down. The second two lines gives the whole work more of a relaxing mood, and the first three lines then give more of an impression of being soothing. Jordan Comish, Fall 2016

I like this tan-renga because it shows someone with lots of distractions in their life. The rain symbolizes all their problems and frustrations, and it is bringing them down. However, when times are tough, the person is able to not let his problems get the best of him and do whatever needs to be done. I've heard this type of advice many times in my life and it is something that I always try to live by. Being able to stay focused on your tasks, no matter what is going on in your life, is something that is essential in order to be successful. Ryan Sikora, Fall 2016

> old man
> the only visitor
> in the cemetery
>
> stepped on my bed
> I'm used to it
>
> Owen Pulver & Douglas Sherrill, Fall 2016

I thought the cap to this haiku was very clever. The original haiku was very sad and lonely, but the addition of the cap made it lonely in a funny way. Instead of feeling bad for the elderly man, the reader can't help but chuckle at the misfortune of the dead, being stepped on continuously. It is still somewhat sad to see how little care we have for those who are gone, but the old man reassures us that some dead still have visitors. Savannah Riestenberg, Fall 2016

Kukai – Mad-verse Kasen or Half-Kasen

Although the students do not fully understand linked verse yet, I introduce them to the fun of spontaneous collaboration by writing a "Mad-verse Kasen" in class. The class sits in a circle and each student folds a blank sheet of paper into eight pages (six for writing verses and one for the front and back covers). I show them how to make the double "cathedral folds" to prepare their paper for writing kasen. This is simply folding the paper in half, then folding each half in half again. Sometimes this is referred to as a "gate fold".

> The paper is folded into 4 pages for each side (cathedral door style).
> Page 1 (outside cover) – title, date, place, copyright, (sometimes authors)
> Page 2 (first fold inside left panel) – first six links
> Page 3 (further inside far left panel) – next six links
> Page 4 (far left inside page panel) – next six links
> Page 5 (right center page panel) – next six links
> Page 6 (far right inside page panel) – next six links
> Page 7 (last fold inside right page panel) – next six links
> Page 8 (back outside cover) – acknowledgments & author links
> optional obi (paper or cloth belt around the folded renga)

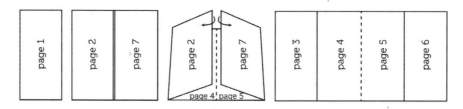

We begin by putting the date on the front page, which will later be the title page. Then we start by writing a hokku (starting verse) on the top of page 2. I usually ask students to bring one of their favorite haiku to serve as the hokku. The student adds their initials beneath the hokku, then passes it to their right. Then the student to the right reads, enjoys and writes a two-link response followed by their initials. Then we pass it right again. Each member of the class has started a mad-verse kasen, and the process continues round robin style. I change the direction of passing (left, second right, second left, etc.) with each page so that students get a variety of linking partners. I also provide short prompts calling for a moon verse in the 5th and 13th and 29th links and blossoms for the 17th and 35th links. We write six links per page, leaving page 8 for details about the authors.

I call this "mad-verse kasen" because the students don't really understand the process, but I want them to enjoy the shared creative process. These are rapid-fire linked verses that violate many of the more traditional rules and guidelines. Sometimes we only have time in class to complete a half-kasen of 18 verses instead of the traditional 36 links.

Here are examples. The first is a half-kasen "The Edges Blur: A Mad-verse Half-Kasen" written by students in the Fall 2018 Global Haiku Traditions class.

The Edges Blur

rock bottom
I turn to the moon
for advice

           ak

she has nothing
to say

           ho

her eyes swollen
with tears
driving on the country road

           es

overweight frog
croaking over the moodiness

           jm

pond water swirling
smiling down on us
the moon

           il

waterlilies float,
disturbed by fish

           dk

●

grandma and grandpa
on an evening stroll
matching walkers

           il

rabid dog chase
who can scoot faster?

           jm

autumn hike
black lab sniffing
every leaf

           es

rainbow inchworm
dangles from silk

           ak

her mother
refuses to hook
her line

           rmb

the worm
wiggles away

           hh

●

staring at Venus
long enough
the edges blur

ak

weeding the garden
smoking the product

jm

handcuffs click
"are you kidding"
damn

dk

disappointing mom
my specialty

ho

falling blossoms
swept off the pavement
by squirrels

il

3 more treatments
and she'll be home   forever

mk

• • •

Authors for this Mad-verse half kasen:

Alissa Kanture = ak
Daria Koon = dk
Emily Sullins = es
Haley Vemmer = hv
Hannah Haedike = hh
Hannah Ottenfield = ho
Isabella Loutfi = il
Isabella Spiritoso = is
Jenesi Moore = jm
Melanie Wilson = mw
Naomi Klingbeil = nb
Rachel Pevehouse = rp
Randy Brooks = rmb
Sophie Kibiger = sk
Sydney Rudny = sr
Zachary McReynolds = zm

Grasshoppers
& Tobacco Spit

scent of lilies
white dress
flows past smiles

kbh

spring breeze extinguishes
the orange flame

bh

a single tear
father's weathered face
beaming

ml

reception delayed
wedding party pictures

lt

soft moonlight
reflects in
the newlywed's eyes

xyz

glassy lake
a fish nibbles our toes

rj

•

tonight's concert
crickets and bullfrogs
opening chord

rj

a lone didgeridoo
echoes in the distance

lh

the yodeler
a long trill sounds
over soft snow

kbh

numb fingers
sculpt her snow fort

bh

a crashing wave
invades castle walls—
erased

ml

feasting on steamed crabs
playful banter

lt

•

family reunion
moon viewing
among strangers

xz

a smile shared
the subway

rj

breathing each other's air
we climb
to the surface

kbh

hard rock
rattles the speakers

bh

crowded park
black boots trample
cherry blossoms

lt

straight-faced troops
march through protesters

xyz

•

TV broadcast
the child struggles
to understand

lt

war in action
reporter rambles on

xyz

beneath the transmitter
a red ant nibbles
the crusty bun

rj

a motherless child
cries for her dolly

lh

painted face
on porcelain bisk
dressed in lace

kbh

her tiny Easter bonnet
stained by jelly beans

bh

•

grimy hands
fumble for colored eggs
among the grass

ml

broken shell
a baby robin motionless

lt

thick smoke
searching for her child
with a broken heart

xyz

crackling fire
first s'mores of fall

rj

harvest moon
sets and rises
between friends

lh

soft talk
gentle laughter

kbh

•

midnight
sisters snuggle
beneath warm blankets

bh

the scent of freshly baked cookies
drifts up the stairs

ml

lemonade stand
a coin drops
in the cup

lt

rain forecast
girls set up an umbrella

xyz

hand in hand
young lovers skip
in the cherry orchard

rj

open eyes
a thoughtful kiss

lh

• • •

Authors for this kasen renga:

Bri Hill = bh
K.B. Hattan = kbh
Lauren Taylor = lt
Liz Hattan = lh
Michele LaBrose = ml
Ryan Jones = rj
Xiu Ying Zheng = xyz

After writing the mad-verse kasen in class, my students read more traditional kasen available on the web. They also read and discuss the previous kasen, "Grasshoppers & Tobacco Spit", written by Bri Hill and friends: K.B. Hattan, Michele LaBrose, Lauren Taylor, Xiu Ying Zheng, Ryan Jones, and Liz Hattan. About half of these collaborators were not in the Global Haiku Traditions class but were guided on writing links by the other students. We discuss favorite links and the overall reading experience of this kasen renga, then the students are assigned to write a traditional kasen renga over the weekend with friends, family, classmates or former haiku students at Millikin. Here are my instructions, including a short guide to key links.

This assignment is a gathering for writing linked verse—if it's nice out you could gather in the park or at someone's house. Allow the spirit of the place where you gather to be a springboard for the haiku, but don't limit yourself to that place once you get into the linking. Let your links go out through time and seasons moving from person (ninjo) focused to non-person (ninjo-nashi) focused in order to avoid too much continuity of people or scenes. Try to avoid more than three ninjo or ninjo-nashi links in a row. Remember, every two links make a new poem. Using the following guide, try writing a kasen-no-renga.

(1) ninjô verses—people or human environment verses (self, other or both)
(2) ninjô-nashi—non-people or things or place or nature or things-only verses

Guide to writing a 36 link kasen-renga:

(1) hokku—sets tone, greets all, establishes season, quiets guests to join in
(2) wakiku—builds on unstated elements of the hokku and maintains season; ends in a noun
(3) daisanku—ends with open-ended image (often transitive verb ING)
(5) usually moon shows up here for the first time
(6) concludes the first page (jo) often written by the official scribe
(7)-(29) heats up the links and leaping (intensification)
(13) moon appears again
(17) blossoms usually show up here
(29) moon's third and final appearance
(30)-(36) kyû—the slow down finale (quiets back down into calmness)
(35) cherry blossoms always here
(36) end with openness and reverberation

After reading several Japanese and English renku, I ask the students why the hokku usually has a kireji, or haiku cut, whereas the other links don't necessarily have a cut. The quick answer is that the hokku starts the linking process within itself . . . it links the first image with the second half. The other verses link to the previous verse. They already have a pause within the sequence of verses so only the hokku needs a pause within itself. As an incomplete verse with some deliberate disjunction, it invites the readers to start imagining "more to the story" which prompts the second verse. Perhaps this is where the haiku tradition of the cut has become such a universal element of haiku.

Here is another example of kasen renga, "Woppy-Soppy", written by the entire class from Spring 2011. For this kasen, after each link we competed with a "mini-kukai" to select the best new link from 4-5 submitted that round. This took almost three class periods to complete.

Woppy-Soppy

open window
letting the papers
fly away

sw

door slams shut
she opens her eyes

es

at breakfast
the aroma
of fresh coffee

cc

under the table
he licks up the crumbs

sw

moon viewing
she's late
again

ke

his reflection
caught in stained glass

bs

•

baptismal pool
a drop of water
clings to my lip

sw

inside his lunchbox
minnows again

sw

walking through
the budding wood
at a turtle's pace

es

abandoned cabin
in the thicket

ac

rusty nails
pin back
the curtains

jk

a flash
in the cracked glass

rb

•

thick moonlit fog
envelops
the crime scene

nk

flinging the evidence
into the river

ke

trudging
into the bar
woppy-soppy

es & ke

I scrape my pockets
for the last dime

sw

she buys flowers
for the cross
on the side of the road

nk

cars fly under a dark sky
silence still

cc

•

first frost
the crack
of dead trees

sw

little footprints
in the snow bank

bs

wedding seed
leftover
for the birds

jk

white silk
re-tying the knot

sw

rose petals
landing
in my wine glass

bs

sunset disappears
a man smokes his pipe

cc

•

standing alone
see you later
instead of goodbye

cc

the wet clothes
cling to her cold skin

sw

icy lake
fish dance
beneath the surface

ke

journal entries waiting
on Alaska's sunrise

nk

beneath their stars
wolves serenade
the cabin

nk

autumn rain hits
the weathered rooftop

jk

•

sun-bleached planks
the old dock slowly
sways

sw

a frog glides
into the reeds

ac

under the bed
postcards from places
I've never seen

nk

Tequila sunrise
in Mexico City

jk

someone
calling my name
in the blossom storm

ac

wooden flute
soothes the restless air

es

• • •

Authors for this kasen renga:

Aubrie Cox = ac
Becky Smith = bs
Cindy Chen = cc
Elise Scannell = es
Jennifer Kibbat = jk
Kate Eagler = ke
Nora Kocher = nk
Randy Brooks = rb
Susie Wirthlin = sw

Kukai – Rengay

After studying and writing Japanese renku, the students are pleased to learn about "rengay" invented by Garry Gay as an alternative English linked verse tradition. As Michael Dylan Welch explains in a short essay, "The renga and renku forms of linked verse have a long, rule-bound, culturally dependent tradition in Japan. Many English writers attempting these forms have questioned the relevance of the many rules in our culture, and sometimes fail to enjoy the stringent renku-writing process. As a reaction to these sometimes-stifling rules and traditions, Garry Gay invented a renga alternative in the summer of 1992: the 'rengay.' The rengay is a collaborative six-verse linked thematic poem written by two or three poets using alternating three-line and two-line haiku or haiku-like stanzas in a regular pattern. The pattern for two people is A-3, B-2, A-3, B-3, A-2, B-3, with the letters representing the poets, and the numbers indicating the number of lines in each given verse. For three people the pattern is A-3, B-2, C-3, A-2, B-3, C-2. Unlike renku, Garry proposes that a rengay stay in one season and develop a single theme." This excerpt is from "Rengay: An Introduction" published in Woodnotes #20, Spring 1994.

I provide my students with the following instructions on writing rengay:

> What is the rengay process? One haiku writer contributes the first link, the hokku, which establishes tone and reverberates with possibilities. After enjoying the hokku, some groups like to discuss possible unifying themes or connections to explore in advance of future links, while other groups like to let the unifying element emerge intuitively from links as they arrive. All partners must agree to accepting the hokku as the starting verse (edits or alternatives can be considered).

> Then the second person comes up with the second link (forming a new poem with the first link), which is then shared and discussed and enjoyed in combination with the first link. Again, if the partners accept the link, then it moves on to the third link, (which forms a new poem with the second link).

> By the end of the third link, a unifying element (feeling, perspective, image, place, time, psychological movement, extension, tone, color, shape, lightness, seriousness) is emerging. This unifying element is heightened or more intentionally intensified over the last three links.

The final step is for the entire rengay to be read and edited for quality, and then a title is selected which invites the reader into the imaginative space of the haiku WITHOUT giving away the unifying element. Titles are not used for haiku because they direct and limit the reader too much, instead of allowing the reader to bring their own imagination to the haiku. In the same way, the rengay title should suggest the unifying element without destroying the reader's imaginative discovery of it.

I provide several examples of rengay with 2 partners and 3 partners, including several by Millikin students. Here are some of my favorites including "The Optimist" and "Field of Dreams" which both happen to be written by twins.

The Optimist

whispers in the dark
sisters speak
of their futures

    nightlight flickers twice
    pitch black

piercing headlights
the widow returns
home to her dog

    keys jingle
    heels on the drive soften

soapsuds
ring the tub
Sunday evening

    red circles cover
    the classifieds

•

by Melanie & Melissa Hayes,
Spring 2001

Field of Dreams

summer wind
dandelion parachutes
dance away

    tranquil seeds
    helicopter to the ground

open meadow
the sun blesses
a perfect picnic

    juicy watermelon
    leaves sticky hands

time to leave
the child searches
for the perfect blossom

    making a wish
    she spreads her dreams in the field

•

by Jason Chmiel, Matt Chmiel, &
Nicole Zabrinas, Spring 2008

Unhinged

falling
through the
looking glass

    smoke-colored wigs
    and demented twins

three quarters
the endless
tea party

    tick tock
    the tail continues
    Cheshire cat grins

hide fading
charm

    the queen's heart
    red as blood

    •

Christa Hunt, Alexa Duncan &
Teresa Brase, June 2016

The Abandoned Lot

a pacifier left
in a parking lot
echoes

    wailing infant
    shopping cart

a mother's last nerve
the freshly removed
wedding band

    the line untanned
    from before he left

echoing footsteps
his signature still wet
divorce papers

    on the court steps
    unsure where to go

    •

Natalie Zelman, Trista Smith &
Danna Herbach, Fall 2014

Reader Response:

"The Abandoned Lot" appeals to me because it has so much depth and emotion within it. When I read this, my heart aches for the family. People get married in hopes of loving each other for the rest of their lives, and sometimes it doesn't go the way things are planned, and as a result, families become broken. I like the turning point and the imagery the second linked verse brings to the rengay. I can see the line of the wedding band on the mother's left hand and I can imagine a signature on the divorce papers. I really enjoy the lines "echoing footsteps" and "his signature still wet." Divorce is a long process and I feel as if the two parties are reminded every day by the stress of it until it gets finalized. I also like how the authors ended this. To me, it can also mean that they are unsure on where to go in life after their divorce. Valina Hoang, Fall 2014

I loved how this one told a story. The rengay tells of the struggles a couple goes through after separation, eventually leading to divorce. The divorce is described through the entire family's point of view. The child is too young to realize exactly what is going on, but (s)he knows that something is not right, and it upsets him/her. The woman is frustrated and fed up with her (now ex) husband. I get the sense that she is also hurt, because she was loyal to him (her wedding ring was not taken off until after they separated), and he betrayed her by leaving them. I feel like the man is just overwhelmed with everything. He didn't necessarily want to leave, but he couldn't stay. It was too much, and he couldn't handle it. That much is evident in his hesitance after signing the divorce papers. He hadn't really thought of a plan; he just had to get away. Mackenzie Peck, Fall 2014

Distant Looks

morning spring mist
from the stem of thorns
a rose

> young girl dances
> around the flower

a woman's cries
from the lone window
neighbors whisper

> the small grave
> on a fresh cut lawn

an old couple sways
to classical songs
ah, to be in love

> looking back
> on a secret affair

•

Alya Saqer, Spring 2007

Reader Response:

My favorite rengay is "Distant Looks" by Alya. I like the way it starts and ends. The beginning contains a rose, but roses are thorny. Then the end kind of parallels that with an old couple, but there was a secret affair. It seems to me that the woman in the middle is the one stabbed by the thorn/hurt by the couple's affair. The whole thing flows really well, keeping each thing separate but tying it all together. Rachel Morrison, Spring 2007

I like the contrast in this rengay that talks of happiness and sadness all at once. I feel like the reader can feel many feelings when reading this and see so many different pictures. I was able to see this all in my mind, a little story of people's different lives. I really like how an old couple finds love again while a woman that I see as being young is widowed. It was by far my favorite rengay this week! Whitney Minor, Spring 2007

Chapter 13

Sharing Collections of Our Haiku

Haiku is for Sharing

Near the end of the semester, I ask the students to create a collection of their best haiku, haibun and renku they have written. Each student is to select only their favorite haiku— a minimum of 10 and usually no more than 30. The collection needs to be written or printed into a booklet to be shared with family and friends in the future. I require that they give the collection a title and write a short author's introduction on the art of writing haiku. I also encourage them to have a reading partner write a short introduction about a couple of their favorite haiku. The students send me a digital copy of the book and bring the physical copy to our last day of class. I collect the copies for my final review and bring them to the final exam, which for us is a public reading of haiku from their haiku chapbooks. After the final reading the students take their collections so that they can share them with others in the future.

On the last day of class, we also have a traditional "signature haiku" gift exchange. Students prepare a copy of their signature haiku on a small gift, often a bookmark, for each other and one for me. This haiku should either represent them in some way or be their favorite haiku—one that they can quickly offer to anyone who asks for an example of their original work.

Since I am asking students for their collections of haiku, one of the last books we read is my own book, *School's Out: Selected Haiku of Randy Brooks*. Students write about favorite haiku by me and enjoy sharing their imagined responses in class. Students often ask for the back story behind a haiku, and once in a while I indulge them with a little story telling. But usually I say that I'd rather leave it to their own imagination. I read each chosen haiku slowly with my "poetry reading voice" to demonstrate how to perform a public reading of your own work. For the final reading, I tell my students to read their work slowly, giving readers time to process each image. I also use their choices to make each student a customized signature gift shikishi of my haiku that they can hang up on a wall. I read and present these at the final haiku reading.

Here are some of the student favorites from *School's Out*, starting with the title poem:

school's out —
a boy follows his dog
into the woods

Randy Brooks, *School's Out*, p. 17

Of all the haiku I have read this semester, I have to say that this is among my favorites. To me, this is the kind of haiku that makes your heart remember. Not only can I see myself following the family dog, but I can also see my brother, and a young Randy Brooks following their dogs into the woods. There really is something special about a friendship between a dog and children. You can trust the dog to take care of a child in the woods. Together, they will have fun adventures. Nathan Heppermann, January 2017

I really liked this haiku because I could imagine the happiness that both the dog and the boy had. The boy is thrilled to finally be done with school for the summer. Now he can play out in the woods, swim and fish with his friends in the river, and do all the other things that country boys love to do. The dog is also thrilled his best friend is free from that prison. Now he can chase him around the woods and swim with him in the river. The dog is happy to be free and with his best friend again. Benjamin Maynard, Fall 2017

This one connects to my childhood. I lived on a big lake with a stretch of woods that were no longer than 40 yards by 30 yards. After school I would always run down to the woods with my dog and friends and we would climb the trees next to the lake and imagine jumping in (which was radical). I like the aspect that the boy just came from school and was learning all day and now he is about to engage in independent studies of his own. I think that some of the best learning that I have experienced in my life came from finding out who I was and what I was interested in through personal studies. Dalton Kauffman, January 2015

> flag on the coffin...
>   her gloves off to hold
>   the child's hand tight

> Randy Brooks, *School's Out*, p. 19

When I first read this haiku, it gave me chills, I absolutely love this haiku. I think it has a lot of different elements to it we can all relate to. I think that we all understand what a flag on a coffin represents, someone who has probably died for our country. This is such a significant yet sad event in history. It also shows the element of loss, and a mother holding her child's hand tight, almost like so she won't lose her child as well. It's like she is grasping on, for their sake, but mostly for hers. The child probably does not understand the gravity of the situation and the mother is so upset for everything in the future, the child growing up without a father, the mother being alone, everything. I get a little teared-up when reading this, but I thoroughly enjoy it! Whitney Minor, Spring 2007

When I read this haiku, I automatically thought of Jacqueline Onassis holding her son's hand at the wake of President Kennedy. Brooks did a great job of capturing a moment that most Americans can identify with. This moment in our history strikes a chord in our hearts, and it is such a touching image to see the love and grief shared by a mother and her child. Although I pictured these specific people, the reality is that this could be anybody from the Civil War era to Vietnam to today's war—nothing has changed, and the cycle of grief continues. Brooks does a good job of capturing the simplicity of this moment in a time of chaos. Alyssa Thompson, Spring 2008

I liked this one because it reminded me of my grandpa's funeral. At his funeral they had the American flag from his service, and it was folded up and handed to my grandmother. What I liked about this haiku was the movement of the text to make a diagonal line, much like the shape of the flag once they fold it. What also adds to the description of this haiku is the mention of the child because it makes it even more sad. Since there is a child involved at this funeral, and the flag indicates that he served our country at some point, this haiku seems to be talking about a funeral for a man that was not yet old enough to pass, that makes it even more upsetting. Lauren Montesano, Spring 2016

dirt farmer's wife
at the screen door—
no tractor sound

Randy Brooks, *School's Out*, p. 20

I really liked this haiku because I was kind of left on the edge. Most of the time I hate when shows, movies, or books leave off with a cliffhanger because you really don't know what is going to happen next. I feel like for this particular haiku it works so well though. With haiku you are supposed to be able to put your own stories and feelings into it and I feel like this sort of cliffhanger does a great job of this. I think of my grandma and grandpa on a Sunday afternoon. This is when my grandfather will go out and get on his tractor and mow the whole yard. When my grandma hears the tractor stop, she is always going to the back door or hopping on her golf cart to go see "what the holdup is". Caitlyn Latshaw, Spring 2017

For me this haiku hits hard and hits home. I am a country raised girl and know that nothing can keep a farmer out of the fields. So immediately I associate the lack of tractor sounds as the death of a farmer. This haiku to me is about a farmer's wife looking out the screen door missing the telltale sounds of her husband's life. It's the little things after someone is gone that we notice and hits us the hardest. There is a sort of sacredness that surrounds a farmer and his job that families respect. This haiku, while completely formed, seems to echo around the loss that this wife feels. Trista Smith, Fall 2018

he opens his cupped palm . . .
a small tadpole with
a little wiggle left

Randy Brooks, *School's Out*, p. 21

I love this haiku because it reminds me of many childhood memories. I think anyone can relate to it from back in their younger days or have experienced something like this with grandchildren. I see this little boy going up to his dad being so proud of his actions and as he opens up his little hands to his dad, he stands there and admires the tadpole. I picture the dad simply acknowledging that his son is enjoying the outdoors but telling him to put it back, so it can live its full life just like he should get to also. Emily Holthaus, June 2016

I enjoyed this haiku because I thought it was very playful. I have memories of holding small tadpoles in my hand when I was younger, and I can remember the slimy, but soothing feeling that it gave me. I especially like the last line of this haiku. I think that the words, "little wiggle" work really well together and add the playful quality that I mentioned. I also find this poem to be very gentle because a tadpole is such a small creature and it is being handled by a much larger being. By using the word, "cupped", it shows that the man is being very calm with the tadpole, showing a great amount of tenderness. Daniel Rausch, Fall 2018

door left open . . .
there he goes
with his kite

Randy Brooks, *School's Out*, p. 22

I love the innocence and playfulness that this haiku brings out. There is a slight tone of disappointment or "Darn that kid," because he didn't close the door, but beneath all that, there is a feeling of joy and contentment that the child is enjoying the precious days of his childhood playing and having fun. Perhaps there is even a feeling of jealousy or nostalgia, as this adult misses the days where there were no real worries, and it was their job to have fun. So many emotions wrapped into less than 10 words! Alissa Kanturek, Fall 2018

First off, I really like the structure of this haiku. The first line, ending in (. . .) leaves the reader hanging onto the last word, "open." Right off the bat, I feel optimistic and (dare I say it) open! The last two lines are said with definite character, and I think that is why I gravitate towards the haiku. "There he goes" is a tongue-in-cheek, cursing phrase to say something without keeping it entirely negative. The second line just throws you into the movement from the boy running out the door; this works well juxtaposed with the first line's ending. The last line, "with his kite" adds a mosaic of imagery—immediately, the reader is thinking about a kite that they once flew, or a kite that they've seen. Even if it's an imaginary kite, it is most definitely flashy and colorful! It doesn't help here that I absolutely LOVE kites, and that I own three of them. But, simply said: if it's the right day to fly a kite, you bet your booty I will be rushing out that door! Kala Keller, Spring 2017

sisters bent over
the heating vent . . .
adult talk below

Randy Brooks, *School's Out*, p. 24

This was probably my favorite haiku in *School's Out*. Immediately after I read it, I had memories of my brother, sister and I at my great-grandparent's house that I had completely forgotten. Every time we went to their house, no matter how long we were there, we ran upstairs to this one room where we could hear through the vent. I remember the vent had a beautiful iron cover over it. The room was directly over the dining room, close to where the adults always were. We would sometimes just sit and listen to their conversation. But, often times my brother or sister would go downstairs to the vent in the dining room, and we would yell back and forth through it. Another cool thing in that same room (unrelated to the vents) was a little closet door inside the main closet. We always halfway pretended-halfway believed that it was a magical little door that led to another world, like in *The Chronicles of Narnia*. It was half as tall as normal doors and rounded at the top. I was always a little nervous to open the door, afraid of what I might find. So, I just let my mind believe it led to another world! It is wonderful to remember these stories! Stephanie Ford, Spring 2002

This haiku was one of my favorites, because it made me think of my siblings and I when we were younger. My sister is only three years older than me, and my brother is only one year older, so we are all very close. We were quite mischievous when we were young and would often eavesdrop. My sister acted as the leader; she would gather us all together and tell us to be quiet as we listened to the voices below us. More often than not, the important discussions we overheard were actually quite insignificant. Our child minds made the "adult talk" seem more important than it actually was. I like that this haiku is able to transport me there, and able to make me reflect on that part of my life. Many of the haiku in *School's Out* are likable for that reason: they are relatable and cause fond memories to resurface. Lane Caspar, Fall 2017

This haiku accurately describes me and my sister when we were younger. Even though my sister and I constantly fought, we would band together and listen through the air vents or at the top of the stairs whenever my parents told us we couldn't be down there for the discussion. Usually it was about what our punishment should be for fighting. My sister and I would eventually run downstairs saying that we had made up and weren't fighting anymore. Also, a lot of times my punishment would be that I wasn't allowed to watch *American Idol*, my favorite TV show, that night, so I would listen to the singers through the air vents. Courtney Buress, Spring 2013

two lines in the water . . .
not a word between
father and son

Randy Brooks, *School's Out*, p. 26

This was my favorite haiku because it portrays a very cherished moment. Any kind of bonding time between father and son is an unexplainable feeling of love, acceptance, and relationship. I love how the haiku was written very simply because that reflects how the smallest moments can mean so much more later on in life. I also like the silence in this haiku because it allows the emotion to be felt instead of spoken. It's much rawer that way. Courtney Ginigeme, Fall 2015

I liked this haiku because there are a couple of different ways that I interpreted it. First, I saw the father going fishing with his son. They are just enjoying a peaceful day on the lake and they are not talking because they just want to really absorb their surroundings and cherish this moment. The other way that I saw it was that the son was mad at the father. Maybe the son got in trouble and got grounded, so he is holding a grudge against his father and doesn't want to talk to him, but it is a tradition for them to go fishing at this time, so he agrees to come. Brandon Januska, Spring 2015

The scene is a perfect example of moments that are too precious for words—a depiction of the unspoken bond between good friends, husband and wife, or in this case, father and son. The son echoes his father's movements exactly, as there is no doubt that his father is the one who taught him to fish. No words between them implies not any kind of tension or discomfort in the connection between the two, but rather that a conversation (most likely a forced one considering the silence and placidity of the situation) would only get in the way of the moment, the situation, the father and son. Brian Blankenship, Spring 2006

first kiss
deep in the woods...
sunbeams filter down

Randy Brooks, *School's Out*, p. 33

I love this haiku. There's a very beautiful moment that is created through the words that are chosen. The initial moment is sweet and tender—the line "first kiss" really sets it up to be this way. Then the last line "sunbeams filter down" changes the moment from being simply tender to magical. It is as though that first kiss ignites the sun and causes the sunshine to come out from hiding. Furthermore, there is a lot of warmth in this haiku— the warmth of the kiss, the warmth of sunshine filtering through the trees, which then creates warmth on the soft padded forest floor. Beautiful. Kersten Haile, Spring 2008

I really liked this particular one because obviously I enjoy this sort of subject matter, but I think it's a great image and it definitely captures that adolescent necessity of hiding anything romantic. I think a lot of us were taught that romantic endeavors were only for people "of age", but most of the time that "age" was never really common knowledge. Consequently, I know I grew up with the idea that anything romantic was basically taboo. So, I really enjoy how this haiku captures that secret element because they're "Deep in the woods" and out of the way of external opinions. The imagery is also just so lovely and picturesque. Who knows if the first kiss was any good or not, but they sure had a perfect setting. Amanda Donohoe, Spring 2017

The intimacy of the scene here is perfect. It almost reminds me of the movie *Twilight*. My mind instantly goes to the scene of Bella and Edward in the little clearing in the forest. They lay side by side in the wild grass, with wild flowers scattered around them. The wind rustles the pine trees, making the birds twitter among themselves. Their eyes never leave each other's gazes. The clouds shift. The sun illuminates patches of the grass through the ancient tree tops. His fingers graze her chin, pulling it closer to his face, placing one gentle kiss upon her lips. Aundrea Marsh, Fall 2015

> end of summer—
> mountain wildflower
> pressed in her diary
>
> Randy Brooks, *School's Out*, p. 35

This haiku was one of my favorites because it made me feel a wide variety of emotions, ranging from joy, pleasure, longing, and sadness. It begins with "end of summer" meaning the end of the girl's freedom and experiences. She is going back to school soon, and the memories of the summer times will be behind her. I was sad about this, because it made me think of all of the summer memories I have had, and how every year, they have to come to an end. However, I felt joy from the fact that she is trying to keep a piece of summer along with her for the rest of the year. She is taking a wildflower and putting it in her diary, which is something she will always carry around. I like the choice of using a wildflower, because I compare it to the freedom that this girl felt during these summer months, but she will ultimately have to close off in her diary. But the memories will always be with her, whenever she looks at this flower. Trey DeLuna, Fall 2017

I really enjoyed this haiku because it amplifies different aspects of my senses. I feel the warmth that is still lingering from the summer, I can smell the mountain wildflower, and can feel the paper under the tips of my fingers. I also like the emotions it brings up of a summer love. There are many memories that this person kept in their diary. All of their words are attempting to capture each memory from the summer, but one memory was unable to be explained in words. Instead, this person kept a wildflower, so they are able to touch their memory. They have something they can go back to and feel again, since the summer is over. This is a precious way of remembering a fond event. It also allows for a multitude of stories to arise for why the person received this wildflower. It could have been a lover, child, or they just picked it up themselves. Erica Forbes, Spring 2016

I have written in a journal since seventh grade. This haiku reminded me of how much of my life I keep in my journal. I have flowers, cards, pictures and many other things in the pages of my journals. I usually do not write very often during the school year because I do not have any free time. However, in the summer I write almost every day. At the end of the summer I have to say good-bye to all the people I do not see during the school year. I write a lot about saying good-bye to my friends and family and about my expectations for the coming year. This haiku reminded me of those summer good-byes. I can understand how much the wildflower meant to someone who would put it in their dairy. It means so much to have all their memories stored in pages and pages of writing. Kerry Hammergren, Spring 2002

Sunday after lunch . . .
the secret of her pregnancy
on each sister's face

Randy Brooks, *School's Out*, p. 38

I really loved this haiku because it reminds me so much of how my family was growing up. It sets up the typical "sisters/women always know" idea with the fact that the pregnancy is a secret, but somehow the sisters can just tell. Maybe this is because they've been pregnant before and can just tell, maybe it's the "glow" that women are supposed to have when they first get pregnant. Maybe it's simply because they're sisters, and they just know. Or maybe, just maybe, they're like my cousins who tell the sisters first before they tell anyone else that kind of news. Regardless, I love the idea of the bonds between sisters that allows for this secret to be shared and for the other sisters to know the one so well that they can immediately tell when something exciting is about to happen. Jessica Golden, Fall 2010

I don't know what it is about this one, but I really like it. I think it's because it can be interpreted in so many different ways. At first, I think this is a really happy haiku. She's telling her sisters before she tells everyone else, which I can completely relate to because my sister told me before she told my mother. I feel like my brother will tell me before he tells everyone else too. However, after reading it a second time, I think secret means more here. Now I see a very young girl, maybe a teen, who has older sisters and she comes from a very family-oriented household. She probably was supposed to be abstinent and now she's worried of what her parents are going to do and say. She goes to her sisters first and she's almost wanting their help. She's scared and now her sisters have to carry around this burden too. Francesca Rios, Spring 2015

the bride's mouth
    stuffed with cake . . . the groom
answers for her

Randy Brooks, *School's Out*, p. 39

This haiku truly melts my heart. It's a wedding, first and foremost. That already brings so much imagery to the mind, seeing nothing but smiles on what's supposed to be the best day of the man and woman's life. When talking about the cake, I could see the bride and groom intertwining arms to eat the first piece of cake, but instead stuffing it in one another's faces, like newlyweds sometimes do. But the fact that the groom answers for her when she can't answer for herself gives this haiku a deeper meaning. To me, it makes me think of one who knows when they found the person for them, if the other person is able to know and feel exactly what he or she is thinking. There's that saying that says, roughly, "you guys just finish each other's sentences". And to me, that's what this haiku is getting at: these two were meant for each other; they're perfect for one another. Maria Klek, Fall 2017

I genuinely enjoyed this haiku because it made me think of many different, rather humorous things. First, I imagined that the bride had been really watching what she ate before the day of her wedding, so she could look just amazing in her dress. Then, when the ceremony was over, she was finally able to just let go and have fun. She has her man, so no need to worry! Second, I imagined that the couple was so in sync that if one person was unable to form his/her thoughts, the other person could just step in and help out. Finally, I enjoyed imagining this beautiful wedding reception, something very classy, with a bride in a lovely white gown and cake frosting on her lips. I found the juxtaposition of the beautiful elegance of the wedding reception and the silly freedom of devouring cake very amusing and enjoyable. Catherine Hixson, Spring 2012

> high as my arms
> can lift him . . .
> the moon still out of reach

> Randy Brooks, *School's Out*, p. 47

I enjoyed this haiku because of the imagery and because of the wonder it brought me. I pictured a little boy being lifted by his daddy, trying to touch the moon, but failing. There is a sense of innocence in this haiku that makes me feel like a kid again, because the boy obviously feels like he is capable of doing anything. He asks his dad to lift him up so that he can touch the moon, but his little arms just can't stretch far enough. While we know this is impossible, I like the determination and the hope that the little boy's innocence brings to this haiku. It reminds us to look at life with a can-do attitude all the time. I also like that it is from the adult's perspective, or whoever is doing the lifting, because it shows their view about the child. It shows that they are touched by this determination and goal. The language is simple, and I like that the lines don't form a sentence exactly but still achieve a complete thought. Kendall Kott, Spring 2015

I usually find the moon to be cliché and over-used in haiku, but I thought it was used in such a beautiful and original way in this haiku, that it turned out to be my favorite. I think what turns me off about "moon haiku" is when the imagery of the moon is the focus, but here that's not the only thing going on. There are multiple layers. I really enjoy the image captured of a father lifting up his son above his shoulders and his son reaching up for the sky, but I also really like the idea conveyed in the poem that a parent can only do so much. Parents can only get their children so far, and the children have to go the rest of the distance themselves as they grow up. I can relate to that idea being a college student who is halfway between a kid and an adult. Morgan Oliver, Fall 2013

This one reminded me of my dad. I remember when I was little, my dad and I used to do this thing where I would walk up his legs while he was standing and then flip over. I loved this trick, because it was a little terrifying but also exhilarating. When I read this haiku, I could just imagine a father holding up his son who is trying to touch the moon but can't quite reach. I can imagine the father smiling lovingly at his son, thinking about how he wants the best for him. My dad and I used to have so much fun goofing around and playing in the back yard. I remember how strong he seemed and how I believed he could do anything. My dad was a super hero in my eyes and he still is. This reminded me of all the times my dad has been there for me, working to give me the moon and holding me up so I can reach. I think this haiku captures this spirit perfectly. Emily D'Ambrose, Spring 2013

> my sister cups her hands . . .
> how the nurse showed her
> the miscarried fetus

> Randy Brooks, *School's Out*, p. 49

Another emotional haiku, and in these closing weeks of school, I think I found one of my favorite haiku of all time. The first line just seems so innocent, and even the second line. Yet, you completely flipped the tone of the haiku with your last line. When I read the last line, my heart dropped to the floor, and my mind somewhat exploded because of the turnaround. I also like the use of the word "fetus" because it was not a baby, but a small life form that will just leave empty questions in the minds of the parents. Joe Pegura, Spring 2016

This haiku is so simple but so powerful at the same time— I got tears in my eyes when I read it. It sums up the preciousness of life that so many people take for granted. For anyone who has experienced this kind of loss, it doesn't go away quickly. Sarah Corso, Spring 2006

> his vomit wiped up . . .
> my bowl of Wheaties
> soggy now

> Randy Brooks, *School's Out*, p. 62

I like this haiku because it reminds me of all of the sacrifices associated with being a parent. The bowl of Wheaties signifies that the author is probably a new parent, because they did not prepare a big hearty breakfast. The vomit, I imagine, is that of a sick child. Before you have a kid, you do not think about all of the little things you will have to give up, such as eating your cereal before it turns to mush. I also like this haiku because the tone of it does not seem angry, but rather understanding. Austyn Krueger, Spring 2015

It is not hard to see that Brooks has taken an active role in his duties as a father and husband. He is not an idle observer but someone who is not afraid to get in the midst of existence. He relishes every moment. Take for example the haiku when breakfast was delayed caring for a sick child. If cleaning up vomit was not enough to spoil the thought of eating, soggy cereal surely was. The image of vomit in this haiku is very poignant. One can hear its sound, as well as, hear the splash of it hitting the floor. The smell of cleaning it up is enough to create a similar action. Then the soggy cereal comes into play. Although this leaves an unpleasant taste in the mouth, the tone of the verse brings memories to mind. What parents have not put life on hold to care for their children's needs? Karen McFadin, April 2007

each stroke of the crayon
his tongue
across his lips

Randy Brooks, *School's Out*, p. 63

For this haiku, I thought of a child concentrating very hard on his drawing. His hand is grasped tightly around the crayon as he tries to make every stroke perfect. As he does this, his tongue comes over up his lip as a symbol of his concentration. This is his usual pose when he truly cares about something, and it is evident in his current work. I found this one interesting because I have always been fascinated by people's various looks of concentration. My brother has a very interesting look of concentration when he plays viola. He puts his lower lip under his upper teeth. I have never seen anyone else basically bite his or herself the way he does. For some reason, I grab my lips when I am concentrating. I never realize I'm doing it until somebody points it out. I wonder what it is about the mental process of concentration that causes us to do these weird, involuntary physical movements. Meg Schleppenbach, Spring 2002

As an elementary school teacher, I love the playfulness of this poem. On many occasions, I have been able to see students in deep concentration and out of the cracks come habits that they probably are not even aware that they have. This scene is an example of one of these times, but it also reminds me of when I was a child. Any time I would truly focus on something, I would stick my tongue out without even realizing it. Sometimes I still catch myself doing this. Alyssa Becker, Fall 2016

home from the funeral
hands in the dishwasher suds
sister-to-sister

Randy Brooks, *School's Out*, p. 67

When I read this haiku, I imagined two sisters in a kitchen after the funeral of someone close to them. One was washing dishes that hadn't been done in a while since they lost their loved one. The other was drying. The two were talking and remembering their loved one. They were telling their best stories and memories. They were sad but couldn't help but laugh at some of the stories that were being told. I liked this haiku because it brought back memories of loved ones that I have lost, both good and bad. It also brought back memories of sharing stories about the loved ones I have lost and hearing what stories others have to share. Benjamin Maynard, Fall 2017

I tend to like the sadder haiku the most. Along with the sadness of the funeral, this haiku also pointed out a positive strong relationship between two sisters. Usually funerals aren't a time to talk much about the sad things, there is either crying, or talk of the happy things that have come about to distract from the crying. After the funeral, these two sisters have to clean all of the dishes of the people who came to the funeral, and they are then connected by the water. Being so close causes them to then open up about all they've had to hide for the past couple days. Funerals are difficult to get through, and these two sisters are doing it together. Lauren Montesano, Spring 2016

she couldn't forgive
what she couldn't forgive—
grave sunken in

Randy Brooks, *School's Out*, p. 73

The first two lines make it seem as if this person has given up their faith for someone else. They gave it their all and the person didn't change so they are stuck with not being able to forgive them. The line after the second line makes me kind of sigh which gives the haiku a feeling of exhaustion from trying to get over a situation and not being able to. The last line is what I love because it has a deep meaning to it. It's a grave but the idea of a grave and how it's dug deep into the ground is what shapes the haiku. It's like the saying you dug yourself a grave and now you won't be able to get out. That is exactly what I get from this haiku and I can connect it to a situation my friends and I have been in. Kate Gebultowicz, Spring 2017

This haiku is of special interest to me because I have gone through a divorce and I can feel the limits that forgiveness sometimes has within that event. Although I always had a good relationship with my former mother-in-law before the divorce, it took her many years to accept me after that. I think some events are so tied to expectations, religion, tradition, etc., that people have a very hard time when they happen. In this haiku, whoever couldn't be quite forgiven had died, or perhaps the person who couldn't forgive had died. That his/her grave has sunken in may refer to the fact that a grave may be unattended or that someone has been to the gravesite so much the weight caused it to sink or that the person who has died has still not reconciled. Betty Hartnett, January 2016

big brother's grin . . .
the last piece of the puzzle
out of his pocket

Randy Brooks, *School's Out*, p. 75

I have never seen a haiku that so perfectly captures the sibling relationship. This is perfect. In these three lines, you get the teasing, back-and-forth, but still caring and loving relationship between siblings, especially the role of the older sibling. Whether an older brother or sister, we, the older siblings, tend to feel that it is our job to make things moderately difficult for our younger siblings. I can imagine this happening in my house so easily. I can see my little brother working diligently on a puzzle or a Lego set and discreetly sneaking a piece into my pocket while distracting him with talk about something unrelated. The payoff, the moment this haiku captures, is such a classic sibling moment—the younger one incredulous and a little bit angry, but also a bit impressed that the elder one managed to sneak it under their nose, while the older one is grinning and trying not to laugh too hard at their sibling's pain. Natalie Zelman, Fall 2018

This haiku makes me smile because it reminds me of my own family. Not only do we have competitive sides to us, but we also used to do puzzles every summer at the beach house together. It was always a competition of who would finish the puzzle with the last piece. Every other summer, my family goes to North Carolina and stays in a beach house on the ocean. Throughout the week-long trip, we take turns during the day putting together a large puzzle. Sometimes 1,000+ piece puzzles. Whoever put the last piece in had bragging rights because "they finished the puzzle" even though that is the easier part of all! It is a nice memory to have and this haiku took me there. Heather Allen, September 2015

coffee shop . . .
    the only empty seat
    still warm

Randy Brooks, *School's Out*, p. 80

This haiku reminds me of a quiet, little coffee shop on the corner of a small town. It is where everyone meets up to do homework or talk. However, the person in this haiku is thinking about the fact that a seat is newly empty. The whole place is crowded with people, but he does not care about that. He only cares about the fact that the one person is now gone. It may have been a stranger that he was admiring from afar, which could indicate a longing to meet them along with the possibility that they may never see them again. It could also be a person who they have always wanted to talk to but don't have the courage to. It also could be the empty seat across from them. They may have been having coffee in this shop with someone and they were just left alone in a crowded place. This haiku brings so many alternate stories along with a warm, busy feeling from the coffee shop. This is probably one of my favorite haiku of all time, honestly. Erica Forbes, Spring 2016

I really enjoy this haiku because of the "homey" feeling I receive from it. I love the atmosphere of coffee shops in general as well—the smells, the music, and the baristas' smiles. The only empty, still warm seat, also tells me this little, quaint shop is packed with business. In my mind, it is the first snow of the year, so everyone is coming in for a hot drink. I enjoy the sensory, behind the scenes, aspects of this haiku. I really appreciate the setting of the first line as well, because it sparks all those senses for me. The normalcy of this haiku is great, giving beauty to a seemingly simple moment. Hannah Gifford, Fall 2012

up late with old friends . . .
    my daughter and her blankie
    out of the dark again

Randy Brooks, *School's Out*, p. 81

This was my favorite haiku because every now and again me and my husband invite friends over at night to play games and have a little drink. I always would put my son to sleep around 10pm and we would forget he was sleeping and get a little too loud and we would hear my son jumping up and down in his crib crying with his blanket in his hand wanting someone to come get him. My son does not go anywhere without his blanket, so it is just funny that this haiku went perfectly with my son. Marshaya Sangster, July 2016

I liked this haiku because it reminded me of all the times I would be awake in my room when my parents and their friends or my aunts and uncles or someone was over. And even though whatever they were talking about was the most boring thing to me, I wanted to be in there. It's like hearing someone laugh and wanting to know the joke so you can laugh to. I liked the use of the word "again", because you now know that this is the third or fourth time that she has been put back to bed. I also liked how the word "blankie" was chosen over blanket because it implies the age of the subject of the haiku. Corinne Cullina, Spring 2006

we walk through
the empty farm house—
her eyes well up

Randy Brooks, *School's Out*, p. 89

This haiku makes me sad. My grandparents live in an old Pennsylvania farm house, and they are getting to the point where they have discussed the possibility of giving up the farm house and moving to a retirement home. I am dreading that day. I grew up with that house—it was my summer home and I have spent several holidays there throughout the years. There are so many memories contained within the house itself and throughout the entire span of property. My siblings and I used to play "house" in the old corncribs and find treasures in the junk shed (including our most prized possession, a smooth glass doorknob), and every evening meant a walk out the back lane to find our special rock—a slab of slate that was big enough for all of us to stand on (until we outgrew it, of course). Rainy days called for attic adventures and swinging on the front porch or playing on the covered balcony. That house has seen it all. My grandma grew up in that house, and my dad and aunt and uncle were raised in that house. I don't want it to be sold out of the family. Mackenzie Peck, Fall 2018

This haiku hit really close to home for me, not because of something that has happened, but because of things that will happen someday. My grandparents live in a log cabin on a farm in Northern Wisconsin. That's where my mom grew up, and where I spent some of the best days of my childhood. Someday soon, either due to the mines that surround the farm or because they will be too old to live there by themselves safely, we'll have to clear everything that they own out of the house and off the farm. I am already dreading the day that it goes up for sale, because I know that it's a part of our family's history. The other reason is because I also grew up in a farmhouse—it's where my family still lives and where I've lived since I was four. We've put a lot of love into that house since we've lived there, from new paint, to an entirely new bathroom, planting apple trees and numerous other projects. I know that one day I will have to officially leave my home there, and my parents will be leaving not long after I will. I can imagine walking through my big brown house with its periwinkle walls, saying goodbye to the rooms that I laughed and cried in, the places where I fought with my brother and spent time with my friends. It's sad, but it's a part of life, moving on, and leaving your past behind. Marah Kittelson, Spring 2016

after all these years
she asks about her mother . . .
I put on another log

Randy Brooks, *School's Out*, p. 91

For this haiku, I really enjoyed being able to feel all of the mixed emotions present in just three lines. The first line implies this growing sense of dread that had faded in the distance but suddenly, the pit in your stomach is back. The second line's ellipses bring on this feeling of hesitation, as if pondering how to touch a touchy subject, and apprehension for all of the emotions to come. The third line brings a sense of awkwardness. People often find bad news easier to break when doing something with their hands. Not only is the character physically fidgeting, but they are also implying that this is a long story that is not easily told. There's a lot of mixed emotions in these three lines. Cori Grzenia, Spring 2016

I like the story this haiku paints. You know that her mother is a rough subject and it doesn't get talked about much, but you don't know why. Did her mother leave or pass away when she was young? "After all these years" suggests that the daughter has had plenty of time to ask about her mom and this conversation could have happened numerous times in the past, so why now? What makes this moment so special? Him putting another log on shows us that the story is long and something that they cannot run through. She deserves the full story, no matter how long it will take, and he is willing to give that to her. Corrin Littlefield, Spring 2016

I have a lot of initial thoughts reading this haiku. I almost wish for more information because I am so confused as to who is the narrator. Is it an adopted parent? Her father? Older sibling? Aunt/Uncle, Grandparent? I wish I knew more. However, I chose it because at first, I think people would believe this to be sad, but I didn't get that feeling. I almost think the girl feels confusion and hesitance. She's never really asked. The person caring for her has always been enough, but now she's wondering. My mom was adopted, and she never had questions until she became pregnant with my sister. She wanted to know family history, diseases, what her nationality was and so on. So, the first line makes me wonder if now this woman is pregnant too and less worried about herself, but for her child. I really wish there was tan-renga verse for this one. Francesca Rios, Spring 2015

> long drive home . . .
> our talk of the past goes
> into the future

> Randy Brooks, *School's Out*, p. 98

I liked this one because it reminded me of a conversation I recently had with my boyfriend. We began our conversation talking about the day we met, and how we started dating, and then we got into a conversation about theoretically what we would do in the future if we ever got married. I liked the visual that was represented with this haiku, and I like the idea of how remembering something from the past can make one think about the future, because I do it all the time. Katelyn Rueger, Spring 2015

I love listening to others' stories and what they have been through. I also love watching their eyes get wide and their six-year-old cheesy smiles when they talk about their biggest dreams. This haiku reminds me of both instances, and how sometimes the best conversations are the ones unplanned and during unconventional times. I never get into a car anticipating really deep and thoughtful conversations, but often, I find myself having those with the people on the ride. We would talk about things that happened in our past and how it made us the person we are today. Those conversations usually lead to conversations about the future and what we think may happen in the next few years or even weeks. I know people are scared to speak up and talk about themselves, so I am very grateful when people close to me open up about their past and their life goals. You get to learn a lot about a person without even trying! Valina Hoang, Fall 2018

Chapter 14

Final Readings & Reflections

Why do we need haiku in our lives?

The Global Haiku Traditions course ends with a public reading of student collections. I introduce each student who reads from his or her collection. Each student introduces their reading by explaining the title of their chapbook and giving a brief summary of their introduction on the art of writing haiku. They often invite friends and family to this final reading and invite partners to help read collaborative works. The final reading is a last gathering for that semester's haiku community—a time of sharing our best haiku and enjoying them together. Students often tap their pens or snap fingers when they hear favorite "haiku friends" again. This is a festive celebratory conclusion to the semester.

The week after the reading I ask students to take some time to think back about what they have learned over the semester about haiku, about themselves, about the literary art of reading and writing haiku. I have two post-semester reflection assignments.

Final Responses to Their Own Favorite Haiku

From the very first day of class, I have asked my students to select and write responses to favorite haiku written by others. For this final assignment, I ask them to write about five of their own favorite haiku written during the semester. In this assignment I simply ask them to write about why these are their personal favorites. Often students start with their signature haiku. Here are examples of final reading responses of their own favorite haiku from the Fall 2018 class.

faded sheet music
passed from mother
to daughter

Daria Koon, Fall 2018

Both my parents have shared a lot of their music tastes with me and have influenced what and how much music I listen to. My mother has also passed along her instruments. Both of my parents play multiple instruments, as well as sing, but my mom and I both sing (a lot of people say I have her voice), play the flute, piccolo, and piano. As a result, a lot of the sheet music I play once belonged to her. A lot of it is yellowed, the pages are worn and soft, the bindings cracking, and pages falling out. These are my favorite songs to play for that specific reason. Not only do I share a connection with the sheet music, but I also share a love for that specific song. In the case of two specific pieces, I have heard her play them as warm-ups my entire life, and I made it my mission to learn how to play them. Those are probably the two pieces of music that mean the most to me, and I have them because of my mom. Writing this haiku, as well as reading it, brings back a host of happy memories of hearing, learning, and playing shared music. Daria Koon, Fall 2018

a B Cup
telling me
im not a woman

Hannah Haedike, Fall 2018

This is something I have struggled with my entire life. I'm too short, I don't have big boobs, I have thunder thighs and I will never be the ideal version of a woman. I've constantly compared myself to the women around me, including friends and family and what women are supposed to look like based on the tabloids and social media. Although the culture industry tells me one thing about how I am supposed to look to be a woman, I find strength and dignity in the fact that I will never look like that. I am a woman no matter what I look like. There is confidence I've found in that. Every woman is different and that's what makes us all so unique and beautiful. Hannah Haedike, Fall 2018

work truck
the boy and his pup
peek over the dusty dashboard

Logan Bader, Fall 2018

This is a haiku that was inspired by my childhood. My dad used to take me on farm calls with him when I was very young, and every time I would go with him, I would take the time to wear my cowboy hat, boots, blue jeans, and cowboy shirt. Sometimes dad would even let me bring our bird dog along as a friend. When I was very young, he would not let me get out of the truck when working cattle because he was afraid that I would get trampled. I would watch over the dashboard of his truck while he would pull calves, pull vaccinations, and more. Every time dad would finish working, I remember getting out and talking basketball and rodeos with the farmers and asking if I could pet their dogs. These were always good memories and it was probably what ultimately got me interested in medicine. Logan Bader, Fall 2018

pumpkin hands
the queen
has arrived

Mary Callaghan, Fall 2018

I simply like this one because it is absolutely ridiculous. I wrote it because I needed more haiku and it was something I did earlier that day, so I wrote a haiku about it. It was ironic because I knew it was a ridiculous haiku yet it was my claim to fame in the class so that was nice. Mary Callaghan, Fall 2018

fox cub
retreating home
bloody paw

Hannah Ottenfield, Fall 2018

I was really happy with this haiku when I wrote it, and it also performed well in kukai. I wrote this one about coming home for a break from college after a recent breakup. My mom and I have an okay relationship, it definitely isn't bad, but we aren't as close as a lot of my friends are with their mothers. However, since I've been away, our relationship has become much better and I feel able to talk to her about things. After my breakup, I just wanted to go home and recover. It's easy to feel like we're real adults in college and completely independent, but the truth is we get hurt, and we find ourselves retreating back to where we started. Hannah Ottenfield, Fall 2018

my tuba boy
if only you knew
the way I blush

Elizabeth Pillow, Spring 2018

At the beginning of the semester I felt so shy about sharing my haiku. I have always felt as though I am not a good writer. People always say that I sound too colloquial in my writing and that it doesn't sound as intelligent as it could. When beginning to write haiku, I was nervous about the criticism of others. I was worried that they wouldn't like what I wrote, or that my poems wouldn't be well received. This turned out to be the opposite. When writing what I coin as my signature haiku, "my tuba boy", I started it as a joke. I remember the prompt being for Valentine's Day, so we were told to write about love, crushes, or so on. As I pondered this prompt, I turned to my friend Molly Compton and said, "How funny would it be if I wrote a haiku about my tuba boy?" To give you some backstory, my junior year here at Millikin I was the assistant stage manager for "Nice Work if You Can Get It". This production had a live band and there was this boy playing the tuba who I thought was SO cute! I turned to my stage manager and said, "Who is that boy playing the tuba?" Her response was, "I have no idea." For a solid year, anytime I would see this boy on campus I would blush and grin ear to ear, and I didn't even know his name. Of course, the only logical name I could give him was "my tuba boy," and that's all she wrote. When writing poems this is the process I would fall into. I would find something that I found amusing, impactful to my life, or something that was bothering me, and I would just run with it. Sometimes this ended in great poems, other times it ended in self-indulgent poop. What I learned most from this class was to trust myself, and to trust that no matter what I am writing, or how eloquent it is, I have something to say. Even if what I have to say is just about the weather outside, I do have something to say, and it matters. As a woman graduating soon, I try to keep this in mind as often as I can. Thank you for helping to remind me that what I have to say matters. Elizabeth Pillow, Spring 2018

Final Course Reflections

The very last assignment is to write a short reflection (1 page) "on how your life has been enriched by learning more about the literary art of reading and writing haiku. What has the art of haiku taught you that will be of value in your professional, social and personal life?" Here are some examples of final reflections by my students.

William J. Higginson once said, "the primary purpose of reading and writing haiku is sharing moments of our lives that have moved us, pieces of experience and perception that we offer or receive as gifts." Our haiku class this semester has really enforced this idea of writing and discussing together, and I liked how haiku brought us to a common ground in almost all facets of life. We could be discussing a softball or bug haiku, yet through haiku, it was somehow made relatable and accessible to the entire class. Mackenzie Martin, Fall 2017

I love haiku. Haiku gives me a short glimpse into split second moments and that's so cool. I've been writing poetry for so long, but now I'm in a haiku rut. I just write haiku continuously. Of course, it's not always good, but it helps relieve stress and pressure from my everyday life to just sit down and write a few short words which sum up a feeling or a moment. To be completely honest, I think my haiku at the beginning of the semester were better than they are now. Which makes me want to switch between haiku, poetry, song writing, and drawing – to keep all of them as fresh outlets where I never get lazy with my artwork but still have the luxury of letting my feelings out onto a page. I'm beyond thankful for taking this class because I looked forward to it every day. Hannah Haedike, Fall 2018

Learning about haiku this semester has been an amazing experience and one that I will take with me for the rest of my time at Millikin, and even the rest of my life. I think that both reading and writing haiku has taught me so much about both the art and my own life. First off, reading haiku takes a great amount of concentration, imagination, and analysis. When you read, you often have to create an image in your head and really get a sense of what that image is telling you. However, there is also a literal aspect to all haiku, and you must take that into account when reading them. Finally, you have to be very open emotionally to them. Often, haiku will make you feel different emotions depending on what they are about or your own experience and what you bring to them. Practicing this with haiku has helped me bring these techniques to my work with plays. I am able to be open to them literally, emotionally, and bring my imagination to the pieces. I am able to better understand what the author is trying to say. Furthermore, I can incorporate this level of analysis into my work on the piece and bring these images and ideas to the audience. What I think I learned the most from haiku, though, is how it is simple, yet so complex and beautiful at the same time. This is because they are just three lines, and not very descriptive, yet they give the reader so much and create such complex images. Even more, they are often about simple things, such as objects, life, people, or nature. They are about things that humans often don't spend much time thinking about. Rather, we tend to take for granted everything around us and don't step back and admire what life has given us. Haiku is very enriching because it reminds people to step back and just observe the things around. It also reminds us to find the beauty in simple things and appreciate what life has offered to us. This is a skill that I can bring to every aspect of my life. Trey DeLuna, Fall 2017

Coming in to the Global Haiku course, I was not sure what to expect. I had heard from other students that Global Haiku was a lot of fun, and that the students in the class enjoyed learning about the topics the course covered. As an English-Writing major, I was hopeful that the course would help me to improve my skills as both a reader and a writer of haiku, because I find haiku to be enjoyable. I was also nervous, because I prefer to write longer works, and had never really attempted to write haiku before taking the course. My knowledge about haiku was very limited prior to this class, which made me feel a bit overwhelmed initially, and I am sure some of my classmates were in the same boat as I was on the first day. However, I did not feel this way for long. The classroom environment was safe, and our ideas were always validated. Soon, I was comfortable enough to share all of my thoughts with my classmates, and I felt like we all lifted each other up. Compared to other competitive classes, this was a great change of pace. Over the course of the semester, we read so many different haiku poets, and discussed their tactics. Prior to analyzing works of different haiku poets, I had no idea just how many different approaches to writing haiku there are. This was fascinating to me, because in only three lines, poets are able to paint such vivid images and circumstances, and by changing minuscule details—such as dashes and periods— poets are able to manipulate the tone or meaning of an entire poem. I liked reading a great number of different poets, but I especially enjoyed reading the haiku written by John Stevenson, who I wrote my craft essay on. Stevenson is definitely my favorite poet out of those we read this semester, because I found his haiku to be both relatable, and well-written. One of the reasons I was a bit concerned at the onset of the class was because I had never written haiku before, except for a few in elementary school— which hardly count. I came to realize that haiku are really whatever you want them to be, and although there are some guidelines, and some haiku are better than others, all it takes is one reader to love a haiku for it to be "born." The simplicity of haiku is what I appreciate the most about it. Writing haiku didn't feel like a chore; I looked forward to the different topics we wrote about for each assignment, and I definitely improved in my haiku writing as the semester progressed. Sometimes it was challenging, but seeing the reactions of classmates to haiku that I wrote made the creative process worth it, despite any writer's block I may have encountered along the way. Over this semester, I have had the opportunity to explain haiku to my friends and family and show them some of the haiku that I've written. I even sparked my sister's interest, who now writes haiku in her journal at the end of the day. That was one of the most enjoyable things about the class; haiku is meant to be accessible to all readers, so it was easy to invite others to join in and either read some haiku, or even help write them. Being able to share an art form with loved ones is a luxury that should not be taken for granted. The Global Haiku course challenged me to break out of my writing comfort zone, and by doing so I now foster great respect for the art of haiku writing. I learned a lot about the process of writing haiku, and different methods that writers employ. I will definitely continue to write haiku in the future, just for myself to enjoy, because I now use haiku writing as a way to unwind after a stressful situation. Global Haiku instilled in me knowledge that I will utilize for many years into the future. Lane Caspar, Fall 2017

My life has been enriched in many ways through reading and writing haiku. I think it has been a wonderful opportunity for me to be able to write haiku because of the outlet it gives me. Through haiku, I can express feelings that are not always easy to express in other ways. It also gives me the chance to use my creative side and appeal to people's emotions. I have always loved creative writing, and I enjoyed the challenge of trying to fit all these emotions and images and sounds into three or so lines. I also thoroughly enjoyed reading haiku. It was very interesting to see how different authors used different techniques and approached their own haiku writing. I enjoyed learning about the variety of styles of haiku as well. It made me realize that a haiku was not just any old haiku, but something carefully thought out and created. *Allyson Isenhower, Spring 2018*

Looking back on this semester of haiku, I can confirm that my life has been enriched and changed for the better. At first, I was skeptical about taking this class because I am not super into literary arts and poetry. Within the first few classes, Dr. Brooks was able to rid me of my skepticism and allow me to embrace haiku. This class has given me a broader range of knowledge and has taught me the value of understanding other people's views after looking at the same thing. Overall, this haiku class has expanded my knowledge. I know a lot of information about mathematics and science, but nothing on the other side of the spectrum. This class allowed me to learn about literary art and broaden my knowledge. I was pleased to learn about the history, formats, and different types of haiku and how to write haiku. This new experience was challenging and beneficial in growing myself as a human being. I believe this class has allowed me to see viewpoints from other people after reading the same haiku. I thought it was amazing to see how differently people interpret the same haiku. Some people see happy things while others see bad. It was incredible to listen to people share what they thought of each haiku. It opened up my eyes to other's ideas and views. This haiku class has actually helped strengthen my relationship with my girlfriend. We were able to sit together and read a haiku book. We told each other what we thought of after reading each. This allowed us to learn more about each other, how positive or negative we are, and our types of creativity. It was a great experience with her, and I feel as though we grew much closer after that experience. Sometimes, we sit and write haiku about anything with each other and share different thoughts. *Austin Taylor, Fall 2017*

Learning the art of haiku has been such an inspiring and enriching opportunity for me. I have been a fan of short form poetry for a while now, and it was really fun for me to learn the intricacies of this artform. I think that I have learned a lot from reading others' haiku. I feel more cultured in that I have read so many poems from poets around the world, and I feel that I have grown closer to my classmates through reading their work. It was such an intimate way to get to know one another on a level that we otherwise would not reach. I also feel that I was able to open up to people that I may not have necessarily known very well on topics that are sensitive for me, and I found it easier through using haiku. I think that haiku has taught me many lessons that can be applied to my daily life. Brevity being one of them, sometimes saying less is saying much more. I've learned to be open and honest and to reflect on the deeper roots of my emotions and why I may be feeling a certain way. I've learned how to take my negative feelings and build them into something positive. I've learned how to be grateful for the small things. I've learned how to connect with other people on a deeper emotional level. I've learned to appreciate poetry that before this class I may not have understood or enjoyed. I plan on continuing to read and write haiku, and I am so incredibly grateful for this experience. This is one of the only classes this semester that I actively looked forward to attending. *Hannah Ottenfield, Fall 2018*

My life has been enriched by learning more about the literary art of reading and writing haiku. We have read many different types of haiku about nature, people, objects, etc. Each haiku is different in its own way, just like people and things you encounter in life. Learning how to write my own haiku was a whole new process than reading and interpreting haiku was. I didn't realize how hard it would be to think of the perfect words to complete my haiku. I have learned how to piece words together and look up new words to use in my haiku. This process has enriched my life by giving me a new outlook on things in life and admiring each little piece of beauty. I have learned how to put a lot of meaning into a few words. This will help me in my profession because when I am a nurse talking to my patients, I will need to keep it short and simple. Being able to think deeply and interpret things I read and hear will also be helpful because communication is key in the nursing profession, like many others. The art of haiku will also help with my social life because I will be able to share my experience from this class and maybe even write haiku with my friends and family. Lastly, my personal life will be affected by haiku because I can think of a haiku when I look at any object. It exercises my mind creating many haiku in my head. *Lexi Doss, Spring 2018*

Before taking this class, I really did not have any experience with reading or writing haiku. The only thing I really knew (or thought I knew) about haiku was that they had to be in a three-line, 5 syllable, 7 syllable, 5 syllable format. This class quickly taught me that this format did not matter at all. I learned to appreciate moments, however small or ordinary they seemed, and try to capture the feelings of that moment. As the semester progressed, I realized I was looking around more, observing and noting what makes each moment special. I am a literature major, so I write a lot every semester, but I found that writing haiku did not feel like work most of the time. When I would sit down to write haiku, it came very naturally and I rarely felt the need to revisit and edit my work, which is something that I do with most of my writing for other classes. I took a creative writing class this semester as well and writing poetry for that class was a very stressful process for me that took hours and dozens of revisions per poem, and I found that I could often capture the same complex emotions in a simple haiku. My favorite haiku that I wrote this semester was the one I named my final collection after, and I wrote a poem, a very short poem, for my writing class that was inspired by the haiku. I did this several times this semester. I have written several cemetery haiku this semester, and I wrote a sonnet for my writing class titled "Cemetery Stroll" that borrowed a few lines from a couple haiku that I wrote. This shows me that whenever I am ever struggling to write something, if I try to write it in a condensed version in a haiku first, it will help me figure out what I am trying to say in a simpler way. Another thing I have gained from this class is the knowledge that punctuation and spacing can be very powerful tools in poetry. I write a lot of poetry in my major, and I never thought much about punctuation or spacing. But this class taught me that, when used properly, punctuation and spacing can change the way that a line or poem is read, which can, in turn, change the meaning or emotion of the poem as a whole. Now when I write poetry, I focus a lot on the way that I use punctuation and the way that I space and break my lines. I think it adds another layer of complexity to the poems that I write. This class was always a highlight of my day, and I made a lot of new friends during the semester. We shared many laughs and inside jokes, and I feel like I got to know all of my classmates very well. At the final reading, when you were giving out awards, I knew my classmates and their writing styles and signature haiku so well that I could guess who each award was going to just based on the name of the award. For example, as soon as you said "best music haiku" I knew it would go to Elizabeth and her signature "Tuba Boy" haiku. The most prominent thing that I will take away from this class and carry with me forever is the appreciation of each moment, and the knowledge that there is always something special and notewor- thy about each moment. I will always remember to slow down, look around, and take in just what it is that makes each moment stand apart, and what emotions are represented in seemingly simple moments. Nicole Wells, Fall 2018

Writing haiku this semester has really been an outlet for me. I enjoyed taking a few minutes to myself each day to reflect on my life and the world around me. Over the course of the semester, I noticed my haiku skills improving, as well as my confi- dence. My favorite thing that learning about reading and writing haiku has taught me is that deep emotions and experiences can be captured in a few simple words. Haiku became a great outlet when I was feeling stressed or even when I was feeling great. Haiku has inspired me to write creatively more, which I haven't had a pas- sion for since high school. Professionally, writing haiku has taught me that my own unique work is important, and following my instincts can sometime produce the best product. I think this is important advice to carry into any professional world. I think it is important to find ways to have fun and put your own personality into your work. Socially, I am more willing to share my writing with others than before. I felt pretty self-conscious at the beginning of this class, but by the end, I was proud for others to know which haiku were mine. I've learned to appreciate and find the beauty in others' experiences and writings as well. I have been able to bond with other people I barely know simply because of the shared human experience that is written into haiku. Personally, exploring haiku this semester has inspired me to continue personal and creative writing and use it as an outlet for myself. It is a re- ally great and enjoyable way to take time away from my usual world of theatre. I like delving into my experiences and feelings in a way different from journaling. It has taught me to appreciate being in the moment, and to enjoy life and the simple things a little more. Haiku has opened my eyes to the beauty of the world and the human experience. I really enjoyed observing many different styles of haiku as well and having the freedom to explore my own style and develop it. Rachel Humphrey, Fall 2018

Global Haiku has impacted my life in so many more ways than I thought it ever would. To be honest, I was upset at first about taking the course. This is only because I really wanted to take "Psych for a Popular Audience" so that I wouldn't have any classes on Thursdays. But now I am more than happy that this is the Honors Seminar that I was blessed to partake in this semester. The art of haiku has taught me so many things. One thing it taught me is that sometimes less is more. I am a very descriptive person, and so coming into this course where I only had 3 short lines to write a poem was hard for me at first. I kept thinking "this isn't enough", "I need to put more', etc. My first round of haiku was fairly rough, but after a few tries, I learned that sometimes less can be more. Haiku is only supposed to give a snapshot into a moment and leave the reader to interpret the rest. This is what makes haiku so fun and impactful. I have now written some pretty good haiku with very few words, but that can still tell an entire story behind them. Another thing haiku gave me was an outlet. I have written some haiku that I never submitted because they referred to some of my personal issues and mental health. Haiku gave me another varied outlet for my feelings, and I will forever be thankful for that. Fi- nally, Global Haiku as a course cured some of my loneliness. Sharing haiku and dis- cussing ideas with people gave me a change in life, where I am usually alone with no one to talk to about ideas, poetry, or anything. Haiku will forever be in my heart and I enjoyed this course dearly. Thanks so much for letting me feel included, like my voice mattered, and like haiku is forever. Thank you! Jenesi Moore, Fall 2018

Being a part of the Global Haiku Traditions class has rebirthed my love of creative writing and enriched my love of noticing the simplicity in smaller moments. This haiku class was a nice slowdown in the middle of my day. Not only did writing haiku help me collect myself but learning how to read haiku and analyze them has taught me a new appreciation for haiku and what it can bring to the art of poetry. I originally signed up for haiku because I absolutely did not want to take a science or math seminar and haiku seemed like a way that I could have a break in my 8 a.m. to 10 p.m. day. However, I have found that it was much more than a class avoidance. This haiku class has allowed me to slow down my very hectic life and fall back in love with the arts. Haiku has been an outlet for me to write about memories I never thought much of and turn them into something not only that brings me joy but to others as well. Sharing my haiku allowed me to get so much closer to classmates I would have never met otherwise. Reading haiku has allowed me to open my mind to more simple and different ways of living. For instance, the "farmku" that was read in class I would have never thought of or imagined because I simply have not experienced it. However, reading the haiku made me feel that I had a better understanding and could at least imagine what it would be like living on a farm. Haiku allowed me to imagine a life I will never live. It also allowed me to note the simplicity in some scenes and that not everything has to be the hustle and bustle of the city. Haiku has allowed me to slow down and have an appreciation for other lifestyles and take notice of old memories that are pushed to the back of my mind. Mary Callaghan, Fall 2018

I went into this semester not really knowing what a haiku was, except like many people, I thought it was the 5-7-5 syllable poem about nature. I was thrilled to discover on the very first day of class that the syllable rule was not real and does not need to be and should not be followed. Instead, haiku should capture a moment, tell only part of a story, and leave the reader simultaneously with a clear picture in their mind and wanting more. I have always struggled with "living in the moment", and I believe that studying, reading and writing haiku has helped me with this. I recall the Haiku Guy story that we read, and how it took weeks and weeks to write just one good haiku. While I cannot entirely relate to devoting entire weeks to just haiku, I definitely received the message. That is, one must be present in a moment to be able to capture it and put it into words. When I was writing haiku, I often thought of something that happened to me that day and tried to remember everything that was going on around me—what I was wearing, what color was the sky, what did the air smell like, who was I with. I found that these seemingly unimportant details often fit really well into haiku. I learned how crumbs in a cup can perfectly describe losing a grandfather, or how the sound of the bird chirping can represent how a trapped woman feels. I found a beautiful connection to the ordinary and the profound, which has enhanced my outlook on life, and my ability to see what is going on around me. Melanie Wilson, Fall 2018

When I started this class back in August, I was in a really weird mental state. I had just gone through a horrible summer of feeling all alone after the constant stimulus that comes with college. All my friends were working their summer jobs and too busy and too tired to hangout afterwards. I worked too, but with boring adults all day long and I was exhausted from the same old same old. I found out that my grandpa was having heart problems that needed further testing, and my grandma had just been diagnosed with breast cancer for which a treatment plan had not yet been determined. When I came back to school on August 6th for First Year Experience Mentor training, quite simply, I was lost. It was during this training that I found out my strengths and through various activities, I felt like I meant something to my peers and to my soon to be students. My birthday came around and ended up being one of the best birthdays I've had in years. Once classes started, I had no idea what to think of my upcoming semester. I was working two jobs, volunteering like crazy, keeping up with a social life, while going through a break up. My class schedule was different than what I'm used to and mainly consisted of non-biology classes. A criminology class, a psychology class, and a haiku class all totally out of my area of expertise. Yet each of these courses made me a more well-rounded individual. I knew little to nothing about haiku aside from the fact that it was a poetry class. I loved poetry, both reading and writing, but truly had no idea what I was getting myself into. Before this class, I had written a little poetry but never had I ever shared it with anyone. When we first started writing our haiku, I wasn't even really sure I was good at it. I was beyond scared to share it with my classmates. During our first kukai, I was excited to see that some of my haiku had made the sheet. When people selected my haiku as some of their favorites, I was shocked, and excited. When I revealed myself as the author, I was still a nervous wreck to admit that I wrote it. Week after week, the nerves grew less strong and I was proud to reveal myself as the author. This class truly taught me the importance of putting my thoughts on paper. Furthermore, turning my thoughts into artwork that others can relate to and appreciate themselves. It also brought forth confidence in owning my artwork and wanting to share it with others without feeling nervous or stupid for it. I loved this class and know for certain that I will continue to write haiku in the upcoming years. Who knows, maybe this will be my backup if graduate school doesn't work out! Naomi Klingbeil, Fall 2018

I have always loved reading and writing. I usually read fiction novels and free verse poetry books. As a writer, I have written short stories, poems, sketches, and monologues. I never properly understood the artform of haiku until this class. I remember learning about haiku in the second grade—it has three lines, with five syllables, then seven, then five again. I believe the one I wrote and presented to the class was about a leaf. Beyond that, I never touched haiku again. I saw this class as an option for an honors seminar and thought, "How fun!" I thought it could be unique and interesting. While this first observation is correct, I learned so much more about haiku's origins and inspirations. This form of poetry has connected with me more than I ever expected. Haiku is very different from the poetry I usually expose myself to—it observes without judgement, it has rules (but they are often broken in creative ways), it shies away from overt emotional expression, and avoids metaphors and similes. I found it fun to learn about the different forms of haiku because I never thought there could be so many (tan-renga, tanka, senryu, etc.) By the end of the semester, I was comfortable playing with the form of haiku in my writing and analyzing other haiku as a reader. I am a performer and writer. Obviously, as a writer, learning about haiku has given me another medium to express myself and my craft. I do not doubt I will write many haiku beyond this class. Haiku has taught me about the value of specificity and expressing oneself in a condensed way – these are very important to actors as well. Socially, it has been exciting to meet people through the class and get to know them through their haiku. Personally, I have started to think of and write down haiku when I find inspiration. It feels as natural to me as writing free verse now. Overall, my learning experience with haiku has been remarkable. Rachel Pevehouse, Fall 2018

I think my life has been enriched by haiku in quite a few ways. I think that haiku has taught me to focus on the little things and notice detail. I learned that you can also find important details in every aspect of your life. Something that might seem insignificant and small actually has meaning and purpose. I learned that I can tell stories within three lines, and that you can fit a lot of details within three lines. I also learned to choose my language wisely, since certain words have many different meanings and others can be more vague than intended. I think that reading haiku has opened my eyes to all of the different things you can write about. In our class alone, we saw haiku about family, romance, death, animals, weather, school, and farms! It showed all of us that haiku can really be anything we want. We can write about whatever we want and tell stories about whatever we want. It was very freeing knowing that haiku can be anything, and it made me interested in what other types of haiku I could read. As for my professional, social, and personal life, I think I will use haiku mostly in my personal life. I enjoy writing quite a bit, and now that I've gotten into writing haiku, I'll probably write a lot more in my time. I could see myself using haiku as a sort of journaling outlet, writing haiku to talk about what I'm feeling or what's happened that day. Throughout this class I've used my haiku to talk about what was going on in my life, and I can definitely see that continuing. I don't see myself using haiku in my social or professional life, just because I'm so busy. But, that's not to say there isn't potential for me to share my haiku with those around me. I already enjoy sharing my haiku with my friends, so I might continue that in my future (if my friends are willing to read them, of course). Haiku has taught me to loosen up a little. I always keep myself extremely busy, and I've learned that I need to sit back and take time to relax. I find haiku very relaxing, so I think I'll work on taking more time out of my day to just sit and write. Socially, haiku has taught me that I can share things with others. I wrote haiku this semester about things I'd never told anyone, and telling people felt really good. I also learned that a lot of art is more social than it seems, especially haiku. Personally, I learned that it's beneficial for me to sit and write haiku. It feels good to get out everything I'm bottling up inside, and haiku is a great way to do that. I think that overall, this class has been very beneficial to me because of all of the things I've learned, and I'm really glad I got to be a part of it! Sophie Kibiger, Fall 2018

Going into this semester, I had never written a haiku poem in my life. If I had, it must've been mandated by a teacher in my late middle school years and it was not an impactful experience for me whatsoever. I believe that I had created some sort of barrier in my head when it came to writing. I felt that I would never be able to express words and ideas as artistically and fluently as others, so I did not even attempt to do so. However, I have begun to realize in this class that creative writing, such as haiku, isn't meant to be perfect. The beauty of haiku is that it is meant to capture the author's experience of a moment in time but is then left to interpretation by the reader. Through this way of looking at it, your writing can't be wrong because it is partially up to what the reader has to offer to the interpretation of the haiku. In becoming more comfortable with writing, I felt like I was able to reflect on my daily life in a new and productive way. I now look at the world through a slightly different lens; there are moments in my day that are incredibly mundane and boring, but I now view them in a different light as something that can be transformed into art. By adding the elements of observation and reflection that come with haiku to my everyday life, I now perceive the world around me to be much more connected and synthesized because it reminds me how the moments of my day are all connected to each other which are also connected to those around me and so on and so forth. This sort of enhanced view of the little details in my day brings more of a focus to my days in my life as a whole. This helps to even the balance between things in my life that seem like a big deal and things that seem insignificant. The balance and synthesis of the overwhelming elements in life and the seemingly miniscule ones make life and the world seem a little less chaotic. I feel that haiku has opened me to new ways of thinking and reflecting on the world around me. My curiosity is now aroused by all moments in my life, no matter how seemingly big or small. The focus and attention to all details in my life has helped me to feel more balanced. I hope that I can maintain this mindset as I continue forward in writing haiku and even in the times that I am not writing as actively. Isabella Spiritoso, Fall 2018

In the past, I have never been a very "poetic" person. It seemed as if it were hard to put together phrases in a way that seem to flow smoothly yet make sense at the same time. I have struggled in the past with my skills in poetry, and thus I have never had a very high appreciation for the topic. However, when learning about writing and reading haiku, there was a certain simplicity to the art that appealed to me. I appreciated how easy it was (for anyone) to write and how quickly I could get my thoughts or feelings into one quick, short poem. I truly feel that this is the reason that I was able to develop some great haiku throughout the semester. The aspect of haiku that I enjoy the most is how personalized it is. Throughout the semester, it was apparent that people have different preferences for writing haiku. I enjoyed the one-lined haiku, likely because I appreciate simplicity. Others liked the creative aspects of haiku and experimenting with various forms that deviated from the typical three-lined structure. Overall, it seemed as if the best haiku that I wrote throughout the semester were based on things that I was passionate about, such as farm life, the outdoors, family, commitment, childhood, and others. It was rewarding to share these passions with others through my haiku writings. Another aspect of haiku that was enriching was developing my reflection skills. By nature, I am typically an introverted person who appreciates deep analyzation and observation before providing my input. Thus, I used reflection skills as one of the main vessels for writing my haiku. Before I would create haiku, I would sit in a quiet room and try to clear my mind of everything. Typically, some topic would remain in the back of my mind, and that is usually what I chose to write about. For example, one day all I could think about was my grandfather. I had just visited him in the nursing home in Centralia, IL over the weekend, so he was especially on my mind. While developing my haiku for the week, I reflected on many aspects of my grandfather, such as his wise advice, what he was feeling while in the home, how the nurses perceived him, my perception of the nursing home as an outsider, and more. This reflection provided me with a lot of great insight to use while writing my haiku for that week, and it also provided me with a sense of comfort as well. Throughout the semester, I found myself enjoying reading and writing haiku outside of the classroom. I would read the haiku collections given out during kukai contests in my leisure time, and I would write haiku for my girlfriend and other friends when they asked for them. I found joy in sharing the subject of haiku with others. While studying or watching movies, my roommates would listen to my haiku. It was a cool experience to watch them develop in their understanding of the art. At first, they struggled to see the point in it. But as I would read them more varieties of my haiku, they began to enjoy it. It was fun comparing the differences between the experiences that inspired my haiku to what images were formed for them when they heard the haiku, and I can also say the same thing about the class activities. The art of haiku has taught me to slow down and pay attention to small details that may seem insignificant. In the present, things sometimes do not always seem important but when reflecting on moments in the future, they can become important or beautiful. I also learned the value of reflection. Reflection, as I stated earlier, was one of the major methods I used in writing my haiku, and I have become more efficient at reflective thought this semester. Finally, I have observed that everyone almost always perceives things differently. When in class, it was amazing to observe how one simple haiku could emit such a strong variety of responses and emotions. Moving into my professional and personal life, I will value these lessons that reading and writing haiku has provided. The idea of slowing down, living in the moment, realizing that everyone is unique, and being able to reflect upon small details will certainly be important in my personal life and also as a physician. It will be important in empathizing with my patients and striving to understand why they may desire certain treatments (or lack of treatments) when I do not think it is the correct path to take, thus creating an atmosphere of respect for the patient as a person. This stems directly from the realization that everyone is different in their beliefs, the way they perceive things, and more. As far as personal life goes, the act of slowing down and enjoying small moments when they present themselves will be key in living a full and satisfying life. Life is short, so every moment is precious. Haiku has taught me to heighten my awareness during these times and appreciate them to a fuller extent. This could be the act of appreciating something small such as my mom making me my morning coffee, or something to the extent of graduation from medical school. I have acquired an appreciation for haiku as an art, but further have gained lots of benefits from it personally. Logan Bader, Fall 2018

I've really grown a lot from being in this class this semester. I think the greatest lesson it has taught me is that humans share so much more in common than things that are different. I not only learned this by writing haiku, but also sharing and listening to others' haiku, and just being in a class where I could enjoy being in the company of really cool people I didn't know before it began. Anyone has the ability to capture life's beauty and hardships in words, and by discovering that, I realized how much we can all relate to one another. As I became more comfortable with writing my own haiku, I noticed that my work was recognized by others and connected with experiences they have had, and I found that this was a major influence on how I wrote my pieces. I became more aware of intentionally listening to others; not just their haiku, but their words and stories. I allowed myself to feel vulnerable and open around people who I may not have normally become friends with, and my life has definitely been enriched by that. I'm not sure if I'll ever just write haiku again for fun, but I'd like to, and if nothing else, I would love to just read haiku from other authors. This class has helped me understand and appreciate what haiku is, and what it can be, and it has forced me to address my human, creative side again. It's made me look at my life reflectively and find beauty in it, even though daily stresses of college life can bog me down. I am so grateful for the art and memories I have made through this class, and I feel like a better human being because of it. More than any other class at Millikin, I felt like I could really be myself and just have fun, and it was a refreshing change of pace. Alissa Kanturek, Fall 2018

When I first added Global Haiku to my class schedule for this semester, I honestly had no idea what a haiku poem was. I briefly remembered writing one when I was in fourth grade, but apart from that ice cream sundae poem, I had never attempted to construct a haiku that meant something. This class has completely changed how I view haiku. I realize now that it is an art form. While a few lines originally seemed like child's play to me in comparison to the novels that people are writing all around the world, they are not simple at all and hardly easy to write. An excellent haiku takes time to form in the writer's mind, in his mouth, and in his hand. I have a greater respect for the haiku community now, for I see the artistry and intelligence it takes to form a haiku. Haiku has taught me that I do not need an abundance of words to communicate my feelings and thoughts. A few words are all it takes. Whether I am writing a paper or giving a speech, excessive wordiness is not called for. Just as I can create a vivid scene in only three lines, I can pour out my thoughts without repeating myself or adding extraneous information. Granted, haiku is not the same as writing academic papers. However, haiku has still taught me how to be concise while still conveying everything I need to. Specific word choice is essential. I look back on my first attempts at haiku during the beginning of this semester, and I want to edit them immediately. I used so many unnecessary words to get my point across. The Writing Center tutor in me made sure that I had articles and adjectives in my haiku. Now that I am at the end of this semester, I know that haiku is not about perfect grammar with capitalization and punctuation. It is about so much more. Haiku shares stories of life and reveals a little of the writer's heart to the audience. Allowing ourselves to have feelings is another point that haiku has taught me. I have so many memories and happy childhood moments I would love to re-live over and over again. Likewise, I want others to experience the joy and cheerfulness I have encountered. I can achieve both of these goals with haiku. However, sometimes sorrow and grief needs to be allowed in these poems. Far too often, society tells us to put on a happy face and ignore our true feelings. With haiku, readers can experience whatever they need to at that moment in time. In class, I love reading others' haiku and finding empathy. While haiku are little, writing them is no small feat. More than anything else, I have learned that haiku requires looking at life through a new lens, such as appreciating the small moments in life and not skipping past the frustration of hard trials. To write haiku, I have had to slow down and consider the people and landscapes around me. The art of haiku unifies cultures through its timelessness and relevance, allowing me to form a greater world-view. While the early Japanese haiku poets spoke a different language and lived during another time, I still can understand what they went through and the messages that their words convey. Haiku is truly a global art form that serves humanity with its honesty. Emily Sullins, Fall 2018

I really hadn't had much experience at all with haiku before this course. I recall having to write a three-line poem with a syllabic pattern of 5-7-5 in second grade and feeling overwhelmed by my inability to properly count syllables. I was delighted to learn from Global Haiku Traditions that these strict rules do not need to exist. While some haiku do follow this pattern, they don't have to. Because of this class, I have fallen in love with free-form haiku! I have always enjoyed writing poetry. From middle school on, I grew to love writing rhyming poems about my feelings and my life. It was a good outlet for me through my angsty years. Because of my slight poetry background, I was very excited to take this class. I figured that we would learn a bunch about the history of traditional Japanese haiku. While this interested me, I was more excited to get comfortable with a new kind of poem. I really like how simple and brief haiku need to be. Every word that is included is there for a good reason. Each word serves a purpose to paint a vivid and emotional picture. While I think of traditional poetry as being filled with metaphors and flowery language that the reader must decipher to find the deeper meaning, haiku lay it all out on the line. Haiku are generally more relatable as well. They capture complex feelings and moments in a few simple words. The brief nature of haiku makes them both easier and harder to write. You don't have much space to write, so there is no need to go too far or get too complicated. This allows the reader and writer to grasp onto a feeling or image immediately. However, because haiku are so concise, the writer is offered a new challenge of picking their words oh so carefully. This concept also relates to my passion for performance and acting as well. In my acting classes, we talk about the "need to communicate" a lot. This is essentially your character's desire to get their point across so that they can achieve their objective. I think of haiku as acting on this need to communicate. They get the point out effectively, but efficiently. While haiku connect to my major, they also provide a really nice vacation from it as well. Acting, singing, and dancing are very emotionally and physically taxing arts. While I love them dearly, it is nice to take a break from them while still accessing a creative side. Like in acting, I can access memories and put them into words for my haiku. The difference is that my haiku can be just for me. Writing haiku has acted a bit like therapy for me. I can take time to reflect on my days and my memories and write haiku about them. I am able to revisit the best moments of my life and reflect on them enough to write about them. It is a very Zen art that I have grown to love. I honestly believe that haiku will begin to take the place of my usual poetry writing. I can't wait to see how my writing grows! Isabella Loutfi, Fall 2018

The Global Haiku Traditions course is very fun, interesting, and educational. Not only did we learn about modern American haiku authors, but we learned about the history of haiku writing and some of the Japanese masters. We learned about the differences in the traditional Japanese works and their incorporation of the moon and nature and cherry blossoms and how American haiku has chosen to branch off. I enjoyed the playfulness and often funny haiku that we read, and I enjoyed seeing the movie a lot. There is a community of haiku lovers, readers, and writers that I had no idea were out there. There are two things that taking this class reminded to do. The first was just a reminder to enjoy it. Even as much as I read, often I get so engrossed in finishing one thing just so I can get on to reading the next thing and the next thing—even though I know there is no way I can read everything. It was nice to hear you say, "take a minute and enjoy the haiku from this book," instead of "read pages 5-10". You reminded me that is a privilege and a pleasure to be able to read good writing. The other thing that this class reminded me to do is tied to enjoyment and that is to slow down. Haiku (and any poetry for that matter) cannot be read quickly one time through. It has to be read slowly with the proper pauses and with time for reflection of the meaning and then maybe read again. I will try to take this lesson to heart, but I know I don't do this well. All learning is valuable and even if I never write another haiku, the knowledge of the traditions of both our own writers and the long tradition of haiku in the world provide an understanding of the connectedness of the world and how different kinds of literary traditions are passed down, changed, branched out, and continued on. Tina Horve, January 2019

When I signed up to take this course, I signed up because friends recommended it to me, and I needed one more course to complete my English minor. I have never been a fan of reading or writing poetry, I would honestly much rather write academic papers all day. I stepped outside of my comfort zone and listened to my friends when they raved about how fun the course was. When I walked in the first day, there were a lot of my pre-conceived thoughts that the course quickly, proved to be false. I was proved wrong on the format, rhyming, and enjoyment aspects. I will always remember leaving the first day with our first assignment to just "write haiku." You didn't give us step by step instructions or hold our hands along the way. In fact, I didn't learn the one cohesive format until almost the end of the course and by that time, everyone was writing with that format. The first day, I thought that a haiku had to be 5-7-5. When you told us that was incorrect, I remember not even knowing how to write. I am always someone who like guidelines. Without any *guidelines I wasn't sure where to even start. I'm sure that, these lack of guidelines, were done on purpose as you wanted us to learn on our own. By forcing myself to just write, I believe that I wrote more freely and didn't try to change the words that my heart wanted to say. I feel like with this new understanding, I can change a lot of my friends' opinions about poetry. Before this course, it was a chore. After this course, it has become something that I subconsciously think about throughout my daily life. See something interesting? Then write a haiku. The last thing that I expected out of the course was to enjoy the actual reading and writing of haiku poetry. When I realized that I could write much more freely than I thought, I began to write for fun. It became something that my friends and I would do when we were out and about. Any funny, sad, or happy events that occurred, we began to write haiku from them. I hope that I will continue to write haiku during law school because it is such a stress relief. Haiku class was hands down my favorite course of the semester. On the first day of class, I kind of felt like people would make fun of one another for writing about their feelings, whether those be happy or sad. I loved that instead, we supported one another, and it was a very open environment. Never once did I worry about writing a haiku and fearing to turn it in because I was afraid that someone would make fun of me. As law school begins in just three short months, I think about what haiku has taught me that I can bring into my social, pro-fessional and personal life. On a social level, haiku has become more of a fun game for my friends and me. We know that if one of us shares something that happened to us, it is up for grabs to be made into a haiku. This is also a way for us to keep track of our college years and remember some of the adventures we went on. In my professional life, first law school and then as a lawyer, I don't think that I will share my haiku with my co-workers and bosses. What I will do, however, is to continue to use the skills that I learned. I learned to look at seven words on a piece of paper, one hundred different ways. Haiku gave me a different perspective for all differ-ent walks of life. Having a different perspective of lives will come in handy when it comes to evaluating courts decisions. In law school, we will do mock trails and this ability to quickly change my lens will help greatly with litigation. As an attorney, this class will help when dissecting why I believe a judge ruled a certain way. The ability to step into the Honor's shoes and view the case as a whole instead of only the side I represent, will be one that I believe will put me a step above the rest. Personally, haiku is something that I will take with me and hopefully write here and there even into the future. I don't foresee myself becoming some haiku author or writing my own books, but I do see myself using it as a social aspect for a fun game and a little bit of stress relief. Thank you for making this course not only my favorite, but the course that I was sad to see end. Breanna Bagley, Spring 2019*

Works Cited

Brooks, Randy & Emily Evans, Melanie McLay, Rick Bearce, Editors. *Millikin University Haiku Anthology*. Decatur, IL: Bronze Man Books, October 2008.

Cox, Aubrie. *Out of Translation*. Somerville, VA: Kattywompus Press, 2015.

Cox, Aubrie. *Tea's Aftertaste*. Decatur, IL: Bronze Man Books, 2011.

Kukai haiku and responses from various Global Haiku Traditions class web pages. Millikin University Haiku: n. pag. <http://www.brooksbookshaiku.com/MillikinHaiku> Web. 14 March 2019.

Lyles, Peggy. *To Hear the Rain: Selected Haiku of Peggy Lyles*. Decatur, IL: Brooks Books, 2002.

Mayfly. Randy & Shirley Brooks, Editors. Battleground, IN: High/Coo Press, issues 1-8, 1986-1989; Decatur, IL: Brooks Books, issues 9-58, 1990-2015; Taylorville, IL: Brooks Books, issues 59-66; 2015- 2019.

Suzuki, Masajo. *Love Haiku: Masajo Suzuki's Lifetime of Love*. Translated by Emiko Miyashita and Lee Gurga. Decatur, IL: Brooks Books, 2000.

Swede, George. *Almost Unseen: Selected Haiku of George Swede*. Decatur, IL: Brooks Books, 2000.

Swist, Wally. *The Silence Between Us: Selected Haiku of Wally Swist*. Decatur, IL: Brooks Books, 2005.

Tipton, James. *Bittersweet*. Austin, TX: Cold Mountain Press, 1975.

Ueda, Makoto, *Matsuo Bashô*. Tokyo & New York: Kodansha International LTD., 1982.

Van den Heuvel, Cor, Editor. *The Haiku Anthology*, Expanded Edition. New York: W.W. Norton, 1999.

Yamaguchi, Tazuo & Randy Brooks, Editors. *Haiku: The Art of the Short Poem*. Film by Tazuo Yamaguchi on DVD. Decatur, IL: Brooks Books, 2008.

About the Author

Brief Haiku Biography

Dr. Randy Brooks is the Dean of the College of Arts & Sciences and Professor of English at Millikin University in Decatur, Illinois. He teaches courses and workshops on haikai poetry traditions including haiku, renga, and tanka. His students' poetry and essays are available on the Millikin University Haiku web site: <http://www.brooksbookshaiku. com/MillikinHaiku/index.html>. Millikin University has hosted two haiku conferences: the Midwest Haiku Festival in 1992 and the Global Haiku Festival in 2000, which featured numerous guest haiku and tanka poets. The Tanka Society of America was founded on campus during the Global Haiku Festival. Dr. Brooks also teaches book publishing, serving as faculty advisor for the student-run book publishng company, Bronze Man Books, founded in 2006.

He and his wife, Shirley Brooks, are co-editors and publishers of Brooks Books and *Mayfly* haiku magazine. Randy and Shirley have been dedicated to publishing books, journals, bibliographies, and online collections of haiku in English since 1976 when they founded High/Coo Press. When they moved to Illinois in 1990, Randy & Shirley changed the name of the publishing company to Brooks Books. For more information about Brooks Books publishing see: <http://www.brooksbookshaiku.com>.

Dr. Brooks serves on the Executive Committee of the Haiku Society of America as the Electronic Media Officer. He serves as the webmaster for Modern Haiku Press and *Modern Haiku* magazine. He is on the editorial board for the annual Red Moon Press haiku anthologies. He also edits the web sampler issues and back issue archives of *Frogpond* magazine published by the Haiku Society of America. He serves as a member of the editorial team for the journal of haiku criticism, *Juxtapositions*.

Randy has won many awards for his poetry including 1st Place in the Harold G. Henderson Award from the Haiku Society of America. He and his wife, Shirley Brooks, co-edited *The Collected Haiku of Raymond Roseliep* which received the 1st Place Merit Book Award from the Haiku Society of America for books published in 2018. In addition to several chapbooks, a collection of his selected haiku, *School's Out*, was published by Press Here (Foster City, California). He and George Swede were co-editors of the *Global Haiku Anthology* published by Iron Press (England). Randy and Lee Gurga were co-editors of the *Midwest Haiku Anthology* published by Brooks Books. He and a team of students and former students were co-editors of the *Millikin University Haiku Anthology* published by Bronze Man Books.

Dr. Brooks has been actively involved in building various archives of haiku publications and currently serves on the board for the American Haiku Archives in the California State Library in Sacramento. In the 1980s he edited and published four editions of *Haiku Review*, a bibliography of haiku books in print and current scholarship.

To facilitate research on contemporary haiku and tanka by his students at Millikin University, he established the Decatur Haiku Collection, with a complete bibliography of all holdings available on the Millikin University Haiku web site <http://www.brooksbookshaiku.com/MillikinHaiku/bibliographies/DecaturHaikuCollection.pdf>.

To facilitate research on contemporary haiku and tanka by his students at Millikin University, Dr. Brooks established the Decatur Haiku Collection, with a complete bibliography of all holdings available on the Millikin University Haiku web site <http://www.brooksbookshaiku.com/MillikinHaiku/bibliographies/DecaturHaikuCollection.pdf>. As Electronic Media Officer for the Haiku Society of America, he maintains the online collections of awards. He also manages the PDF library of back issues of *Frogpond*. As web editor for Modern Haiku Press, he edited and designed a digital archive of the first ten years of *Modern Haiku* magazine, available on a CD. He has also completed digital archives of all issues of *High/Coo: A Quarterly of Short Poetry*, *American Haiku* magazine, and the growing web archive of *Modern Haiku* magazine.

Haiku & Tanka Collections by Randy Brooks

The Art of Reading & Writing Haiku: A Reader Response Approach. Brooks Books, (Taylorville, IL), 2019.

Walking the Fence: Selected Tanka of Randy Brooks. Brooks Books, (Taylorville, IL), 2019.

Broadside. *Haiku With Legs.* Brooks Books, (Taylorville, IL), 2015.

Common Time: Photo-Haiga. Limited edition of photography by Priscilla Meddaugh and haiku by Randy Brooks, Blue Connections Studio. (Decatur, IL), 2008.

Unmasking Us: Photo-Haiga. Limited collector's chapbook gift edition with photography by Priscilla Meddaugh and haiku by Randy Brooks, Blue Connections Studio. (Decatur, IL), 2007.

School's Out: Selected Haiku of Randy Brooks. Press Here, (Foster City, CA), 1999.

Broadside. *Crows Talking Crow,* Press Here, (Foster City, CA), 1999.

The Homestead Cedars. The Virgil Hutton Haiku Memorial Chapbook Competition, (Normal, Illinois: Saki Press), 1999.

In Her Blue Eyes: Jessica Poems. (Decatur, Illinois: Brooks Books), 1998.

Online Book. *Black Ant's Journey to Japan: A Modern Tanka Journal.* (Gualala, CA: AHA Online Books), 1998.

The Collected Haiku of Randy Brooks. Boston Macintosh Users Group CD, Volume 2, Discovery Systems, (Dublin, Ohio), 1990.

Me Too! High/Coo Press, (Battle Ground, Indiana), 1985.

The Last Quarter Mile. Grey Whale Press, (Florence, Oregon), 1981.

Barbwire Holds Its Ground. High/Coo Press, (Battle Ground, Indiana), 1981.

The Rosebud Bursts. High/Coo Press, (Battle Ground, Indiana), 1979.

Where Will Mockingbird Nest? Juniper Press, (LaCrosse, Wisconsin), 1977.

Index of Haiku Authors & Readers

Naomi Klingbeil, Fall 2018 – 26, 32, 106, 124, 155, 158, 175-176, 209-210
Natalie Perfetti, Spring 2009 – 43, 145, 167
Natalie Smith, Spring 2016 – 23, 93, 129, 133
Natalie Zelman, Fall 2014 – 46, 129, 184, 197
Nathan Bettenhausen, Spring 2010 – 25
Nathan Heppermann, January 2017 – 47-48, 143, 188
Nicholas Kemp, Spring 2017 – 152
Nicholas Sanders, Spring 2015 – 45, 46, 85, 94, 153, 156, 166
Nicholas Scarpinato, Fall 2015 – 100, 130, 132
Nicole Wells, Spring 2018 – 44, 67, 208
Nicole Koch, Spring 2015 – 157
Nicole Silverman, Spring 2005 – 140
Nicole Zabrinas, Spring 2008 – 106, 118, 183
Nora Kocher, Spring 2011 – 180-181
Norman Mears, July 2017 – 127

Ocamie Outlaw, November 2014 – 42
Olivia Birkey, Spring 2010 – 163-164
Olivia Cuff, Fall 2014 – 20, 167
Olivia Gonzalez, Spring 2017 – 55, 69, 159
Owen Pulver, Fall 2016 – 90, 108, 173
Paige Dorsel, Spring 2017 – 137
Pat Thompkins – 17
Patrick Steadman, Spring 2006 – 17, 81, 142
Peggy Lyles – 36-52, 73-76, 165, 168-169
Philip Koberlein, Spring 2007 – 97
PMF Johnson – 18

R.A. Stefanac – 73
Rachel Cook, Spring 2006 – 97-98
Rachel Humphrey, Spring 2018 – 48-49, 80-81, 115, 144, 208
Rachel Morrison, Spring 2007 – 160, 185
Rachel Pevehouse, Fall 2018 – 34, 53, 80, 109, 120, 123, 125, 172, 175-176, 210
Rachel Walker, Spring 2005 – 118
Ramey Sola, Fall 2013 – 104
Randi Mehrmann, Spring 2013 – 134
Randy Brooks – 34, 58, 136, 166, 175-176, 180-181, 187-200
Raquel D. Bailey – 19, 20
Rebecca Coutcher, Fall 2014 – 33
Renee Sample, Fall 2016 – 69, 139, 167
Rob Spurling, Fall 2012 – 103, 143
Roberta Beary – 131
Rory Arnold, Spring 2018 – 131
Ryan Fraedrich, Fall 2012 – 166
Ryan Jones, Spring 2003 – 87, 176-178
Ryan McDonald, Spring 2018 – 124, 131
Ryan Murphy, Spring 2009 – 145
Ryan Sikora, Fall 2016 – 173

Sabrina LeBlanc, January 2018 – 47
Sam Miller, Spring 2017 – 111-112, 152
Samantha Bies, January 2016 – 121

Samantha Miles, Fall 2010 – 99, 134
Samantha Parks, Fall 2010 – 80, 140
Samantha Sinkhorn, Fall 2008 – 162
Sandy Fitzgerald, February 2010 – 59
Sara Siegfried, Fall 2014 – 116, 132
Sarah Bassill, Spring 2005 – 77, 140
Sarah Corso, Spring 2006 – 98, 195
Sarah E. Kisly, Spring 2013 – 40
Savannah Riestenberg, Fall 2016 – 105, 113, 116, 133, 144, 167, 173
Seth Harshman, Fall 2012 – 163
Shannon Hackl, Spring 2007 – 49
Shannon Kroner, Spring 2002 – 56, 61
Shannon Netemeyer, Fall 2016 – 167
Sierra Shaw, Spring 2009 – 118, 168
Skya Gentle, Fall 2012 – 78
Sonia Sanchez – 130, 131
Sonja Chargois, July 2016 – 146
Sophie Kibiger, Fall 2018 – 34, 61, 109, 125, 144, 172, 175-176, 211
Stacey Longfellow, July 2013 – 40
Stacey Orr, Spring 2003 – 87
Stefanie Davis, Spring 2012 – 84-85
Stephanie Dietrich, Spring 2006 – 65
Stephanie Ford, Spring 2002 – 190
Susie Wirthlin, Spring 2010 – 25, 64, 101, 106, 115, 171, 180-181
Sydney Brangenberg, January 2017 – 51, 73, 96, 103
Sydney Rudny, Fall 2018 – 154, 175-176

Tammy Maxwell, February 2010 – 59
Tara Goheen, Spring 2012 – 172
Taryn Pepping, Spring 2016 – 42, 71, 91, 152
Taylor Hagerdorn, Fall 2014 – 38, 43, 167
Teresa Brase, June 2016 – 184
Therese O'Shaughnessy, Spring 2013 – 60, 104
Thomas Friend, July 2017 – 57
Tina Horve, January 2019 – 123, 215
TJ Holmes, Spring 2014 – 18
Travis Meisenheimer, Spring 2004 – 88, 135
Trey DeLuna, Fall 2017 – 38, 65, 128-129, 137, 192, 204
Trista Smith, Fall 2014 – 33, 131, 184, 189
Tyler Lamensky, Fall 2010 – 63
Tyler Trzcinski, Spring 2016 – 142

Uriah Walker, January 2016 – 63
Valina Hoang, Fall 2014 – 184, 200
Wally Swist – 67-76, 157, 168
Whitley Sapp, Spring 2019 – 66
Whitney Gray, Spring 2016 – 22, 70, 90, 114
Whitney Minor, Spring 2007 – 160, 185, 188
Will Frankenberger, Spring 2009 – 145
Xiu Ying Zheng, Spring 2003 – 62, 176-178
Yunek Moore, Spring 2017 – 54-55, 65, 128, 136
Zachary McReynolds, Fall 2018 – 39, 134, 175